Posted

Check Mr Thomas

any unitarian church in Ruabon
Wrexham or Johnson City

Cross-street chapel

Check St Marks Munn Trip
for picture of St Marks

$2\frac{1}{2}$ miles thru
$2\frac{1}{2}$ n back
The long walk is
part of the gift

British Unitarians
against American Slavery,
1833–65

British Unitarians against American Slavery,

1833–65

146 M

Douglas Charles Stange

Rutherford ● Madison ● Teaneck
Fairleigh Dickinson University Press
London and Toronto: Associated University Presses

Associated University Presses, Inc.
440 Forsgate Drive
Cranbury, NJ 08512

Associated University Presses Ltd
25 Sicilian Avenue
London WC1A 2QH, England

Associated University Presses
2133 Royal Windsor Drive
Unit 1
Mississauga, Ontario
Canada L5J 1K5

To James Luther Adams
In memory of Harry Lismer Short

Unitarian preceptors of Harvard and Oxford

Library of Congress Cataloging in Publication Data

Stange, Charles Douglas.
   British Unitarians against American slavery,
1833–65.

   Bibliography: p.
   Includes index.
   1. Slavery—United States—Anti-slavery movements.
2. Abolitionists—Great Britain.   3. Slavery and the
church—Unitarian churches.   4. Unitarians—Great
Britain—Political activity—History—19th century.
5. Unitarian churches—Great Britain—History—19th
century.   I. Title.
E449.S78   1983   973.5   82-48436
ISBN 0-8386-3168-1

Contents

Acknowledgments

"Remember the ladies," declared Abigail Adams to her husband, John, confronting his conscience with the needs and contributions of women relative to justice in the Constitution of the United States. Women are firstly remembered here not out of deference to traditional social convention, but because women have been preeminent in making possible this modest offering toward an understanding of the history of religion and reform. What contribution it makes toward such an understanding, they (and obviously my male mentors) are to be thanked, what errors in fact, judgment, and style it perpetrates I solely am to be blamed.

Jutta Eva Blaesing Stange, my beloved wife, provided the ever-patient support and encouragement that enabled this study to see life. Maria Grossmann of the Andover-Harvard Theological Library and Kathy Swift and Barbara Smith of the Manchester College (Oxford) Library afforded generous access to, and indispensable assistance in, the Unitarian book and manuscript collections under their care. Elisabeth Jupp of the Harrow School in London offered superb instruction in English history as well as sensitive criticism on the use of the English language. Dolores J. Lawrence, Sharon Peplinski, and especially, Annette K. Davis of Central Michigan University all contributed their professional skills to produce typescripts for me of the highest quality. Finally, Mary Zeiss Stewart, my sister co-worker at Central Michigan University, shared the kind of collegial support that a professor who teaches hundreds of undergraduates must have to persevere in scholarship. Her friendship and humanitarian ideals inspire.

I am deeply thankful to these women. I shall always remember them.

My thankfulness and remembrance is equally manifested toward those men who have given of their time and labor to instruct me and share with me in the telling of the story of the Unitarians and antislavery reform. At the top of the list of my benefactors are John McManners, Regis Professor of Ecclesiastical History and Chairman of the Department of Modern History, Oxford University, and Conrad Wright, John Bartlett Lecturer on New England Church History and Professor of American Church History, Harvard University. John McManners offered gentle, patient, and sagacious advice at all stages of writing this book. Conrad Wright generously read each chapter and helped me immensely by correcting my infelicities of style and ensuring my accuracy and fairness in regard to Unitarian history. No student of Unitariana ought to hazard publication without first securing a critique from Professor Wright. Others who read a portion or all of the manuscript were David Brion Davis, Bruce Findlow, Winthrop Jordan, Leon Litwack, H. G. Nicholas, C. Duncan Rice, and Howard Temperley. I am grateful to these scholars for their interest and assistance.

A host of librarians, archivists, historians, clergy persons, colleagues, et al. aided me by locating materials, offering suggestions, influencing opinions, and refreshing my spirit in bringing this project to completion. They are listed here without regard to rank or gender and my respect for them and my appreciation of them is uniform. To each of them will come a letter of thanks and a copy of these acknowledgments. Some of the institutions they represent are listed in the bibliography. My thanks and every good wish to Alan Seaburg, Elizabeth Shenton, Rodney G. Dennis, Kathleen A. Major, A. S. Bell, Laura V. Monti, F. E. Leese, M. R. Perkin, Glenise Matheson, Virginia J. Renner, C. J. Wright, Kenneth A. Lohf, James Tyler, John D. Stinson, Anthony W. C. Phelps, Karl Kabelac, Mary L. Robertson, Mary E. Williams, Jean R. McNiece, James Lawton, John C. Broderick, E. Basil Short, Ian Sellers, A. T. Milne, Andrew M. Hill, Arthur J. Long, Clare Taylor, K. R. M. Short, F. Kenworthy, Allen L. Shepherd, Ken Folkert, Baird Tipson, Roger Hatch, and the Hibbert Trust.

Lastly, I reaffirm my appreciation of the British Unitarian abolitionists. My recounting of their story is my memorial, however deficient in design and execution, to their incarnate divinity.

Douglas C. Stange
Coldwater Lake, Michigan

Prologue

The British Unitarians, a "sect everywhere spoken against," said Joseph Priestley, or "theological negroes," as they called themselves, were a small, highly educated, financially respectable, politically aggressive and articulate denomination that exerted an influence far beyond what their numbers, some 60,000 members in Great Britain and Ireland, would ordinarily command. It was an influence they exerted under the duress of being ostracized as infidels by England's orthodox Christians. Still they had an unbounded enthusiasm for reform and were drawn to almost every movement for social justice, particularly the antislavery movement. They were "anti-everything-arians," said one of their opponents, yet it would be closer to the truth to say that they were "pro-everything-arians" if one thinks in terms of quality of life, justice, peace, equality, liberty, freedom, and tolerance. Sadly, much of what they wrote and tried to accomplish has been ignored by scholars. Their contribution, however, is too interesting and important to remain ignored. This book is the story of their contribution to the thirty-year war against the "master sin of the world" and "the crime above all crimes"—American slavery.

It is a story that begins with a description of the background of the Unitarians both in the United States and Great Britain. The American Unitarians had emerged from the Congregationalist state churches of New England and were linked to the established order. An English contemporary declared that in a sense they were "torified." The British Unitarians on the other hand were "hereditary nonconformists." They emerged primarily from the English Presbyterians, with a few congregations joining them from the Independents, General Baptists, Methodists, and Anglicans. Neither the American

Unitarians nor the British were able to grow beyond a few hundred congregations. Both groups were considered heretics by their fellow Christians, but whereas American Unitarians suffered no political or social liabilities, the British Unitarians did experience political liability and social ostracism. They did not achieve political toleration until the Trinity Act of 1813 and social toleration continued to be for them an elusive goal throughout the nineteenth century. However, the prejudice they endured had the positive effect of propelling them into reform, particularly into the antislavery movement. Reform to them became the solvent of heresy's stain.

The Unitarians did their part in the achievement of British Emancipation and then redirected their energies into the American antislavery movement. In focusing on the American situation, a transformation in their thinking on slavery took place. For several reasons they passed from a rather moderate stance on antislavery to a radical abolitionism. They developed an affinity for the radical abolitionists in America, the followers of William Lloyd Garrison, partially as a result of the common odium that the Garrisonians experienced in America and that they as "infidels" experienced in Great Britain. They were also influenced by the writings of Harriet Martineau; the charisma of Garrison, whom many of them met at the World's Anti-Slavery Convention in London in 1840; and the Garrisonian evangelism of Samuel May, Jr., an American Unitarian abolitionist minister, who visited England and Ireland in 1843. Their commitment to radical abolitionism seemed complete when the denomination's newspaper, the *Inquirer,* became a Garrisonian vehicle through the conversion of its editor, William Hincks, and when Samuel May successfully secured remonstrances against American slavery from British and Irish Unitarian associations. These remonstrances provoked the American "Unitarian Protest Against Slavery" in 1845, which 173 ministers of the American Unitarian Association signed. Unfortunately, the protest dictated no course of action.

The British Unitarian abolitionists continued their pressure upon their American brethren, but their attempts to solicit additional antislavery protests from the Americans were unsuccessful. These attempts by the abolitionist stalwarts to make every Unitarian a bona fide abolitionist began to provoke controversy and reaction set in. When the Anti-Slavery League was founded in England as a national organization to preach the Garrisonian Gospel of immediate emancipation, it did not prove to be popular. Although many Unitarians were active at its foundation and in its activities, it failed to receive wide support and soon collapsed.

In the mid-1840s a storm arose over the appointment of a slaveholder to the Board of Vice-Presidents of the American Unitarian Association. When several ministers of the AUA issued an invitation to their British brethren to attend their anniversary meetings, an intense debate ensued in Britain and Ireland on whether the invitation ought to be accepted. Although the abolitionists were unable to encourage the British and Foreign Unitarian Association to take official action on the so-called Boston Invitation, they independently composed a reply. Only sixty ministers signed it. The acrimonious debate over the invitation severely damaged the abolitionists' reputation and crediblity. Instead of continuing in the hope of making every Unitarian an abolitionist, they were faced with the task of keeping their own numbers and enthusiasm intact.

In the first half of the decade of the 1850s the emotional commitment of the Unitarian abolitionists was intensified in the surge of antislavery activity actuated by the Fugitive Slave Law controversy, and then in reaction to the wide dissemination in Great Britain of Harriet Beecher Stowe's sensational novel, *Uncle Tom's Cabin*. This was a period in which British Unitarian antislavery reformers achieved their highest level of activity. However, after the mid-1850s a turnabout occurred; antislavery enthusiasm in Britain generally diminished and Unitarian interest decreased accordingly. There were several reasons for this decline. Of primary importance was the increasingly complex political nature of the antislavery struggle in the United States. In the face of the Kansas-Nebraska Act, the Brooks-Sumner Affair, the 1856 presidential election, the Dred Scott Decision, and John Brown's Raid on Harpers Ferry, antislavery reformers in Britain felt more and more helpless to influence Americans morally to end slavery. Unitarians experienced their own special difficulties. Their antislavery activity was seriously hampered by the death of two of their most important antislavery leaders. Moreover, they were plagued by an orthodox attack upon the alleged infidel opinions of Garrison. Lastly, many Unitarians believed that America had become so totally corrupt that her redemption and reform were necessary before she could corrupt Great Britain. Their belief gradually evolved into the idea that America was so morally corrupt that only her isolation or quarantine could contain her sins of slavery and racism. Some Unitarians simply lost interest in the movement and withdrew.

The advent of the American Civil War renewed the interest of British Unitarians in American problems. In general, they hoped that somehow the conflict would bring an end to American slavery. At the same time, they abhorred the war as a wanton waste of life and property. Most strove to be neutral, although a few chose sides. All cheered the war's conclusion, lamented the death of Lincoln, and greeted emancipation with a generous outpouring of money and supplies for the freedmen.

Several observations can be drawn from this story of the British Unitarians. As one would expect, to seek reform in a foreign country is an extremely complicated and frustrating process. Results are usually sporadic and slow in coming. In their campaign against American slavery, the Unitarians revealed themselves to be international Christians and citizens of the world, who were devoted to the common welfare of the human race, to racial tolerance, and to participation in reform as an ecumenical endeavor. Their motivations for antislavery reform in particular, and reform in general, arose out of a liberal theology that sought to prove its moral superiority; a minority status and consciousness that sought social acceptance; a strange and surprising evangelical warmth (typical of only some Unitarians and alien to the denomination as a body) that fired an emotive drive against social evils; a capitalist ideology that believed in a liberating progress; a political philosophy that favored freedom, honesty, and benevolence in government; a nationalism within an internationalism that proclaimed England's manifest destiny to be the protection and encouragement of human liberty at home and abroad; and a familial attachment to the members of their faith and reformers of their persuasion that was mutually supportive and rewarding. This book seeks to prove that the nineteenth-century Unitarians are worthy of scholarly investigation and analysis, and suggests that the study of their motivation, commitment, vitality, and perseverance in the fight against American slavery can enhance our understanding of the role of religion in reform.

Protestation of American Slavery

——— 1 ———

Reform as the Solvent of Heresy's Stain:
Unitarian and Abolitionist as Synonyms—Genesis

Unitarians Defined: Reformers, Heretics, Monsters, Jacobins, Radicals

The Unitarian denomination has always esteemed a reform interest as one identifying characteristic of its membership. Had it not made its birthplace of eastern Massachusetts America's "historical center . . . of morality and culture [and] even, to some extent, of progress"?[1] This observation for the nineteenth century, however, is accurate only so far as the history of *individual* Unitarians is concerned. They indeed were in the vanguard of the movements for prison reform, temperance, peace, education, women's rights, and antislavery. Their denominational body, the American Unitarian Association, was not. The AUA, James Martineau (1805–1900) declared, was "the most conservative body of Unitarians in the world." Its leadership preached law, order, and the preservation of the status quo. It was perturbed by radical reformers who disturbed the good order and possible growth of the AUA by

17

insisting that the denomination denounce America's social evils.[2] Still, it did not hesitate to take credit for their success. It might be disturbed when individual Unitarians plunged into waters of reform too turbulent for the denomination to hazard, but if they were successful in challenging those waters, it would be there to welcome them ashore. In other words, while their reform activity was disruptive the reformers were held at arm's length. When their reforms succeeded and American society acknowledged them as heroes, the denomination blessed, claimed, and embraced them.

This was particularly true when some individual Unitarians campaigned against slavery in the 1830s. They found their pleas for antislavery pronouncements from their denomination resisted. The denomination did not want to bind the consciences of its membership to contested pronouncements. It did not wish to offend the Boston elite whose business ties, political concerns, and Southern contact drove them to seek neutrality on the issue of slavery. Lastly, it did not want to jeopardize its missionary outreach in Massachusetts or in the Southern states. It knew that reforming zeal in respect to abolitionism would lose its opportunities to make converts in the South and among the patricians of Boston. By 1860, however, its numbers in Massachusetts had increased very little and its few churches in the South were closed or moribund. The antislavery cause was being proclaimed by nearly everyone. Two Unitarian abolitionists who had unsuccessfully pleaded with their denomination to speak thirty years before, now were chosen to draft an antislavery statement representative of the denomination's newfound antislavery consensus![3]

The rejection and eventual glorification by the AUA of the individual American Unitarian abolitionists was essentially duplicated by the Unitarian denomination in Britain. Many British Unitarian individuals worked vigorously to end America slavery. They tried to influence their own denominational organization, the British and Foreign Unitarian Association, as well as the AUA. Like the Americans, however, they found the BFUA resisted their efforts. It detested their enthusiasm and was reluctant to make antislavery pronouncements that it believed had little effect on ending slavery in the United States. The British Unitarian abolitionists were not deterred. They were dedicated to the idea that a commitment to reform was a Unitarian belief. They believed that their devotion to the abolitionist cause would win them adherents to the Unitarian faith. Eventually, the BFUA honored their work.

It was one of those extraordinary coincidences of history that the very same day, 26 May 1825, that the American Unitarian Association was formed in Boston, the British and Foreign Unitarian Association came into being in London. Neither group knew of the existence of the other until some weeks later. The histories leading up to their foundation, as well as the constituencies they served, were rather different.

The American Unitarians were an indigenous group that had Arminianism as a mother and supernatural rationalism as a father. They grew up on the rocky soil of New England in the midst of the established church of Congregationalism. Dr. Conrad Wright has expertly drawn their family tree. He has demonstrated that they were progeny of religious liberals whose social standing and influence made them chafe under the dogmatic and rigoristic Calvinism of the Congregationalist state church. They could not accept a bleak theology in which the majority of the human race was consigned to hell. They found comfort in the Arminian view that all men and women had the opportunity under God's guidance, and through their own moral discipline, to overcome sin and achieve salvation. Supernatural rationalism taught them that unassisted reason could establish the essentials of natural religion, but that natural religion ought to be supplemented by biblical revelation. They were labeled "Arminian" because they held views similar to the Dutch Remonstrant, Jacobus Arminius (1560–1609). Their supernatural rationalism was a reworked version of the deism of the Age of Reason. They could not find support, clearly stated or otherwise, for a Trinitarian doctrine in the Bible and they were called by their enemies, much to their consternatioin, Unitarian.[4]

It was a religion of aggressive, ambitious, and financially successful Americans and when New England Congregationalism began to be sundered by schism, the social prominence of the Unitarian party was conspicuous. Harriet Beecher Stowe, visiting Boston in the 1820s, was amazed to see that "Unitarianism reigned . . . [and] all the elite of wealth and fashion crowded Unitarian churches." When the division in the Congregational Church was completed, all but one Congregational church in Boston had become Unitarian. In all, the Unitarians had approximately 125 churches; 100 of these were in Massachusetts, mostly in or near Boston; twenty elsewhere in New England; and only five outside that region.[5] Unitarianism popularly became known as the denomination that believed in "the Fatherhood of God, the Brotherhood of man, and the Leadership of Jesus." Its orthodox opponents sarcastically added—"in the vicinity of Boston."

In the enthusiasm over their birth as a denomination some Unitarians believed that their sect would prosper unaided, that it would spread naturally with a growing America. But others were pragmatic enough to realize that to advance their cause, a cooperative agency was necessary. They established the American Unitarian Association. By 1850, the Unitarians had approximately 230 churches.[6] Their growth was not spectacular; it never would be. However, they did have influence. At the time of the establishment of the AUA the Unitarians held the highest social standing attainable in the United States. Their leadership in politics was undisputed in Massachusetts and recognized on a federal level; a few of their number even captured the presidency. They filled every judgeship in Massachusetts but one. They held a controlling influence over education in Massachusetts and in much of New England. American's most renowned university, Harvard, was under their control.[7] In eastern Massachusetts they were the establishment and their theology carried with it no social or political liability.

The British Unitarians were predominately upper-middle-class managers, merchants, and manufacturers. The bulk of their congregations were, and are today, found largely in industrial areas: Manchester, Birmingham, Leeds, Sheffield, Leicester, Nottingham, and Newcastle. Unitarians took a very active part in developing the textile industry, and many Britons will recognize the names of Brunner in chemicals, Osler in glass, Partington in paper, Tate in sugar, and Wedgwood in pottery.[8] They once had in the eighteenth century a broader spectrum of support from the titled to the poor. However, the social escalator carried many of their elite up and away from their congregations, while dry intellectual sermons drove their poorer brethren not necessarily down, but certainly out.[9]

Their numbers were small. According to the Census of 1851, they had only 229 places of worship in England and Wales. They had at most 30,000 active members. The Reverend John Relly Beard (1800–76), writing about *Unitarianism Exhibited in Its Actual Condition* in 1846, cited five Unitarian ministers at work in Scotland, but only one Unitarian chapel, St. Mark's,

Edinburgh. He counted thirty-six anti-Trinitarian congregations in the North of Ireland and generously guessed their membership to be 30,000.[10] Denominational cohesion was almost nonexistent, a situation that Unitarians perpetuated for the sake of theological independence, but found detrimental to their church's numerical growth and missionary expansion. The British and Foreign Unitarian Association, founded to give the Unitarians a national identity, was a loose collection of congregations, district associations, and individual subscribers. At no time, however, did more than eighty congregations belong to it between its founding in 1825 and 1867, when congregational and district representation were abolished.[11]

Still, despite the denomination's small numbers, scattered congregations, and stunted growth, it could always boast in the nineteenth century that most of its members were highly educated, financially respectable, and politically aggressive. They exerted an influence far beyond what their numbers would command. They served in Parliament, became mayors of English industrial centers, and pressed for political and social reforms.[12] It was not all work and no play for the Unitarians. There was no severity in their religion; they could dance, play cards, and attend the theatre.[13] Their theology, unlike that of their American coreligionists, did carry with it severe social and political liabilities.

The British Unitarians traced their beginnings to the year 1662, when 2,000 ministers were ejected from the Church of England for refusing to accept the Act of Uniformity. They gave up their living rather than to submit to episcopacy and what they thought was a corrupted church. These Dissenters included mostly Presbyterians, but 194 were Independent or Congregationalists, and nineteen were Baptists. Among the Presbyterians was Richard Baxter (1615–91), a hero to many Unitarians because he eschewed sectarianism and proclaimed a comprehensive or catholic church that included all Christians. Comprehensiveness was an eternal ideal of most Unitarians and all had to wait until eternity to see it in practice. Few of the Dissenters were Arian, let alone Socinian or Unitarian. But as they built their own chapels, they founded them on a congregational polity and on "open" or nondoctrinal trusts. Since subscription to no particular creed was required and no central body existed to enforce orthodoxy, the foundations of these chapels were not high enough to escape the tide of rationalism in the eighteenth century.[14] Some of the Dissenters, however, sought the "higher ground" of an enforced orthodoxy. When the waters receded, the battered Presbyterians who remained were, to these orthodox, "dead carcass[es] to which all the obscene birds of bygone heresy—Arian, Socinian, Unitarian— gladly flew."[15] At the end of the eighteenth century Presbyterian in England was nearly equivalent to Unitarian.

The evolution of Unitarianism among the liberal Presbyterians was complex. The two forms of anti-Trinitarianism that flourished in England were Arianism and Socinianism. Arianism taught that Jesus Christ preexisted before the creation of the world, was somewhat divine, but not consubstantial with God the father, and "atoned" for the sins of humankind. Some liberal Presbyterians never went beyond Arianism. But in their Christology other liberal Presbyterians took another step— Socinianism—which denied Jesus Christ's preexistence, divinity, and atonement. However, it did maintain that Jesus was worthy of adoration. The final step for many liberal Presbyterians was Unitarianism and when the greatest of the liberal Presbyterians, Joseph Priestley (1733–1804), declared that Jesus was as "divine as a loaf of bread," that step fell with a thump.[16] The term *Presbyterian* had indeed evolved. It no longer meant presbyterian in communion, but catholic; no longer presbyterian in polity, but congregationalist; no longer presbyterian in theology, but unitarian. It was all very confusing. "We agree in nothing but this," wrote Priestly, "that we equally reject all human authority in matters of religion."[17]

Traces of Arianism, Socinianism, and Unitarianism were found in other Dissenting churches as well as the Church of England, but it was to the "carcass" of liberal Presbyterianism that the "obscene birds" of these heresies flew. As a result, the Unitarian denomination in the nineteenth century could follow almost half of its congregations back to Presbyterian (or mixed Presbyterian-Congregational) meetinghouses. But in addition to these, there were congregations that could be traced back to the liberal ministers and congregations of Independent, General Baptist, Methodist, and Church of England origins.[18]

Some scholars have cogently argued that the theology that bound these groups to the liberal Presbyterians was not a common anti-Trinitarianism, but Arminianism. The latter had been at the beginnings of American Unitarianism and it was the theological focus of the British liberal Presbyterians as well as the groups that came over to their party.[19] They valued highly the Arminian emphasis on personal effort and discipline in achieving one's salvation. This liberal view satisfied the merchants, industrialists, managers, artisans, and intellectuals, who filled their meeting houses.[20] They possessed money, property, and intelligence and they believed that they held in their hands a carte blanche, signed by God for talents unlimited. Orthodox Dissenters might view them as obscene birds of bygone heresy, but they saw themselves as a phoenix rising above the ashes of the burned-out hellfire of Calvinism.

Much of their self-confidence and liberality of thought could be attributed to the education many of them received in the Dissenting academies. Scholars have agreed that these excellent schools stimulated "independent thinking" and a "scepticism of tradition and authority."[21] Liberal Dissenters cultivated close friendships at these academies where minister and layman studied side by side. Friendship and family were extremely important to them because it was crucial to know whom they could trust; at times it had been necessary for their very survival.[22] Along with the orthodox Dissenters they bore the burden of oppressive legislation, but as anti-Trinitarians they bore a heavier share. All Dissenters were barred from public office by the Corporation and Test Acts. They were turned away from the Universities of Oxford, Cambridge, and Durham. They also faced onerous legislation that impeded their very life cycle: the registration of their births, the validity of their marriages, and the disposition of the dead. The Unitarians, however, did not share in the minor relief of the Act of Toleration. On the contrary, along with the Roman Catholics they were excluded. And whereas the Quakers and the Jews were granted some special dispensation, they were handed the Blasphemy Act, which threatened them with imprisonment. Unitarians were not "tolerated" until 1813 when an act gave relief to those "who infringe[d] the doctrine of the Holy Trinity."[23]

It would be incorrect to maintain that, since some of these laws were inconsistently enforced, and others not at all, the Unitarians did not suffer anxiety over them. The last heretics burnt in England and Scotland had been anti-Trinitarians and, although they perished in the seventeenth century, the awful memory of them still lingered.[24] They knew that their fellow subjects looked upon them, in the words of Thomas Belsham (1750–1829), as "monsters," and their worry over the potential harm to their persons and property was valid. They found themselves "outstanding in political and social unpopularity" and it had a strange effect on them.[25] Robert K. Webb has written that

> any beleaguered group develops certain characteristics directly arising from persecution. If the group is composed of intellectuals, the characteristics are likely to be especially striking—and Unitarianism was attractive to a great many intellectuals. Any group excluded from power and prestige is likely in time to make a virtue of exclusion, to find a moral superiority in the socially or politically inferior position they must occupy.[26]

Such an ambitious, intelligent, well-educated minority had but one place to turn for satisfaction, politics, and that meant— given their proclivities and the enormity of the tasks at hand— radical politics.

Before the end of the eighteenth century they were guided in their radical political quest by two of their most brilliant leaders, Richard Price (1723–91) and Joseph Priestley. These two men preached to them a philosophy of personal liberty, religious toleration, and social progress. Price, an Arian in theology but a bearer of the Unitarian label, taught his flock to be the "best citizen[s] of this World." To be such they had to be completely free and the state ought to provide them "equal and perfect liberty." Men and women were not cattle nor slaves, "the sovereignty [of] every country belong[ed] to them." Price was a warm, humble, generous minister who served the Unitarian chapel in Hackney, a chapel with a name unique, and to the orthodox appropriate—Gravel Pit.[27]

Priestley, an energetic Unitarian publicist, has been called "the most important name in the History of English Unitarianism."[28] In addition to theology, he delved into science, languages, and history. His theological views clashed with those of Price. He saw Arianism as a "capital corruption" of Christianity; Jesus was a good man, but as common as bread.[29] Unlike Price, who wanted humanity to have total freedom under God's guidance to work out its salvation and build a moral universe, Priestley saw humanity bound to a Divine Plan that included a prescribed salvation and a moral universe already built. Priestley was committed to the necessarian philosophy of David Hartley, but transformed it into a doctrine of necessity under God's direction. Men and women were free to make decisions only within the context of God's predetermined plan—a prescription for Divine Progress that all had to swallow. Belief in the Plan made one happy because one had faith that he or she was building God's Kingdom here on earth.[30] It was Calvin's doctrine of double predestination cleaved in half. The reprobates and Hell were dispensed with and the saints and the Heavenly Jerusalem were retained. It was all very positive and optimistic. Priestley was as much a millenarian as the simple white-robed yeoman who sat on his thatched roof awaiting the Second Coming of Christ. "For Priestley the necessarian," wrote Anthony Lincoln, "the ultimate millenium on earth had all the certainty of the last term of a scientific series." He lived in "a fever of expectation" and charted current events as harbingers of the "glorious and paradisaical" eschaton to come.[31]

Obviously, to Price, the prophet of "equal and perfect liberty," and to Priestley, the diviner of God's Indubitable Progress, the American and French revolutions were wonderful executions on earth of plans made in Heaven. During the year that the Americans declared their independence, Price published a sermon entitled *Observations on the Nature of Civil Liberty.* It sold 60,000 copies and was condemned by some for spreading the "democratical principles" of the Unitarians. He and Priestley preached pro-American sermons on the public fast days set aside by the British government. They worked for the relief of the American prisoners of war. All the Unitarians appear to have been on the American side: they mourned for the "victims of Lexington," toasted General Washington and his army, and cheered the Americans on to victory. Price became as millennial as Priestley in his perception of the war. He saw it as the "Lord's doing" to accomplish great things. "Perhaps I do not go too far," he announced, "when I say that next to the introduction of Christianity among mankind, the American Revolution may prove the most important step in the progressive course of human improvement."[32]

Price preached as eloquently at the advent of the French Revolution. He delivered one of the most important sermons in British history: "A Discourse on the Love of Country." It was another "democratical" oration that probably caused some of the "Church and King" crowd to lament that Unitarianism was no longer a capital crime. It displeased Edmund Burke immensely and he spread his anger over a year in writing his famous reply, *Reflections on the Revolution in France.* Priestley also praised the revolution from his pulpit and published his remarks for circulation. The tutors and students at the

Unitarian academies of Warrington and Hackney immitated their leaders' enthusiasm. There seems to be no record that any of the known Unitarians of the time opposed the revolution.

Such unanimity on revolution brought them difficulty and unhappiness. Their theology had gained them the name "monsters," their politics now gained them the name "Jacobins." At first there was only ridicule, then violence. In Birmingham, a mob of boys mocked Priestley in the streets, then a mob of men sacked his home. They made a funeral bier of his life's work— books, papers, and experiments—and burned it to the ground. Unitarians were terrorized throughout England. The Unitarian chapels of New Meeting, Old Meeting, and Kingswood, all located in or near Birmingham, were burned to the ground. Several laymen had their homes in the same city put to the torch. Cross Street Chapel in Manchester was attacked and Unitarians in Liverpool were harassed. Unitarian homes and chapels in smaller towns had their grounds vandalized and their windows broken. It appeared that God's Divine Plan, as far as it concerned the Unitarians, had gotten out of hand. Price did not live to see the riots; he died in 1791. Priestley, having lost everything, departed for the United States in 1794, and died in peaceful Pennsylvania ten years later.[33]

The Unitarians, greatly inspired by Price and Priestley, had worked to free the Dissenting interest from the disabilities that they suffered under the law. They had done their part to press members of Parliament to repeal the Test and Corporation Acts. Any progress they had achieved was temporarily dashed by their adulation of revolution. Repeal and reform had to wait for the nineteenth century for success. Still, they continued to fight. So involved were they in the political battles between 1790 and 1832 that they were accused of not being a religious group at all. "The Unitarians," remarked a contemporary journal, "are a political rather than a religious sect—radicals to a man."[34]

Unitarians Despised: "A Sect Every Where Spoken Against"

Entering the nineteenth century, the liberal Presbyterians (or Unitarians, as they were increasingly being called) were in a much weakened state. During the evangelical revival that swept Britain in the eighteenth century they had chosen to maintain their religion of the head rather than to admit a religion of the heart. Whereas the revival directed other denominations into a drive for new recruits, the liberal Presbyterians held back. Many of them still believed in a comprehensive church and that belief dampened missionary fervor. The extent of their support for evangelism was recruitment by example.[35]

At first glance it is difficult to see how the evangelical revival could have affected the Unitarians. Among the denominations of Great Britain they were "free from the least tincture of enthusiasm."[36] Still the evangelical revival of the eighteenth century was an international phenomenon that struck Germany, America, England, and Wales with tremendous force. In England and Wales it was manifested primarily in the work of the Methodists, but Owen Chadwick believes that it affected "every denomination" and Kitson Clark tells us that it "spread into every class and corner of England, from the lowest to the highest." And in view of the romantic attitudes that it engendered throughout England, it is doubtful that the Unitarians could have escaped its influence.[37]

They certainly did not escape contact with the Methodists. It was hate at first sight. The Unitarians lamented John Wesley's political convervatism, especially his opposition to the Americans' revolution and his lack of sympathy for the Unitarian's agitation to repeal their political disabilities.[38] Moreover, they saw that Methodist evangelism and its infection of orthodox Dissent pushed them toward the periphery of the denominational spectrum. They discovered themselves shoved to the end of a theological continuum that had orthodox Dissent (Independents, Baptists, or orthodox Presbyterians) in the middle, and, if diagramed, appeared as follows:

Anglicans—Methodists—orthodox
Dissent—Quakers—Unitarians.

However, in light of church comprehension, they had always seen themselves in a very different continuum, namely:

Anglicans—Unitarians—orthodox
Dissent—Quakers—Methodists.

Aside from a few liberal Anglicans, no other Protestant church conceived the denominational continuum their way. In fact, orthodox Dissent and most Anglicans had been for some time pushing the Unitarians toward the edge of Christianity—many, for example, refused them the name *Christian*. The Methodists merely joined in driving them over the edge, all the time singing lustily:

Stretch out thy arm, thou Triune God!
The Unitarian fiend expel,
And chase his doctrines back to Hell.[39]

Unitarians could have heard this hymn sung in their back-
yards for the Methodists pushed into the very industrial areas
where Unitarians were numerous. Unitarian mill owners had to
contend with Methodists' converting their operatives.
Unitarian employer, Methodist employee, the contrast between
them paralleled the contrast between the two denominations.
Methodists were tightly knit together in conferences, circuits,
societies, and classes.[40] Unitarians were constantly unraveled
and probably the least associational of all Britain's denominations. Methodists were ruled by strong leaders, at first under
the autocratic direction of John Wesley and later under lesser
tyrants such as Jabez Bunting.[41] Unitarians could not unanimously follow Jesus Christ, let alone obey mortal men. Methodist ministers preached personal sanctification and checked the
daily piety and habits of their flocks.[42] Unitarian ministers
preached personal liberty and rarely pried into the private lives
of their people. Methodists (except the Calvinist followers of
George Whitefield) taught an Arminianism of the heart. Unitarians taught an Arminianism of the head.[43] Methodists talked a
lot about death and life in heaven.[44] Unitarians talked a lot
about living and life here on earth. Despite these major con-
trasts, some Methodists went beyond their Arminianism of the
heart and became Unitarians. Few Unitarians went the other
way.[45]

Although painful relations existed between the Unitarians
and Methodists, some cordiality might have been expected between the Unitarians and the Independents and the Baptists.
After all these denominations had had a common origin in the
Great Ejection of 1662. However, the Independents and the
Baptists had themselves grown apart. Under the impulse of the
evangelical movement they both had experienced expansion in
numbers. This expansion had not been obtained without the
loss of old commitments. Their congregational polity had encouraged a free exchange of preaching assignments and lay
cooperation. This fluidity between congregations was now com-
promised by the institution of county unions and associations
on the Methodist model. Cooperation gave way to denominational rivalry.[46] The Independents favored an educated ministry, an outreach "to the great middle section of the country,"

and a moderate Calvinism. The Baptists tended to have ministers who were not well educated, served a lower section of the community, and taught Calvinism less moderate.[47] However, both the Independents and the Baptists had something in common: an ever-increasing animosity toward and suspicion of the Unitarians. The Independents had lost about six congregations to the Unitarians and were perturbed that the Dr. Williams's Library, which they considered to be *their* library, was now in Unitarian hands. The Baptists had seen the Arminian element in their denomination, the General Baptists, drift over to the Unitarians.[48] These losses were absorbed, but not forgiven. By the mid-nineteenth century the Baptists had 2,789 congregations and the Independents, 3,244. The Unitarians struggled along with their 229.[49]

The Unitarians' lack of growth resembled the decline the Quakers were experiencing: during the first half of the nineteenth century they lost thirty percent of their membership. There were other similarities between the two groups. They shared the title "the aristocracy of Dissent."[50] They encompassed similar constituencies; for every Tate and Wedgwood among the Unitarians, there was a Barclay and Lloyd among the Quakers.[51] They shared a common philanthropic outlook.[52] Yet along with these similarities, there were major differences. The Quakers were tightly controlled. Their meetings and members were closely supervised. Marriage to non-Quakers was prohibited.[53] They suffered fewer political disabilities than the Unitarians. They faced less social ostracism. Educated Britons found their eccentricity in dress and their personal demeanor interesting and Anglicans and orthodox Dissent saw their theology as nonthreatening. The Quakers were neither anti-Trinitarians nor Christ-deniers. In fact, they abhorred Unitarianism. They adamantly condemned the Hicksite or Unitarian heresy that had corrupted the American Quakers.[54] The Unitarians could not even find friends among the Friends.

The denominational efforts at union in the early nineteenth century helped to further the isolation of the Unitarians. The Baptists organized the Baptist Union in 1812. They reorganized it with a new constitution in 1832, the same year that the Independents founded the Congregational Union. Both groups built upon the county unions and associations that had been functioning for several decades. They desired national unions in order to secure greater doctrinal agreement, to encourage evangelism at home and abroad, to develop a religious publication program, and to try to match Methodist success in organization and efficiency. They were also reacting to the Anglican criticism of their fragmented condition. With the Methodists and Quakers tightly organized and the BFUA's giving the Unitarians an organizational identity, the denominations of England were clearly differentiated. This became especially true when the few remaining orthodox Presbyterians formed a synod in 1836. Unhappily, jealousy, competition, and often suspicion increased among the denominations. The Unitarians usually found themselves the odd men out.[55]

There had been another reason behind the efforts at union. Owen Chadwick has called it the "centripetal force," that is, the political disabilities experienced by the Dissenters. Orthodox Dissent realized that forceful opposition to these disabilities necessitated a united front. They recognized that the Unitarians had political sagacity and influence and that their participation would facilitate victory. The Unitarians had "the ear of the Ministers," declared the *Eclectic Review*, "they were the only class of Dissent known to the political coteries or clubs." Thus, the orthodox Dissenters cooperated with Unitarian allies to secure the repeal of the Test and Corporation Acts in 1828 and to pass acts on registration and marriage in 1836.[56]

The Unitarians also lent their aid to secure the Reform Bill of 1832 and the Municipal Corporations Act of 1835. Under the latter act, Unitarians were extraordinarily successful in being elected mayors and aldermen. They had long been volunteers on the municipal boards of commissioners that dealt with city lights, sanitation, streets, and sewers. Moreover, they had given generously to build city libraries, museums, and art galleries. Orthodox voters forgave the Unitarians their theology in recognition of their record of public service and philanthropy. Following the Municipal Corporations Act, the first mayor of Manchester, the third of Liverpool, the first five of Leicester, the first two of Bolton, the first of Derby, the second of Leeds, and the third of Birmingham were Unitarians. So many mayors came from the Unitarian Chapel in Bristol that it was called "the Mayor's Nest."[57]

On several controversial political issues the Unitarians clashed with the orthodox Dissenters, or Nonconformists, as they were now usually called. One issue of controversy was the emancipation of Roman Catholics in Britain. On this issue they proclaimed to orthodox Nonconformity: "Be Just and Fear

Nothing"! The Unitarians firmly supported the Catholic Emancipation Act of 1829 and most of them also endorsed the Maynooth (Roman Catholic) College Grant in 1845.[58] Another controversial area was the campaign to abolish the church rates and to disestablish the Church of England. Unitarian support for the former was rare and for the latter almost nonexistent. Most Unitarians continued to revere church comprehensiveness and some thought the national church was still the vehicle for it.[59] Yet another issue of political controversy was the extension and improvement of British schools. Unitarians, along with Roman Catholics, found themselves barred by other Nonconformists and the Anglicans from playing a role in the administration and staffing of the schools. Some exceptions to this exclusion occurred in the communities where Unitarians (or Roman Catholics for that matter) had considerable influence or large numbers.[60]

These controversies were minor skirmishes compared to the major war being fought between the Unitarians and some Nonconformists over the deeds to the Unitarian chapels. With the Trinity Act of 1813 Unitarians obtained legal possession of their chapels, of which nearly 200 had originally been orthodox. The orthodox challenged their possession. Since Unitarianism was illegal before 1813, the orthodox hoped to regain the chapels. They also challenged Unitarian control over a fund established by Lady Hewley in 1704. Although the Unitarians distributed three-fourths of the income from the fund to orthodox "preachers of Christ's holy gospel, or their widows," the orthodox wanted all of it. The Hewley case and a few other suits involving their chapels went against the Unitarians. There was a genuine threat that more suits against them would produce similar results.

The Unitarians comprised only two percent of the Nonconformists, but they demonstrated that their political influence and acumen had not diminished. They lobbied a bill through Parliament in the face of ferocious opposition against them, firstly on the part of Independents and Baptists, who had a stake in the legislation, and secondly on the part of Anglican Evangelicals and Methodists, who did not. The second group was driven solely by their hatred of the Unitarians. An intense debate ensued in Parliament in which one member declared that rather than further Unitarianism, the orthodox men who had founded the disputed chapels would "have had their right hands cut off." However, with the help of Roman Catholics (who owed the Unitarians a favor), moderate Anglicans, and various "sensible persons" the Unitarians secured passage of The Dissenters' Chapels Act in 1844. Thereafter, their chapels were safe in their hands, but their place in British society yet remained one of duress.[61] They remained "a sect every where spoken against."[62] The "outbreaks of bigotry," against them, confided an English Unitarian to an American friend, did "not diminish."[63]

Unitarians Destined: Reform as the Solvent of Heresy's Stain

Ian Sellers, a Unitarian historian, has written about the Unitarians' "spiritual isolation and social magnificence." Constantly, they tried "to break down the unnatural barriers that divided them from their compeers in the Establishment" (and he could have added, "and in Nonconformity"). But their "ever-current failure" had a most beneficial effect. "For it was their minority-consciousness, their sense of unique mission, the fearlessness which sprang from their exalted and unshakeable position in the social hierarchy which enabled them to defy social conventions" and to work for social reform. The Reverend Henry William Crosskey (1826–93) mentioned the "ostracism and neglect" his Unitarianism brought him when he was a young man, and the prejudice endured during his first ministry. "Some years [it] was extraordinary," he confessed, "but I thoroughly enjoyed the combat against it, and it put me in high spirits." And if persecution strengthened and hardened Unitarians as Spartan individuals against orthodox dogma and political and social injustice, it united them as comrades in arms. "There was a strong bond of union," declared Sir John Bowring (1792–1872), the dedicated Unitarian layman and member of Parliament, "between those [of us] who professed an unpopular and heterodox faith."[64]

However, the prejudice that made Unitarians efficient at self-defense and aggressive against evil lessened somewhat when their theological opponents saw their reforming zeal or joined them in the cause at hand. Persons, for example, who were normally repelled from cooperating with one "whom they regarded as outside the pale of Christianity" were drawn to the labors of the social reformer and antislavery advocate, Mary Carpenter (1807–77). Her brother, the Reverend Russell Lant

Carpenter (1816–92), a friend of Frederick Douglass, re-marked that his colleagues in reform never shunned him be-cause he belonged to an "unpopular church." However, their father, Lant Carpenter (1780–1840), actually felt compelled to hold back from some reforms to which his "heart was devoted," lest his "stain of heresy be baneful, if not destructive, to the success of them."[65]

Possibly some Unitarians participated in reform efforts in order to gain social acceptance. Theophilus Lindsey (1723–1808), the founder of the first Unitarian chapel in London, believed that Unitarians who fought against the slave trade would "soften prejudices" against them even with the "very orthodox men" such as abolitionist Granville Sharp, who de-nied them access to heaven if they failed to change their senti-ments before they died. Therefore, some Unitrians might have seen reform as a solvent of heresy's stain. Clearly, the optimism in their approach to reform was unyielding. "In the Religion of the Unitarians," wrote Crosskey, the world was "regarded as a possible Kingdom of Heaven." And to the Unitarians, all things were possible. They were destined for reform. Had not Priest-ley preached to them that God marched unwaveringly toward social and moral perfection in this world, and that they, des-tined to be *"workers together with God,"* marched in His van-guard?[66]

Recently, Robert Kiefer Webb canonized Priestley as the pa-tron saint behind all British Unitarian reform interest in the nineteenth century.[67] However, Webb failed to mention the other schools of thought among the British Unitarians. Harry Lismer Short wrote about two of the schools, both of which went beyond the views of Priestley. One was an "anti-supernatural school, hostile to miracles and to the uniqueness of Christianity." It was radically liberal and worshiped man more than God. Its representatives usually drifted away, or were ejected from Unitarianism. Frequently their major contri-bution to reform followed their departure. The other was an "esthetic" school that reveled in an intuitive, mystical, almost pantheistic Christianity. It built Gothic churches, wrote inspira-tional hymns, and treasured altars, liturgies, and vestments. This was the school of James Martineau (1805–1900) and its interest in reform was anemic. It maintained, explained Short, "an aristocratic and paternal attitude to social questions." Unitarian reformers, particularly the abolitionists among them, found its feeble interest in reform "distressing."[68]

There was another school of the Unitarians that contributed greatly to the Unitarian ranks of reformers. One usually has to read non-Unitarian historians to discover it as well as the name its members bore—"the evangelical Unitarians." This Unitarian school, Owen Chadwick tells us, was represented by "Bible Protestants, orthodox and rigid, accepting miracles and plenary inspiration, fervent in religious life, distinguished from evangelical dissenters only by the conviction that the Trinity was not a doctrine of scripture." In the words of William R. Ward they possessed a "naturalised evangelicalism."[69] Presumably he means that an evangelicalism became the accustomed view of certain Unitarians. He names none. But this present study will tell the story of several of them. They were for the most part Arians, the theological relatives of Richard Price. They were warm, pastoral, and mission-minded. They were lovers of Jesus Christ and committed to reform. Reform gave the evangelical Unitarians a theatre of operations. They were not preoccupied, as were many orthodox evangelicals, with personal piety and sanctification. They were quite smug about their own personal achievement. Entirely free of the burden of morbid introspection, they could turn their attention outward and toward social improvement and political justice. Evangelicalism has been cited as the primary impetus for reform among the Quakers.[70] No one has said that about the Unitarians. This lack can be partially attributed to the Unitarian denomination's own design. To a liberal denomination that prided itself on a dispassionate and rational theology, an evangelical Unitarian was a contradiction, an aberration, an embarrassment. Lant Carpenter's persistent talk of his "Lord Jesus Christ," for example, fired false rumors that he was converting to the orthodox.[71] Unitarians loathed the term *evangelical Unitarian* and were prone to refer to such a person as one whose theology "leaned to the conservative side."[72]

Thus, while not denying that Priestley's influence on Unitarian reform activity was great, one could argue that the evangelical Unitarians' was just as great. Each influence probably reinforced the other. For all Unitarians clearly shared several common prespectives that promoted reform activity. The first was their dedication to the "individuality of the individual."[73] This emphasis on individuality freed a Unitarian reformer to respond to reforms at any time and in any way he or she saw fit. It was not necessary to wait upon their whole denomination for approval or action. Admittedly, however, it did make united action by the denomination difficult to obtain. Second, they all believed in the efficacy and morality of political action. One of their ministers who took an active interest in political affairs declared that he did "not lose [his] right of citizenship when [he] became a minister of the Gospel." They fought in the political arena without qualms and they fought very well.[74] Third, they saw themselves as citizens of the world. Quakers believed that the "real Christian [was] a citizen of the world." Unitarians concurred. Crosskey never forgot that he was "a citizen of England and the world." Unitarians worshiped, declared another Unitarian minister, "not the God of Britain merely, but the God of the whole earth."[75] Last, all Unitarians made universal brotherhood a cardinal tenet of their theological faith and doctrine. They expressed concern, Priestley declared, not only for their own countrymen or for Europeans, but for "the distressed inhabitants of *Asia, Africa,* [and] *America.*" Lant Carpenter, in a commemorative sermon on the coronation of Queen Victoria, told his congregation that the principles of international justice were founded on the "common relation of all to the Universal Parent," who willed "mutual equity" among the human family, and on the teachings of Jesus, who taught "love to all, without distinction of race, or clime, or colour." Unitarian associations in passing antislavery resolutions invariably reaffirmed their denomination's belief in the "Universal Father [who had] made of one blood all nations."[76]

Unitarians, therefore, had the theological and philosophical direction to guide them into reform movements. Henry Solly (1815–1903) could have spoken for his denomination when he said that he had "an overpowering desire to right all the wrongs of the universe." No wrongs escaped their attention. They supported the rights of women and worked to obtain education and the ballot for women. They were one of the first groups in Britain to admit women to the ministry.[77] They enlisted in the cause of temperance, many going so far as to sign the pledge of total abstinence.[78] They believed that drunkenness enslaved the minds and souls of men and women. Such enslavement contradicted their theology of personal freedom and self-discipline. The bondage of drunkenness, Russell Lant Carpenter preached, was more disgraceful than the bondage of Negro slavery. Negro slavery was involuntary, liquor slavery was voluntary. Moreover, liquor slavery enslaved the soul. In the temperance movement Unitarians worked in harmony with

Roman Catholic, Anglican, and Primitive Methodist coworkers. Solly wrote that the same orthodox who refused to patronize a "Socinian grocer" or "Unitarian jeweller," and who disdained him as a "theological leper," "cordially invit[ed] and accept[ed his] aid" in the cause of temperance.[79] As far as the cause of peace was concerned, the Unitarians left the vanguard to the Quakers. They opposed aggressive war, but "abjured" the philosophy of nonresistance.[80]

In the area of economic reform the Unitarians were free traders. They perceived free trade as consistent with free religion and free thought.[81] Also the great number of merchants and manufacturers among them confessed free trade as dogma. The Unitarians, Raymond Holt has written, discerned the abolition of the Corn Laws as "a religious crusade." And in this crusade their orthodox adversaries became comrades in arms. Solly and his fellow Unitarian ministers were welcomed at a Manchester rally against the Corn Laws attended by "700 ministers . . . of all denominations." Solly was even given the opportunity to address the gathering.[82]

Like so many other denominations in Britain, whether Anglican, Independent, or Quaker, the Unitarians believed that commerce and industry operated under the gospel of Divine Economic Law. They were seriously divided on movements that were beneficial to what James Martineau called the "white slaves" of England: factory legislation and trade unions.[83] In this area they followed their own philosopher of laissez-faire economics—Joseph Priestley. Economically, he saw a bright future for England, if only the government held aloof and permitted his necessarian doctrine to proceed unimpeded. If it did so "progress" would be "unlimited."[84] Unitarians accepted the concepts of the notorious wage-fund theory, the Malthusian view on population, and the free marketplace. They professed that the relationship between employer and employee, the dynamics of labor and production, and the differential between costs and profits followed natural laws impervious to alteration. They observed without censure manufacturers who impressed children from poorhouses and orphanages, operated machinery without safety devices, stretched work days beyond the light of day, and paid a pittance for the life labor of men, women, and children.[85] Many of these manufacturers were dedicated Unitarian laymen. Raymond Holt in his book *The Unitarian Contribution to Social Progress in England* has tried to be just in judging these men. He explained how government inspectors at the time determined the conditions in factories owned by Unitarians to be of the "better type." Yet even the best type was not too good and praiseworthy conditions might have been affected by the desire to contain strikes, rather than to extend benevolence.[86]

All discussions of Unitarian manufacturers invariably lead to a consideration of Josiah Wedgwood (1730–95). David Brion Davis has compared factory discipline of the operatives in Wedgwood's potteries to plantation discipline of slaves in the West Indies. He concluded that Wedgwood was an "autocratic master." Others have judged Wedgwood a "benevolent despot": a 'good' employer in the sense that a 'good' modern employer in South Africa might look after 'his boys.'"[87] In his philosophy of economics Wedgwood assuredly profited from his friendship with Joseph Priestley. He was one of the few courageous individuals who stood by the Unitarian minister after the Birmingham riots.[88]

Wedgwood's economic ideas were formed in the eighteenth century and hammered out in the heat of the Industrial Revolution. In evaluating Unitarian manufacturers, Wedgwood's autocratic rule and wage slavery ought to be measured against the attitudes and conduct of a nineteenth-century Unitarian industrialist, John Fielden (1784–1900). As a successful manufacturer of woolen goods and a member of Parliament, Fielden supported a variety of measures to improve the lot of the working classes in England. He could be numbered among the "evangelical Unitarians," having been converted in 1818 by one of the rare Unitarian missionaries who circulated among England's working people. Fielden had been a Quaker, an Anglican, and a Methodist, before he discovered from a Unitarian missionary the truth regarding "the mind of Christ." He served his new faith by teaching a Bible class and becoming the superintendent of his chapel's Sunday school. Fielden knew personally the effect of ten hours of labor on a child of ten years, for at that age his father had sent him to work in the family's woolen mill. In 1836, he published "The Curse of the Factory System." He lobbied in Parliament for a limitation on factory hours and encouraged the formation of trade unions, even among his own workers.[89] In his reform efforts, Fielden was opposed by the Quakers, who were always the "inveterate opponents" of the limitation of factory hours, and by some of his fellow Unitarians.[90] He was aided by the Baptists, Independents, Catholics, Evangelical Anglicans, and Unitarians such as John Relly

Beard, Henry Solly, and William Crosskey, who attempted to reach out to workingmen and bring them into their congregations.[91]

Most Unitarian ministers and congregations who felt a sense of duty to working men and women, favored separate domestic missions for them. They established these in Birmingham, Bristol, Leeds, Liverpool, London, and Manchester. Their objectives were to improve the prospects of the poor through self-help; to educate their children and "to shelter them from corrupting agencies." They sought not to add more Unitarians to their rolls, but to increase the number of respectable citizens in their community. William R. Ward has said that the missions intended to place "the poor on the same escalator as the rich."[92] If the poor applied themselves, they might someday share a pew with a manufacturer or a merchant. Those Unitarian congregations that could not finance a domestic mission assisted their local poor in other ways. They distributed no gifts. The Bridgwater Chapel, for example, provided "the poor with useful articles *at a reduced price*" and lent them blankets in the fall to be returned in the spring.[93]

One frequent accusation against Unitarian reformers by the poor and working classes of England was the apparent inconsistency of fighting to end plantation slavery abroad, while permitting and supporting wage slavery at home. It was also directed against the Quakers, who were asked to explain, for example, why Quakers in Bradford in 1833 gave £1,000 to the antislavery movement, but only £3 to the factory movement.[94] Unitarians let the Quakers defend themselves, but based their own defense on the testimony of Priestley. He had argued in his sermon against the slave trade that in Christian theology all men and women were "equally the subjects of God's moral government here, and [the] heirs of immortality hereafter." This principle, he explained, did not remove the inequalities among persons in society, yet it ought to promote "equal, at least sufficient, advantages" for each person to improve his or her nature and to prepare for immortality. In this respect rich and poor, master and servant, employer and employee could be equal. But not master and slave. The slave was reduced to a "mere brute" and had no opportunity to benefit from the power of reason or Christianity.[95] In this neglect lay the difference between plantation slavery and "wage slavery"—the capacity for free thought and free action. The wage slave possessed it, the plantation slave did not. The latter deserved one's attention, the former did not. The dichotomy was attractive and probably eased the consciences of some Unitarians. It was a naïve assessment, however, of the degree of freedom factory operatives were supposed to have had under the masters of industry.

As a denomination, the Unitarians were severely divided in their views on reform efforts for England's working classes. In the area of antislavery reform they were also not united as a body in the kinds of measures, or the amount of effort or time, they ought to employ. But they were united in the belief that they ought to be antislavery. In this reform the work of several Unitarian individuals was impressive. Unfortunately, it is not well known. It may have been the numerical insignificance of Unitarianism in Great Britain or its relative lack of organizational or institutional expression that caused historians of past generations to ignore the Unitarian contribution to the antislavery movement.[96] However, given the influential position of the Unitarians in the nineteenth century, size and denominational precariousness do not account for their being lightly treated. The probable reason is that, like women's history and black history, Unitarian history was the history of a subjected, oppressed, and despised minority that frequently was not properly or sympathetically recorded. Raymond Holt has explained that many distinguished Unitarians of the past were not recognized as such because of the intense prejudice against their faith. Some nineteenth-century biographers, he said, "often felt that to have been a Unitarian was a stain on the reputation of the subject of their biography and in characteristic fashion strove to conceal this stain. So what began as persecution and persisted as prejudice now survive[d] as ignorance."[97]

The perception of a person such as George Armstrong (1792–1857), a Garrisonian abolitionist and a Unitarian minister, that he and his colleagues were Britain's "theological negroes,"[98] could help partially to explain why he and so many other Unitarian individuals were so earnest in their attack on slavery. They themselves had experienced prejudice and ostracism. They had felt slavery's shackles in the civil disabilities that law and social practice imposed upon them. They could not help but be aware that there were social benefits in participating in antislavery reform. An American Unitarian minister, George Bradburn (1806–80), who visited Great Britain in 1840, remarked that there was "scarce anything . . . more likely in England to mar a . . . man's reputation than to be thought opposed or indifferent to the cause of abolition."[99] The Unitarians could enhance their reputation by being supportive of or committed to the cause.

That was not the case, however, if one lived in Liverpool. When William Roscoe (1753–1831), the "greatest of Liverpool's citizens," advocated the abolition of the slave trade, the education of slaves, and gradual emancipation, he gained few friends and a legion of enemies. When Roscoe was baptized at the Unitarian Chapel of Benn's Garden, in 1753, there were very likely a dozen slave traders connected with the congregation. By 1798, only one remained, a reduction probably the result of Roscoe's work. His first published protest against the slave trade, in 1771, was a poem called *Mount Pleasant*, but his most eloquent plea for abolition was his *Wrongs of Africa*, published in 1787. He wrote for the "friendless and injured negroes," in an attempt to draw public attention to the trade. He offered the profits from the poem's sale to the newly founded London Society for the Abolition of the Slave Trade. In so doing, he pleased the Evangelical Anglican and abolitionist Thomas Clarkson, who was encouraged that help could actually come from Liverpool. The city controlled five-eighths of the English slave trade and to oppose her commerce in men and women was "tantamount to treason."[100]

Roscoe followed with *A General View of the African Slave Trade, Demonstrating Its Injustice and Impolicy: with Hints toward a Bill for Its Abolition,* a pamphlet that caused violent anger among the Liverpool slave traders. This was succeeded by still other pamphlets, and when he represented Liverpool in Parliament, he helped to pass the Abolition Bill on 25 March 1807. He faced a riot when he returned home, but escaped unharmed. His work, combined with the fact that nearly half of the members of the Liverpool Anti-Slavery Society were Unitarians, caused many Liverpool citizens to look upon *Unitarian* and *abolitionist* as synonyms. This was an exaggeration, of course, for it was only their cooperation with Evangelical Anglicans and Quakers in Liverpool that secured success. As a group, they deserved to be included, declared Thomas Clarkson, "among the forerunners and coadjutors in [the] great cause."[101]

Some other Unitarians who assisted the antislavery movement at this time were Price, Priestley, Wedgwood, and William Smith, M.P. (1756–1835). Price preached that the slave trade was "shocking to humanity, cruel, wicked, and diabolical." Priestley's forty-page pamphlet, *A Sermon on the Subject of the*

Slave Trade, in 1788, sold well, but how widely is not known.[102] Josiah Wedgwood was an enthusiastic member of the governing committee of the Society for the Suppression of the Slave Trade. His famous cameo, "Am I Not a Man and a Brother?," became the shield of the whole antislavery movement not only in Britain, but in America as well. William Smith became a Unitarian sometime before 1791, but remained close to his former Evangelical friends. He had a "passion for the cause" and Thomas Clarkson cited him as the first person outside their original Abolition Committee to join them in combatting the slave trade. His biographer has written that his opposition to the trade "came directly from his religious conviction" that God had made of "one blood all [the] nations of men." The Anglican Evangelicals tolerated Smith's religious views in part because he was a most useful bridge between them and the "more liberal and radical supporters of Abolition." His friendship with William Wilberforce grew warmer as the years passed and he worked with him for the cause in Parliament.[103]

The abolition of the slave trade having been achieved in 1807, antislavery reformers worked to have any attempt to continue trade in slaves declared at first a felony, then an act of piracy. The movement to achieve the abolition of slavery in Britain's colonies began in 1823. In January of that year William Smith, together with William Allen, Thomas Fowell Buxton, and Zachary Macaulay, laid the basis for the Anti-Slavery Society. Their Anti-Slavery Committee, which lasted until 1839, when the British and Foreign Anti-Slavery Society was established, continued the metropolitan leadership of the British antislavery movement. The predecessors of their society had been the London Society for the Abolition of the Slave Trade (1787–1807) and the African Institution (begun in 1807 and operating, concurrently for a time with the Anti-Slavery Society, until 1827). All these organizations were usually directed by laymen, some of whom were members of Parliament, and all of whom were invariably Quakers or members of the Dissenting denominations. Auxiliary organizations, also dominated by the Quakers, operated in the provinces collecting funds for the national organization and educating their localities in antislavery matters. Josiah Wedgwood served on the Committee of the Anti-Slavery Society, and William Roscoe led its auxiliary in Liverpool. It printed and distributed antislavery propaganda and lobbied for emancipation. Reviewing one of its pamphlets, the *Edinburgh Review* was pleased with its work in Liverpool, a city famous for the "enormities of the slave traffick," which was now trying "to make amends for its horrid fruits." The "venerable" William Roscoe, said the *Review*, headed the society there "to adopt all lawful and peaceful measures" for slavery's "ultimate abolition," and everyone ought to pray for his success.[104]

Roscoe had not been acknowledged as a prophet by his own city, but now he had been by his nation. It proved that the Unitarians' antislavery work did have a salutary effect on their reputation. Thomas Clarkson wrote affectionately of their antislavery labor and Wilberforce counted one of their company, William Smith, as an intimate friend. Wilberforce had written against the theology of the Unitarians and Lant Carpenter thought him "greatly prejudiced against their views of Gospel faith." But Carpenter still believed that he and Wilberforce held common views as "to Gospel practice."[105] The Unitarians' gospel practice or belief in reform provided them with the opportunity to work with other denominations in the antislavery cause: Evangelical Anglicans, Quakers, Methodists, Baptists, and Independents. Priestley had been "particularly happy" that in preaching against slavery, he could "join heartily with every denomination of Christians in the country, the Catholic, the members of the Establishment, and Dissenters of all denominations."[106] Antislavery reform was a rather special solvent to heresy's stain.

Notes

1. Daniel Walker Howe, *The Unitarian Conscience: Harvard Moral Philosophy, 1805–1861* (Cambridge, Mass.: Harvard University Press, 1970), p. 11.

2. James Martineau to Charles Wicksteed, n.p., 23 April 1857, James Drummond, *The Life and Letters of James Martineau, LL.D., S.T.D., Etc.*, vol. 1 (New York: Dodd, Mead & Co., 1902), p. 320; Douglas C. Stange, "Abolition as Treason: The Unitarian Elite Defends Law, Order, and the Union," *Harvard Library Bulletin* (April 1980): 152–63; Douglas C. Stange, *Patterns of Antislavery among American Unitarians, 1831–1860* (Rutherford, N.J.: Fairleigh Dickinson University Press, 1977), pp. 183–186.

3. Stange, *Patterns of Antislavery*, pp. 171–227.

4. Conrad Wright, *The Beginnings of Unitarianism in America* (Boston: Starr King Press, 1955), pp. 1–8; Earl Morse Wilbur, *A History of Unitarianism in Transylvania, England, and America* (Boston: Beacon Press, 1969 [1st edition, 1945]), p. 380.

5. Wilbur, *A History of Unitarianism*, pp. 433, 435–36. See p. 436 for the quotation by Stowe.

6. Ibid., p. 464.

7. Ibid., pp. 435–36, 441, 455.

8. Raymond V. Holt, *The Unitarian Contribution to Social Progress in England*, 2nd revised ed. (London: Lindsey Press), pp. 30–31, 36, 65–66.

9. William Reginald Ward, *Religion and Society in England, 1790–1850* (New York: Schocken Books, [1973]), p. 65.

10. Owen Chadwick, *The Victorian Church*, Part 1 (New York: Oxford University Press, 1966), p. 396; John Relly Beard, *Unitarianism Exhibited in Its Actual Condition; Consisting of Essays by Several Unitarian Ministers and Others; Illustrative of the Rise, Progress, and Principles of Christian Anti-Trinitarianism in Different Parts of the World* (London: Simpkin, Marshall & Co., 1846), pp. 174–76, 209, 330–37.

11. Harry Lismer Short, *The Founding of the British and Foreign Unitarian Association*, Supplement to *Transactions of the Unitarian Historical Society* 16 (October 1975): 14, 21.

12. John D. Gay, *The Geography of Religion in England* (London: Gerald Duckworth & Co., 1971), pp. 181–182.

13. Robert Kiefer Webb, *Harriet Martineau: A Radical Victorian* (New York: Columbia University Press, 1960), p. 46.

14. Francis E. Mineka, *The Dissidence of Dissent: The Monthly Repository, 1806–1838* (Chapel Hill, N.C.: University of North Carolina Press, 1944), pp. 11–12; Michael R. Watts, *The Dissenters* (Oxford: Clarendon Press, 1981), p. 219; Henry Gow, *The Unitarians* (London: Methuen & Co., 1928), pp. 43–46.

15. Anthony Lincoln, *Some Political and Social Ideas of English Dissent 1763–1800* (New York: Octagon Books, 1971 [1st edition, 1938]), p. 30.

16. Mineka, *Dissidence of Dissent*, pp. 8, 14–15; Watts, *The Dissenters*, p. 371; Wilbur, *A History of Unitarianism*, pp. 318–19; Gow, *The Unitarians*, pp. 18–19; Joseph Priestley, "An Appeal to the Serious and Candid Professors of Christianity (1770)," *The Theological and Miscellaneous Works of Joseph Priestley, LL.D., F.R.S., etc. with Notes*, vol. 2, John Towill Rutt, ed. (London: George Smallfield, 1806–[32?]), p. 414.

17. Priestly quoted by Lincoln, *Some Political and Social Ideas*, p. 19.

18. Jeremy Goring, "Introduction," *English Presbyterianism: From Elizabethan Puritanism to Modern Unitarianism*, [Jeremy Goring and Roger Thomas, eds.] (London: George Allen & Unwin, Ltd., 1968), p. 19.

19. Ibid., p. 22.

20. Holt, *The Unitarian Contribution*, p. 308.

21. Watts, *The Dissenters*, p. 465; Holt, *The Unitarian Contribution*, p. 309; Horton Davies, *The English Free Churches*, 2nd ed. (London: Oxford University Press, 1963), p. 103.

22. Holt, *The Unitarian Contribution*, p. 331; Erik Routley, *English Religious Dissent* (Cambridge: Cambridge University Press, 1960), p. 145.

23. G. I. T. Machin, *Politics and the Churches in Great Britain 1832 to 1868* (Oxford: Clarendon Press, 1977), pp. 2–3; Mineka, *Dissidence of Dissent*, pp. 9, 12–13; Chadwick, *The Victorian Church*, pp. 80–81; Gow, *The Unitarians*, p. 98.

24. Holt, *Unitarian Contribution*, pp. 16, 178; Wilbur, *History of Unitarianism*, p. 178; Lincoln, *Some Political and Social Ideas*, pp. 240–41.

25. Lincoln, *Some Political and Social Ideas*, pp. 29, 61.

26. Webb, *Harriet Martineau*, p. 66.

27. Lincoln, *Some Social and Political Ideas*, pp. 101, 126, 148; Watts, *The Dissenters*, pp. 471, 474.

28. Gow, *The Unitarians*, p. 82.

29. See note 18, above.

30. Lincoln, *Some Social and Political Ideas*, pp. 151–52, 155–57.

31. Lincoln, *Some Social and Political Ideas*, pp. 172, 173. Cf. also 152–53.

32. Watts, *The Dissenters*, pp. 479–80; Lincoln, *Some Social and Political Ideas*, pp. 24–

25, 44, 48, 49, 133; Harry Lismer Short, "Presbyterians under a New Name," in *English Presbyterianism*, p. 226; Richard Price, "Observations on the Importance of the American Revolution, and the Means of Making It a Benefit to the World," *Richard Price and the Ethical Foundations of the American Revolution*, Bernard Peach, ed. (Durham, N.C.: Duke University Press, 1979), pp. 182, 183.

33. Holt, *Unitarian Contribution*, pp. 105–14; Watts, *The Dissenters*, pp. 486–87; Ward, *Religion and Society*, pp. 23–24.

34. *The Christian Remembrancer* quoted by Mineka, *Dissidence of Dissent*, p. 22.

35. Goring, *English Presbyterianism*, p. 27.

36. Lincoln, *Some Social and Political Ideas*, p. 21.

37. Watts, *The Dissenters*, p. 394; Chadwick, *Victorian Church*, p. 5; G. S. R. Kitson Clark, "The Romantic Element—1830 to 1850," *Studies in Social History: A Tribute to G. M. Trevelyan*, John Harold Plumb, ed. (Freeport, N.Y.: Books for the Libraries Press, 1969 [1st edition, 1955]), p. 231; Routley, *English Religious Dissent*, pp. 149, 162, 168; Ward, *Religion and Society*, p. 67.

38. Watts, *The Dissenters*, pp. 480–81; Machin, *Politics and the Churches*, pp. 8, 14; Mineka, *Dissidence of Dissent*, p. 142.

39. John Briggs and Ian Sellers, eds., *Victorian Nonconformity* (New York: St. Martin's Press, 1974), p. 3; on the Unitarian-Anglican Broad Church connection, see Dennis G. Wigmore-Beddoes, *Yesterday's Radicals: A Study of the Affinity between Unitarianism and Broad Church Anglicanism in the Nineteenth Century* (Cambridge: James Clarke & Co., 1971); verse from hymn 431 of the]Methodist] *Large Hymn Book* quoted by Mineka, *Dissidence of Dissent*, p. 19.

40. David M. Thompson, ed., *Nonconformity in the Nineteenth Century* (London: Routledge & Kegan Paul, 1972), 20; Davies, *English Free Churches*, p. 139.

41. Watts, *The Dissenters*, pp. 443–45; Ward, *Religion and Society*, p. 5; Chadwick, *Victorian Church*, p. 374.

42. Watts, *The Dissenters*, p. 404; Ward, *Religion and Society*, p. 5.

43. Watt, *The Dissenters*, pp. 439–40.

44. Ibid., pp. 413, 415.

45. The interaction between the Methodists and the Unitarians has been charted by Herbert McLachlan. See his *The Methodist Unitarian Movement* (Manchester: The University Press, 1919).

46. Ward, *Religion and Society*, pp. 70–72.

47. Chadwick, *Victorian Church*, pp. 400–401, 412–13; K. S. Inglis, *Churches and the Working Classes in Victorian England* (London: Routledge & Kegan Paul, 1963), pp. 14, 15.

48. Watts, *The Dissenters*, pp. 464, 469.

49. Thompson, *Noncomformity*, pp. 148, 150.

50. Ward, *Religion and Society*, pp. 63, 67, 69; Alan D. Gilbert, *Religion and Society in Industrial England: Church, Chapel and Social Change, 1740–1914* (London: Longman, 1976); p. 41; Thompson, *Nonconformity*, p. 13.

51. Chadwick, *Victorian Church*, p. 424; Davies, *English Free Churches*, p. 110.

52. Chadwick, *Victorian Church*, p. 424; Elizabeth Isichei, *Victorian Quakers* (Oxford: Oxford University Press, 1970), pp. 212–57.

53. Watts, *The Dissenters*, pp. 300–302.

54. Chadwick, *Victorian Church*, p. 423; Isichei, *Victorian Quakers*, pp. 280–82; Watts, *The Dissenters*, p. 462; Davies, *English Free Churches*, p. 109; Ward, *Religion and Society*, pp. 66–68.

55. Chadwick, *Victorian Church*, pp. 399, 401; Briggs and Sellers, *Victorian Nonconformity*, pp. 29, 143; Watts, *The Dissenters*, pp. 297–98.

56. Chadwick, *Victorian Church*, p. 144; Briggs and Sellers, *Victorian Nonconformity*,

pp. 120–21; Ward, *Religion and Society*, p. 21; *Eclectic Review* quoted by Machin, *Politics and the Churches*, p. 57.

57. Machin, *Politics and the Churches*, pp. 54–55; G. Kitson Clark, *The Making of Victorian England* (Cambridge, Mass.: Harvard University Press, 1962), p. 101; Holt, *Unitarian Contribution*, pp. 23, 214–22, 270–74.

58. Machin, *Politics and the Churches*, p. 172; Ward, *Religion and Society*, pp. 115, 121; Russell Lant Carpenter, ed., *Memoirs of the Life of the Rev. Lant Carpenter, LL.D., with Selections from His Correspondence*, (Bristol: Philp and Evans, 1842), p. 322.

59. Machin, *Politics and the Churches*, pp. 161–63, 306–7; Ward, *Religion and Society*, pp. 133, 134; Chadwick, *Victorian Church*, pp. 155–56; Holt, *Unitarian Contribution*, p. 347.

60. Ward, *Religion and Society*, p. 42; Holt, *Unitarian Contribution*, pp. 262, 328.

61. Ward, *Religion and Society*, pp. 203–4; Chadwick, *Victorian Church*, pp. 392–95; Machin, *Politics and the Churches*, pp. 165–66.

62. Joseph Priestley, "The Use of Christianity, especially in difficult Times. A Sermon, delivered at the Gravel-Pit Meeting, in Hackney, March 30, 1794, Being the Author's Farewell Discourse to his Congregation (1794)," *Works*, 15: 556.

63. Mary Carpenter to the Rev. A. A. Livermore, 27 July 1846, J. Estlin Carpenter, *The Life and Work of Mary Carpenter*, 2nd ed. (London: Macmillan & Co., 1881), p. 75.

64. Ian Sellers, "Social and Political Ideas of Representative English Unitarians, 1795–1850," B. Litt. thesis (Keble College, Oxford, n.d.), p. 185; Richard Acland Armstrong, *Henry William Crosskey, LL.D., F.G.S., His Life and Work* (Birmingham: Cornish Brothers, 1895), p. 20; John Bowring, *Autobiographical Recollection of Sir John Bowring*, with a Brief Memoir by Lewin B. Bowring (London: Henry S. King & Co., 1877), pp. 3, 387.

65. William B. Carpenter, *Sketch of the Life and Work of Mary Carpenter of Bristol* (Bristol: Arrowsmith, 1877), p. 21; R. L. Carpenter, *Memoirs*, p. 461. Russell Lant Carpenter wrote that the "influence of the profession of an unpopular faith [was] to strengthen the character. [His father's] wish '*to be*, not to appear, the best' was fostered, by the misapprehensions which surrounded him, and by the reproaches that were cast on him as a denier of that Saviour whom he loved and obeyed." See ibid., p. 460.

66. Herbert McLachlan, *Letters of Theophilus Lindsey* (Manchester: The University Press, 1920), pp. 92–93; Armstrong, *Henry William Crosskey*, p. 226; Joseph Priestley, "A Sermon, on the Subject of the Slave Trade; Delivered to a Society of Protestant Dissenters, at New Meeting, in Birmingham (1788)," *Works*, 15: 387.

67. Webb, *Harriet Martineau*, p. 88.

68. Short, "Presbyterians," pp. 256–59, 261; Holt, *Unitarian Contribution*, p. 343.

69. Chadwick, *Victorian Church*, pp. 396, 397; Ward, *Religion and Society*, p. 67.

70. Watts, *The Dissenters*, p. 462–63; Isichei, *Victorian Quakers*, pp. 12–13, 214.

71. Short, *Founding of the BFUA*, p. 19.

72. See Robert Henderson, "Memoir of the Late Rev. George Armstrong, of Bristol," *Christian Reformer* 14 (August 1858): 470, and Herbert McLachlan, *Records of a Family 1800–1933: Pioneers in Education, Social Service and Liberal Religion* (Manchester: Manchester University Press, 1935), p. 16.

73. Henry Solly, *"These Eighty Years" or, the Story of an Unfinished Life*, vol. 1 (London: Simpkin, Marshall & Co., 1893), p. 279.

74. Holt, *Unitarian Contribution*, pp. 144–45; Gow, *The Unitarians*, pp. 96–97; William McMillan, *A Profile in Courage, Henry Montgomery (1788–1865)* (Newry: E. Hodgett, Ltd., 1966), p. 19.

75. Isichei, *Victorian Quakers*, p. 245; Armstrong, *Henry William Crosskey*, p. 127; Holt, *Unitarian Contribution*, p. 125.

76. Priestley, "Sermon on the Slave Trade," *Works*, 15: 368; Lant Carpenter, *A Dis-*

course on Christian Patriotism: Delivered to the Society of Protestant Dissenters in Hanover Square, Newcastle-Upon-Tyne, on the Sunday after the Coronation of Her Majesty; . . . (London: Longman, Orme, Brown, Green, and Longmans, 1838), p. 25; "Resolutions of the Newcastle and North of England Unitarian Christian Tract and Missionary Society" [title supplied], *Christian Register*, 11 September 1847, p. 146.

77. Kathleen Woodroofe, "The Irascible Reverend Henry Solly and His Contribution to Working Men's Clubs, Charity Organization, and 'Industrial Villages' in Victorian England," *Social Science Review* 40 (March 1975):17; Mineka, *Dissidence of Dissent*, p. 158; Holt, *Unitarian Contribution*, pp. 19, 147; Armstrong, *Henry William Crosskey*, p. 127.

78. Herbert McLachlan, *The Unitarian Movement in the Religious Life of England* (London: George Allen & Unwin, Ltd., 1934), p. 207; Russell Lant Carpenter, ed., *Memoirs of the Life and Work of Philip Pearsall Carpenter, B.A., London, Ph.D., New York, Chiefly Derived from His Letters*, 2nd ed. (London: C. Kegan Paul & Co., 1880), pp. 62, 64, 98; Armstrong, *Henry William Crosskey*, pp. 52–53.

79. Russell Lant Carpenter, *Personal and Social Christianity: Sermons and Addresses . . .*, J. Estlin Carpenter, ed., With a short memoir by Francis E. Cooke (London: Kegan Paul, Trench, Truebner & Co., 1893), p. 240; Estlin Carpenter, *Life and Work of Mary Carpenter*, p. 72; Solly, "*These Eighty Years*," 1: 2, 36 and 2: 337.

80. Solly, "*These Eighty Years*," 1: 329.

81. Ursula Henriques, *Religious Toleration in England 1787–1833* (Toronto: University of Toronto Press, 1961), p. 35.

82. Holt, *Unitarian Contribution*, pp. 26, 197–200; Solly, "*These Eighty Years*," 1: 371–72.

83. Holt, *Unitarian Contribution*, pp. 25, 26, 165, 189; Isichei, *Victorian Quakers*, pp. 247–48; Thompson, *Nonconformity*, p. 121; Anthony Burton, *Josiah Wedgwood: A Biography* (New York: Stein and Day, 1976), p. 187; [Frances H. Bradburn], *A Memorial of George Bradburn* (Boston: Cupples, Upham and Co., 1883), p. 49.

84. Lincoln, *Some Social and Political Ideas*, pp. 175–77.

85. Holt, *Unitarian Contribution*, pp. 52–53, 165–68, 206.

86. Holt, *Unitarian Contribution*, pp. 42–43, 51–57, 66–67

87. David Brion Davis, *The Problem of Slavery in the Age of Revolution 1770–1823* (Ithaca, N.Y.: Cornell University Press, 1975), pp. 460–61; Burton, *Josiah Wedgwood*, pp. 40, 93.

88. Burton, *Josiah Wedgwood*, pp. 213–14.

89. Holt, *Unitarian Contribution*, pp. 183–86, 204.

90. Ibid., pp. 187, 189–90; Isichei, *Victorian Quakers*, p. 247.

91. Holt, *Unitarian Contribution*, pp. 179, 203, 262; Ward, *Religion and Society*, pp. 207–8; McLachlan, *Records of a Family*, pp. 15–16; Solly, "*These Eighty Years*," 1: 334; Armstrong, *Henry William Crosskey*, p. 50.

92. John Webb, ed., *The Unitarian Almanac for 1854* (London: Edward T. Whitfield, n.d.), pp. 27–33; Gow, *The Unitarians*, p. 157; Ward, *Religion and Society*, p. 66.

93. *Report of the Western Unitarian Christian Union with the Resolutions Passed at the Second Half-Yearly Meeting, Held at Plymouth, Wednesday, September 30, 1846* (Bristol: H. C. Evans, n.d.), p. 11, italics mine.

94. Holt, *Unitarian Contribution*, p. 188; Isichei, *Victorian Quakers*, pp. 231, 247–48, 284.

95. Priestley, "Sermon on the Slave Trade," *Works*, 15: 376–77.

96. The two "best accounts" of British antislavery work before 1833 do not mention the Unitarians at all. See Reginald Coupland, *The British Anti-Slavery Movement* (London: Frank Cass & Co., 1964 [1st edition, 1933]), and Frank J. Klingberg, *The Anti-*

Slavery Movement in England: A Study in English Humanitarianism (n.p.: Archon Books, 1968 [1st edition, 1926]). Roger Anstey's excellent study on the Atlantic slave trade identifies only two Unitarians who were against the trade. See Roger Anstey, *The Atlantic Slave Trade and British Abolition 1760–1810* (London: Macmillan Press, 1975), pp. 261–262. The best published account of British antislavery activity after 1833 by a scholar of the present generation does recognize in a few pages the Unitarian contribution. See Howard Temperley, *British Antislavery 1833–1870* (London: Longman Group, Ltd., 1972), pp. 213, 237.

97. Holt, *Unitarian Contribution*, p. 14.

98. "[The Twenty-second Annual Meeting of the] British and Foreign Unitarian Association," *Inquirer*, 29 May 1847, p. 348.

99. Bradburn, *George Bradburn*, p. 66.

100. Jean Trepp, "The Liverpool Movement for the Abolition of the English Slave Trade," *Journal of Negro History* 13 (July 1928): 265, 268; Ian Sellers, "Liverpool Nonconformity, 1786–1914" (Ph.D. diss., University of Keele, 1969), p. 205; William Roscoe, *The Wrongs of Africa. A Poem*, Part the First (London: R. Faulder, 1787), 4; Anne Holt, *Walking Together: A Study of Liverpool Nonconformity, 1688–1938* (London: George Allen & Unwin, Ltd., 1938), pp. 155–56; Henry Roscoe, *The Life of William Roscoe*, vol. 1 (Boston: Russell, Odiorne, & Co., 1833), pp. 54–72.

101. Trepp, "Liverpool Movement," pp. 268–70, 272, 274, 283–85. For the quotation by Clarkson, see p. 273; R. V. Holt, *Unitarian Contribution*, p. 135; A. Holt, *Walking Together*, pp. 158–59.

102. Price, *Richard Price and Ethical Foundations*, p. 213; R. V. Holt, *Unitarian Contribution*, pp. 133–34; Priestley, "Sermon on the Slave Trade"; McLachlan, *Letters of Theophilus Lindsey*, 92.

103. Betty Fladeland, *Men and Brothers: Anglo-American Antislavery Cooperation* (Urbana, Ill.: University of Illinois Press, 1972), p. 49; Burton, *Josiah Wedgwood*, p. 199; R. V. Holt, *Unitarian Contribution*, p. 134; Richard W. Davis, *Dissent in Politics 1780–1830: The Political Life of William Smith, MP* (London: Epworth Press, 1971), pp. 55–56, 105, 109–110.

104. Charles Booth, *Zachary Macaulay: His Part in the Movement for the Abolition of the Slave Trade and Slavery* (London: Longmans, Green and Co., 1934), p. 68; Davies, *English Free Churches*, p. 252; Harold Temperley, "Anti-Slavery," in *Pressure from Without in early Victorian England*, Patricia Hollis, ed. (London: Edward Arnold, 1974), p. 27; R. V. Holt, *Unitarian Contribution*, p. 135; "Review of *Negro Slavery*," *Edinburgh Review* 38 (February 1823): 177.

105. Thomas Clarkson to William Smith, n.p., 1 September 1833, in Edith Hurwitz, *Politics and the Public Conscience: Slave Emancipation and the Abolitionist Movement in Britain* (London: George Allen & Unwin, Ltd., 1973), 174; William Wilberforce, *A practical view of the prevailing religious system of professed Christians, in the higher and middle classes in this country, contrasted with real Christianity* (London: T. Cadell, jun., & W. Davies, 1797); L. R. Carpenter, *Memoirs*, p. 376; Lant Carpenter, *Sermons on Practical Subjects* (Bristol: Philp and Evans, 1840), p. 147.

106. Raymond G. Cowherd, *The Politics of English Dissent* (New York: New York University Press, 1956), pp. 52, 54; Watts, *The Dissenters*, p. 479; Priestley, "Sermon on the Slave Trade," p. 385.

2

"Theological Negroes" as Garrisonians: From Moderate to Radical Antislavery—1833–45.

British Emancipation: Honest, Judicious, Gradual, Safe.

During the years 1787–1807 the goal of the British antislavery movement was the abolition of the slave trade; from 1823 to 1833, it was emancipation. In the spring of 1823, Thomas Fowell Buxton introduced a motion in Parliament that "the state of slavery [was] repugnant to the principles of the British constitution and the Christian religion, and it ought to be gradually abolished throughout the British colonies." In the debates that followed a Unitarian and an antislavery pamphlet attributed to him were sometimes mentioned. The Unitarian was the Reverend Thomas Cooper (1791/2–1880), a minister who had the unique experience for his denomination of having been a missionary to West Indian slaves. He had served a two-year period on the Jamaica plantation of a distinguished Unitarian, Robert Hibbert (1770–1849), a man who later established a trust to fund Unitarian projects. Although Cooper admitted that his patron was the "best of masters," his observations on the plantation's slavery contained descriptions of gross immorality and brutality. They were at first published in the *Monthly Repository*, a Unitarian publication with a modest circulation, but were subsequently reprinted in a widely distributed pamphlet called *Negro Slavery*. The pamphlet was published by the "Society for Mitigating and Gradually Abolishing the State of Slavery throughout the British Dominions," or, as it was popularly known, The Antislavery Society. Cooper's observations comprised only a part of the pamphlet, but the sensation they produced fastened his name upon it. Outside of Parliament, the former missionary was referred to in company with such abolitionist celebrities as Buxton, William Wilberforce, and James Stephen. Moreover, the pamphlet, *Negro Slavery,* was cited as possible "proof of the triumph," of those promoting emancipation. These observations were compounded error. Cooper was no Wilberforce, and the promoters of emancipation experienced no triumph. Following the debates, the government only instructed the colonies to legislate improvements in the slaves' condition, advice that was defiantly ignored.[1]

Lant Carpenter represented the conservative view that the question of emancipation had to be met by the West Indian proprietors themselves. He expressed his opinion in a letter to a friend and member of Parliament who had spoken disparagingly of Cooper's observations. Defending Cooper, Carpenter declared that if blacks were not educated for freedom, "incalculable evils" would result. Perhaps that was why he drafted his petition to the House of Commons for gradual emancipation in the spring of 1824.[2]

However, most abolitionists feared that "the slave society could not reform itself." In 1825, Macaulay, of the London Committee of the Anti-Slavery Society, reported that many of his colleagues wanted to undertake new courses of action. Tensions arose over demands to apply greater pressure on Parliament and to engage in greater agitation. To further the goals of emancipation, the society financed antislavery lecturers, held large public meetings, and established, in 1826, the *Anti-Slavery Reporter.* Greater publicity increased antislavery membership and influence. By 1830, the amelioration of the slaves' condition no longer meant timid policies of improvement, but emancipation. A combination of factors too complex to be detailed here, such as a Whig government's coming into power in 1830, disturbances in Jamaica, the Reform Bill of 1832, economic instability in the West Indies, the evolution of a religious abolitionism that advocated immediate action, and so on, aided the abolitionists in securing passage in Parliament of an Emancipation Act in 1833.[3]

Cooper had testified before the two Committees on Emancipation in Parliament, in 1832. He was among the twelve antislavery witnesses, eight of them ministers, in the House of

Commons. He told the M.P.s that the blacks would be industrious wage earners if given the chance, that peace would follow emancipation, but that the education of the blacks without emancipation would assuredly bring insurrection. He was among the eight antislavery witnesses in the House of Lords. He told the Lords that emancipated slaves would make a "happy and useful peasantry." He included in his testimony, of course, many personal recollections of slavery. The *Anti-Slavery Reporter*, delighted over Cooper's testimony, advised its readers to read *Negro Slavery*, the pamphlet that had produced a "most powerful effect" a decade before, and was in fact, "the precursor of all the Anti-Slavery efforts which [had] since been made."[4]

In 1833, Unitarian congregations presented to Parliament four petitions, containing 425 names, in favor of emancipation. Congregationalists submitted 205 petitions (26,080 signatures), Baptists, 188 (26,287), and Wesleyan Methodists, 1,953 (229,426). Thus, Unitarian activity in the petition drive for emancipation was disappointing. Moreover, Hibbert, who had thought the abolition of the slave trade to be beneficial, now presented *anti*-emancipation petitions to both houses of Parliament. The petitions opposed emancipation without "full compensation" to the proprietors. When Parliament approved 20,000,000 pounds to compensate the planters, an uproar arose over paying those who had robbed the "poor negroes" of years of labor.[5] Lant Carpenter, however, supported the compensation measure as money well spent. In letters to newspapers and to members of Parliament he recommended a gradual and "safe" emancipation, believing that an "immediate, unprepared, and unrestricted emancipation" would have been "culpable rashness." His constant regard for moderation cast upon him the "odium of being lukewarm in the cause," a charge that hurt him deeply, for he saw himself as an "ardent friend of freedom."[6]

His moderation could be traced partially to friendships with planters from his days in Liverpool. It was also influenced by the observations of his son's stay in the British West Indies. William Benjamin Carpenter (1813–85) had joined John Bishop Estlin (1785–1855), the eminent ophthalmologist and member of his father's congregation, in a visit to the Island of Saint Vincent, in 1833. They stayed on the estate of a master who had discarded the whip and was solicitous of his slaves' physical comfort. The young Carpenter achieved a greater understanding of the planters, once having seen the difficulties that surrounded them. After four months on the island, Estlin also formed opinions of slavery that were markedly different from those of Thomas Cooper. He saw blacks who were not whipped, and who frequently laughed, sang, and danced. He believed that perhaps they were "*too* well off," when one regarded their laziness and immorality. Slavery's greatest evil was not cruelty, which had been grossly exaggerated, but the "want of religion." Estlin was "no advocate of slavery," but he was convinced that a sudden change from slavery to freedom would produce "distress, suffering, and most formidable evils." He therefore favored an "honest," "judicious," and "gradual" emancipation. Strange words for the future radical abolitionist, but as a friend later commented on this period of his life, Estlin had not sounded the depths of slavery as he would afterwards.[7]

The Emancipation Bill became effective on the first of August 1834 and 800,000 slaves began a "judicious" and "gradual" emancipation that required a period of apprenticeship. The Reverend Edwin Chapman (1798–1875) preached a thanksgiving sermon at the Stamford Street Unitarian Chapel in London, in honor of the "glorious deed." Members of all sects and parties, he explained, had brought it about. "Christian principle" had conquered British slavery and would overcome it elsewhere, especially in that nation which boasted "free and glorious institutions."

In 1838, with abolitionist help, the process of apprenticeship ended earlier than planned, and the Reverend John Relly Beard preached a commemorative discourse. He attributed emancipation to the "genius of Christianity," and believed that only Great Britain could have achieved it. The extinction of slavery "was a God-like work" that would have a beneficial impact throughout the world. He too called attention to America and ominously predicted that "before many years slavery will either be destroyed in the United States, or,—which God avert—it will bring desolation and dismay over that flourishing and happy country."[8]

Lant Carpenter had linked the hope inherent in the first of August to "that great nation," America, united to England in so many ways. The date did become a common festival of international patriotism and humanitarianism for the abolitionists in the two nations. Samuel J. May (1797–1871), an abolitionist Unitarian minister in Syracuse, New York, saw the first of August as an "event more auspicious to the cause of the poor and oppressed, than any other event since the advent of the Messiah"! American ministers such as May used the date to inspire America to imitate England "in her repentance." It carried a particularly hallowed significance for Unitarians, for Channing honored the anniversary with what was to be his last public address.[9]

Channing's "Noble Trust": Abolitionism as Moderation

During the next twenty-five years or more, allegiance to the first of August and common testimony to the unity of origins, language, interest, and goals of their two nations were often acknowledged by Unitarian antislavery coworkers in Great Britain and America. Partially, this unity was attributable to the common odium that the radical abolitionists, the followers of William Lloyd Garrison, experienced in America, and that the Unitarian believers experienced in Great Britain. The treatment received in Great Britain by Lucretia Mott, a Garrisonian Hicksite Quaker, was most revealing. Her difficulty in being seated at the 1840 World's Anti-Slavery Convention was, in the opinion of one observer, a matter of religious rather than sexist prejudice. The "real cause" for her not being admitted, he declared, was prejudice because she was a Hicksite (and therefore unitarian in her theology). She carried the mark of the beast on her forehead in the view of Calvinist Dissenters: "Unitarians in their eyes [were] the most odious of heretics." Garrison, on his third trip to England in 1846, was gratified by the reception he received from the Unitarians. Their faith was as odious in England as "infidelity" was in America, he wrote to his wife, but they had been the ones who had "most zealously" espoused his mission.[10]

American Garrisonian abolitionists and their British Unitarian supporters were not drawn together immediately. For some time the latter held to a gradualist view of emancipation. Their work in ending slavery in the British West Indies influenced their thinking. They had helped to achieve emancipation there through political change and compensation to the slaveholders. Only after some time did they see that a similar program was exceedingly difficult, if not impossible, in America. They were also influenced by the writings of William Ellery Channing (1780–1842) and awed by his honored place among Unitarian heroes. Armstrong, for example, said that he was attracted to American antislavery reform by Channing's "noble trust."[11]

Channing represented a type of philosophical abolitionism that thought of slavery in abstract terms, desired to have a modifying effect upon the more radical abolitionists, particularly the Garrisonians, and favored a gradual, cautious emancipation program accompanied by compensation. Joseph Blanco White (1775–1841), the Spanish expatriate and former Roman Catholic priest, who became a Unitarian in the early 1830s, called Channing's voice against slavery one of "greatest moderation and justice." Channing frequently poured out his feelings against slavery in his correspondence with friends and supporters in England. He sent them his antislavery writings, which were moderate, carefully reasoned, and sensitive discussions of the various issues. They comprised about a half dozen works, starting with *Slavery* in 1836, and ending with his address on the anniversary of British emancipation, given shortly before his death in 1842. English and Scottish editions of his works were enthusiastically noticed in Unitarian periodicals. The *Christian Reformer*, reviewing *Slavery*, rejoiced: "Channing may be, under Providence, the Emancipator of the American Slaves!"[12]

Channing's moderate antislavery position received a sort of official sanction by the British and Foreign Unitarian Association. They included two of his antislavery works, *Remarks on the Slavery Question* and the Lenox Address, in their list of tracts for sale and distribution. Oddly enough, their counterpart, the American Unitarian Association, never did distribute his individual antislavery writings. In their attempt to radicalize the BFUA and prod the AUA, the radical abolitionists expended a good deal of work and energy. How they themselves evolved into radical abolitionists and how they tried to demonstrate that Garrison, not Channing, was destined to be the Liberator, or "Emancipator of the American Slaves," is important to understanding British Unitarian participation in the trans-Atlantic battle against slavery.[13]

Signs of a New Era: From Moderation to Radicalism

One of the earliest transformations in British Unitarian antislavery thinking took place in regard to the colonization schemes. Early in the 1830s reception of such schemes from

America was mixed. In 1834, the Reverend Edwin Chapman, editor of the *Unitarian Magazine and Chronicle* and later a Garrisonian, praised the American Colonization Society. He declared that the society's principles were "wise and benevolent." He believed that criticism of it had been fully answered, and he strongly recommended its work. A contrary opinion was voiced by William Turner, Jr. (1761–1859), minister of the Hanover Square Chapel, Newcastle-on-Tyne. He could not recommend it and believed its proposal to return American blacks to Africa was the wildest fantasy that a rational person could compose. Russell Carpenter originally favored the society, then backed off when he learned that it only sought to make "colonization a safety-valve to [the slaveholders'] terrible machine for crushing humanity." Aside from questions regarding the possible ulterior motives of the colonizationists, the impracticability of their schemes lost them what little British support they might have had. John Bishop Estlin later pointed out that the American Colonization Society had sent to Africa in sixteen years no more blacks than were born in America in two weeks! In 1841, James Haughton (1795–1873), a Dublin merchant, wrote that almost no defenders of colonization still remained in Britain or Ireland.[14]

The transformation from a gradualist view of emancipation and an interest in moderate schemes of action such as colonization to radical and immediatist views of the Garrisonians was in part related to the rise of revivalist evangelical thinking in Britain and America. "As a kind of surrogate religion," David Brion Davis has written, "antislavery had long shown tendencies that were pietistic, millennial, and anti-institutional. By the 1830s it had clearly marked affinities with the increasingly popular destinies of free grace, immediate conversion, and personal holiness."[15] This evangelical revivalism did not pass over the Unitarians, and the Reverend George Harris (1794–1859) best typified the evangelical tone among them.

Harris was one of the originators of the Scottish Unitarian Association in 1813, and a supporter of "old biblical Unitarianism." In addition to serving Unitarian congregations at first in Glasgow, and later in Newcastle-on-Tyne, he traveled about Scotland and the north of England like a Methodist circuit rider. He denounced slavery, capital punishment, war and intemperance—but particularly slavery. To him, Unitarianism was the one faith that could destroy it, as well as undermine the "tyrannies of the world."[16] To further Unitarianism, he performed "unabating toil" and achieved an "extraordinary pulpit eloquence."[17] He inspired James and Lucretia Mott as an "eloquent vindicator of his injured fellowmen," and he opened his pulpit to Lucretia Mott when they visited him in Glasgow in 1840.[18] He was one of the British Unitarians for whom Garrison felt a "strong personal friendship."[19]

Reviewing Channing's *Slavery* in his own magazine, the *Christian Pioneer,* Harris denounced the "gigantic evil" of slavery, and praised the nation infected by it: America was his "first vision of liberty." From childhood he had looked to it as "the refuge of oppressed conscience, the land of equal rights, and social blessedness." The Declaration of Independence was his "political catechism and creed." Although slavery tainted the soil of America, he explained, it did not taint the principles of her declaration. For the document had given America her life, but not her slavery. That was Great Britain's "gift"; Great Britain had "branded that curse upon the country she misgoverned," and it was a curse that the British people still had to share. To be an antislavery reformer in Great Britain, Harris wrote, "was comparatively an easy task," but the radical abolitionists in America faced difficulties.[20] Perhaps his support of the radicals was out of respect for their difficulties or perhaps it was out of admiration for the comprehensiveness of their reform interests.

In another review in his magazine, he advocated inspiring men and women through antislavery and reform sermons. He belittled "metaphysical discourses" and "dry abstract moral essays" and extolled sermons on one's "everyday duties" to people of "all climes, colours, and nations."[21] This was an international Christian outlook, and he based it upon a Christ-centered, evangelizing approach to the world. Sedate, smug, aristocratic Unitarians of Boston and London would feel terribly uncomfortable around Harris's "Christian philosophy of Politics," and advocacy of "mission circuits" of ministers and lay preachers serving the "masses."[22]

Not surprisingly, Harris instigated the first collective protests against American slavery by British Unitarians. His Scottish Christian Unitarian Association censured American slavery at its yearly assemblies in 1837 and 1840. Other "evangelical" churches were sending antislavery protests to their co-religionists in America and condemning Christian fellowship with slaveholders, why not Harris's? Whether his antislavery activities ever approached being a surrogate for religion might be questioned, but that his religion might be seen as a surrogate for an antislavery society was unquestionable. The appeals of British Christians to American friends and fellow believers were appreciated by the Garrisonians. Said Wendell Phillips, in 1839, the "sympathy and brotherly appeals of British Christians are the sheet-anchor of our cause."[23]

Another influence upon the transformation of British antislavery thinking was the observations and writings of Harriet Martineau (1802–76). Although she claimed to have ceased being a Unitarian "in the technical sense" in 1831, she constantly had to tell her "old co-regligionists" that she "disclaimed their theology *in toto*."[24] She had studied under Lant Carpenter while a young girl and "worshipped" him. Under his influence she became a "devout and devoted Catechumen, . . . desperately superstitious, living wholly in and for religion, and fiercely fanatical about it." In 1830 she won prizes from the British and Foreign Unitarian Association for three essays on how to carry the Unitarian Gospel to Roman Catholics, Moslems, and Jews.[25] Thus, despite her withdrawal from the denomination the following year, and her non-Unitarian and antireligious posture in later years, Unitarians paid a great deal of attention to what she said. Being the sister of James Martineau (1805–1900), Great Britain's most distinguished Unitarian theologian, also enhanced her influence.

What she said regarding the American abolitionists was based upon her experiences while traveling in the United States in 1834 and 1835, the very years of George Thompson's antislavery mission to America. It was while attending a meeting of the Female Anti-Slavery Society besieged by antiabolitionist rioters in Boston, that she experienced her baptism in Garrisonian abolitionism. The women's courage so impressed her that she confessed to them her full agreement in their abolitionist principles. When the Boston elite ostracized her for participating in the meeting, she moved still closer to the radical abolitionists and became their staunch supporter. To her, the abolitionists were the "blameless apostles of a holy cause," and Garrison, their leader, was the "most bewitching" person she had met in the United States.[26]

Along with George Thompson, she played a very important role in supplying information to the British public on the American antislavery movement. Their pro-Garrisonian views greatly influenced the unknowing and uncommitted. Her antislavery report, "The Martyr Age of the United States," was exciting reading. Although her brother James always disapproved of the Garrisonian approach to reform, and admired (and adopted as his own view) the "Independent position" of Channing, his lack of public statements on antislavery naturally did nothing to counter those of his sister. In the various controversies that pitted one part of antislavery reformers against the Garrisonians, Harriet Martineau invariably took the side of the latter. In 1841, at the height of the internecine war among antislavery partisans in America, she wrote that any true friend of the slave who knew the facts of antislavery history would would aid Garrison and his band.[27]

Not everyone, however, became caught up in Martineau's praise of the "kingly Abolitionists," and her attacks upon antiabolitionist clergymen infuriated some. "We dislike Miss Martineau's intolerance," wrote Unitarian minister James Freeman Clarke (1810–88) in Louisville, Kentucky. Her judgment of Unitarian clergymen according to her Garrisonian standard probably disturbed him the most. For she had even gone so far as to reclaim Unitarian membership to make more credible her attack on American ministers, whom she felt were deficient in antislavery matters. "As a body they must," she wrote in 1837

> though disapproving slavery, be ranked as the enemies of the abolitionists. Some have pleaded to me that it is a distasteful subject. . . . Some say that their pulpits are the property of their people, who are not therefore to have their minds disturbed by what they hear thence. . . . Some think the subject not spiritual enough. . . . So while society is going through the greatest of moral revolutions, . . . the clergy, even the Unitarian clergy, are some pitying and some ridiculing the apostles of the revolution.

She could speak of the Unitarians, she declared, because—forgetting her denominational apostasy in 1831—she was a "Unitarian [her]self." No wonder the Boston *Advertiser,* published by a conservative Unitarian layman, denounced her as a "foreign carpet-bagger."[28]

The affinity of British Unitarian antislavery reformers for the Garrisonians was deepened as a result of the controversy arising out of the World's Anti-Slavery Convention in 1840. Although he could not attend, Channing saw the meeting as a "sign of a new era," wherein men on both sides of the Atlantic would be united in the cause of humanity. But Channing had not said men "and women," and when the convention met, a majority of the men there also demonstrated no perception of a union with women in the cause of humanity. American women were furious at being refused places and they had some sympathetic male supporters at the convention. Dr. James Bowring, for one, upheld their right to attend as full delegates. Unitarian James Stansfeld (1820–98) was so "profoundly affected" by the uproar that he dated from that hour his lifetime support of equal rights for women. James Haughton felt that the English abolitionists were "mean and despicable" to refuse places to women "long known as zealous [reformers]." Garrison, arriving late, created a stir when he chose to sit with the exiled women in the gallery.[29]

The excitement of the controversy at the convention and the debates following it engendered significant interaction between American Garrisonians and British Unitarians. The Reverend William James (1808–76), and two theological students, Francis Bishop (1813–69) and Henry Solly (1813–1903) found Garrison a great inspiration. James Haughton judged him as "one of the most right-minded men" he had ever met, and became one of his most dedicated disciples. Other Unitarians fell under the spell of James and Lucretia Mott. Besides George Harris, John Bowring, James Haughton, William Rathbone (1787–1868) of Liverpool, and the Reverends Joseph Hutton (1790–1860) of London, William James of Bridgwater, Hugh Hutton (1795–1871) of Birmingham, William Hamilton Drummond (1778–1865) of Dublin, and other Unitarian celebrities opened their homes and chapels to the abolitionist couple. Harriet Martineau also became their friend. As an honorary life member of the Massachusetts Anti-Slavery Society, she was upset that the Anti-Slavery Convention had rejected women and she wrote to Lucretia Mott:

> I cannot but grieve for you, in the heart-sickness which you must have experienced. . . . We must trust that the spirit of Christ will in time enlarge the hearts of those who claim his name—that the whites, as well as the blacks, will in time be free.[30]

It is likely that the convention accomplished at least three things for the Unitarian antislavery reformers. It expanded their consciousness of being citizens not only of Great Britain but of the world, it caused some of them to see the resemblance between religious oppression and sexist oppression, and it drew them closer to the Garrisonian camp. As citizens of the world, their condemnation of American slavery became more strident. Two years after the convention, Haughton exclaimed in *The Liberty Bell,* "Shame on you [Americans]! Your blotted escutcheon is the scorn of the world," and George Armstrong in his memorial sermon for Channing cried out, "WIPE OUT THE SHAME [Americans,] which renders [you] a scorn among the nations of the earth!"[31]

Unitarians could not help consider some of the parallels between their religious oppression and the oppression of women, when Lucretia Mott traveled about Great Britain and Ireland conversing often on the Unitarian faith. She probably discussed with Unitarian leaders the accusation that her Unitarian proclivities counted as much in denying her a seat at the convention as did her being a woman. Quaker abolitionist William Smeal told her that he deprecated the treatment of George Harris and their Unitarian friends by the orthodox."[32]

Finally, how could British Unitarians not help "sympathize quite strongly" with Garrison, when his opponents, including some members of the British and Foreign Anti-Slavery Society, were labeling him a Unitarian? That label was "sufficient reason," wrote a friend, for casting both him and the American Anti-Slavery Society "beyond the pale of union or sympathy." Garrisonianism, Howard Temperley has written, "would appear to [have] held a particular attraction for Unitarians."[33]

The Inquirer *on Antislavery*

The Garrisonian biases of the Unitarian abolitionists were reinforced by the reporting and editorial stance of the newspaper of their denomination, *The Inquirer.* It began publication in July, 1842 as a champion of "Truth—Freedom—Charity" under the editorial direction of the Reverend William Hincks (1794–1871), an old companion of Roscoe in the Liverpool Anti-Slavery Society. He had served the Renshaw Street Chapel in Liverpool, and had come to the *Inquirer* from a professorship in natural history at the Unitarian College in York. Until 1847, when he left the paper, he gave antislavery news a prominent place, wrote many antislavery editorials, regularly reported the meetings of the American Anti-Slavery Society and some of its auxiliaries, and reprinted articles from the *National Anti-Slavery Standard*. American antislavery news, in other words, meant news by and about the Garrisonians.[34]

In his many editorials on American slavery Hincks clearly revealed that not only his mind, but his emotions were in tune with the Garrisonians. His "blood boil[ed] with indignation" and his "cheeks tingle[d] with shame" when he wrote about some of the atrocities in America's "very irreligious and detestable system" of slavery. The Garrisonians seemed to him to be the only ones who could secure the "regeneration of the national character" of the United States.[35]

The chosen method of the Garrisonians to end slavery was by moral means and Hinck's comments on two issues revealed his commitment to their method. One issue was the use of England's naval squadron to stop the slave trade. He opposed the squadron's role for he had no faith in "physical force agencies."[36] The other issue was the debate in England on whether to remove the duties protecting sugar grown in the British West Indies. Free traders said yes, some abolitionists said no. Hincks was drawn into the debate when James Haughton criticized the *Inquirer* for not opposing the introduction of slave-grown sugar. The Dublin merchant had long favored the price subsidies on British West Indian sugar, even though he was a strong advocate of free trade. But he believed that the products of slave labor were stolen goods and not "lawful . . . commerce." Hincks answered that he fully agreed with Haughton's antislavery enthusiasm. Yet, among the three means to overthrow slavery—moral, financial, and forceful—only the first was permissible. Force was out of the question, and financial coercion could provoke nations into war. Moreover, he believed that the exclusion of slave-grown sugar would effect nothing because other nations would purchase it. Increased trade increased international understanding and progress, and these in turn would bring the "abandonment of the slavery system."[37]

Casting Stones across the Water: Two Antislavery Addresses to Brethren in America

Back in 1843 when the *Inquirer* had been preaching Garrisonianism, it announced that another World's Anti-Slavery Convention was being held in London. This second World's Convention was less exciting than the first. For one thing, Garrisonians were not invited, a fact that the *Inquirer* either ignored or did not know. The paper welcomed the "philanthropic strangers" whom the "great," "glorious," and "holy" cause had attracted to England. One of these "strangers" was Samuel May, Jr. (1810–99), a Unitarian minister from Leicester, Massachusetts, and a rabid Garrisonian. May, of course, was not a delegate to the convention, but he took advantage of the heightened awareness regarding antislavery reform to lobby immediately among his coreligionists in behalf of his favorite brand of abolitionism. He found a very receptive audience. George Armstrong, William James, Mary Carpenter, Joseph Lupton (1816–94), sometime mayor of Leeds, Mary Estlin (1820–1902), and her father, John Bishop Estlin, were among those he secured for, or encouraged in, Garrisonianism. Estlin was perhaps his greatest prize. Wendell Phillips congratulated May in winning over to the Garrisonians their "ablest and best helper of recent years."[38]

May attended Unitarian meetings throughout Great Britain and Ireland, and shocked his audiences with tales of proslavery Unitarian ministers in the United States, or at least men whose silence encouraged slavery's respectability. In his address before a crowded meeting of the Western Unitarian Christian Union in Taunton, he asked Unitarians of Great Britain to address an "earnest appeal and remonstrance" on slavery to their "brethren in America." Subsequently, at a meeting in Glasgow, he repeated his wish. At a meeting in Dublin, he learned that the Reverend Dr. Drummond and James Haughton had already prepared an address and dispatched it to America. May took no credit for it, but it was probable that his "wish" preceded his arrival in Dublin. May had effectively mesmerized the Unitarian abolitionists, and their Garrisonian commitment, at least for most of them, was now complete. No persons perhaps were more hypnotized by May than Armstrong and James.[39] Shortly after his departure from England for a tour of the continent, May received a request from Armstrong to prepare a "statement of the facts and names" relating to the Unitarian pro-slavery perfidy in America. Before he could reply, Unitarian newspapers and journals began to carry the "Address of the Irish Unitarian Christian Society to Their Brethren in America."[40]

The address was stern. Slavery was a "plague-spot" in America, a "cancer which must be boldly cut away." It was a "compilation of the greatest crimes against God and man." It was sin to enslave the "image of the living God." They had "heard with sorrow" and "indignation" (from Sam May, no doubt) that American Unitarians were guilty of "this wickedness." They hoped the report was only "one of the vile calumnies" uttered against Unitarians in America and England. To them "virtue and vice" were not "more opposite to each other" than "Unitarianism . . . and slaveholding." They alluded to the "sad doings" by Unitarians in the slave states. A Unitarian minister, George F. Simmons, had been run out of Mobile, Alabama, for preaching antislavery sermons, and another minister, Mellish I. Motte, had been denied the pulpit of the Unitarian congregation in Savannah, Georgia, for fear that he *might* preach antislavery sermons. Could the "persecutors" of these men possibly be Christians, asked the Irish Unitarians, and did good men hold fellowship with them? They closed with the ringing appeal that Unitarians worldwide ought to be for "civil and religious liberty for all, the black man as well as the white man."[41] A letter by James Haughton accompanied the publication of the Address in the *Inquirer.* He hoped for similar remonstrances from other British Unitarians.[42] Despite the reminder by the *Christian Register,* the newspaper of American Unitarians, that the British had a "great work near at hand," and an insinuation by others that perhaps the abolitionists had somewhat exaggerated the Simmons Affair, George Armstrong, for one, had already begun to take up the question in a way very pleasing to Haughton.[43]

Armstrong had received a reply from May to his request for information. The American abolitionist had answered: with the exception of a few outstanding individuals, May believed that American Unitarians were chargeable with "having done nothing, *nothing* in comparison to their influence and ability" to expose slavery's horrors and to work toward emancipation.[44]

Armstrong had circulated an address of his own to American Unitarians for signatures. Harriet Martineau cheerd him on. Unhappily, not all of his Unitarian brethren were so supportive; some were "fastidious and shirking." They all wished him well—"*in the abstract—but etc., etc., etc.,*—the old song!" Yet many did sign and he hoped the address would have a wide circulation among the Unitarians particularly and the American public generally.[45]

"The Address from Unitarians of Great Britain and Ireland to their Ministerial Brethren of the Unitarian Churches in the United States of America" was dated 1 December 1843, and printed as a broadside. It praised the American abolitionists. It admitted that American Unitarians probably acknowledged the "deep wrong" of slavery, but it worried that "inconvenience and sacrifice" promoted inaction. They who signed it were well schooled in "sacrifice," for as professors of a "faith everywhere spoken against," they could "witness to the difficulty of bearing . . . testimony to unpopular truth. Though tolerated, [they] were *stigmatized* by the State," and "singled out . . . for HER-ESY." Thus circumscribed, and because the question was "bound up with the honor of [their] faith," they hoped that their American brethren could be foremost in protesting slavery, and thus could help to vindicate for "UNITARIANISM her just position among the beneficent agencies in the world." The address was signed by nearly 200 Unitarian ministers.[46]

Some prominent ministers refused to sign it. Some stated that they were "not sufficiently familiar with the subject of slavery" to sign. Philip Carpenter refused because he believed the address would accomplish nothing. Unitarians in England had not done so much at home that they could lecture their American coreligionists. The most distinguished minister who refused to sign was James Martineau. He had the greatest sympathy with the cause, but he felt the address would have "no power of influence and some danger of provocation."[47] He too believed British Unitarians had too many obligations at home to "rebuke . . . others, without hearing the whisper, 'Let him that is without sin cast the first stone.'"[48]

Most Unitarian publications in England and America published the address. Criticism varied. George Harris suggested in his *Christian Pioneer* that it ought to have condemned "slavery in all its shapes," including "class distinctions." The American journal, the *Christian Examiner*, doubted the propriety of the action. The English failed to understand America's domestic institution and, counseling in "ignorance," probably ought to have remained silent. However, Samuel May assured Armstrong that it had been a boon to the American abolitionists. Armstrong himself believed that benefits were likely to result from it.[49]

Two Replies and a Protest

Although some American Unitarians passed the British address off as an "impertinence," its first benefit was to force them as a body to discuss slavery openly. At a meeting in Boston, fifty Unitarian ministers debated long and hard, then voted to respond to the address. They drafted a letter and sent a copy to every Unitarian minister in the United States. Only 130 signed it. Like the British address, it lacked the names of many prominent ministers.[50]

The letter labeled slavery a curse and claimed "no difference of feeling or opinion" existed between the British and Americans on the question. But because it was a domestic institution protected by state law, the Americans had about as much right to interfere as did British citizens. They could only appeal to the "conscience and hearts" of the slaveowners. They asked "counsel and sympathy for themselves and for the slaveholders, and trusted that eventually slavery would no longer "stain" their "national character."[51]

To debate whether they ought to reply to a fraternal address was disappointing, but their reply itself was even more disappointing. They expressed great solicitude for themselves and the slaveholders, but ignored the slaves. "We laymen," wrote Estlin to Samuel May, "do not think our ministerial *papas* have been very civilly treated as to . . . their Anti-Slavery Address. I suppose it was unpalatable food, and not easy of digestion?"[52]

Several Unitarian conservative ministers in Massachusetts had found the address so unpalatable that they felt compelled to send their own reply and to meet censure with censure. Their letter was sarcastic and insulting. They accused the British of misinformation. They advised instruction in the workings of the American Constitution, and declared that antislavery feeling in New England was generally "as strong and as religiously held" as that in old England. If they preached on slavery infrequently, it was because their parishioners were not slaveholders. What their duties were on the slavery question they themselves were the "most competent" to judge. Ten conservatives, including Francis Parkman and Orville Dewey, signed the letter.[53]

Hincks was shocked by the letter's tone. He protested in the *Inquirer* that British Unitarians had not acted in ignorance, nor written in a reproachful or arrogant spirit, but simply in "zeal for a holy cause." Armstrong was especially irritated. America was the example for the hopes of constitutional reform *everywhere*," but slavery was paralyzing her influence. Why could not her "CHURCHES OF CHRIST . . . lift their voices?" Haughton likewise asked: Was it not just to call upon all Unitarians to oppose zealously so "infernal" a system? If Unitarianism were foremost in antislavery, the denomination's growth would need no missionary campaigns.[54]

Although the British address stimulated no comment at the annual meeting of the British and Foreign Unitarian Association in May 1844, it caused intense excitement at the annual meeting of the American Unitarian Association. Samuel May introduced some antislavery resolutions that led to a separate meeting and three days of protracted debate. May called "feeble" the final resolutions that emerged. However, they did declare that slavery subverted Christian brotherhood; that slavery was an accumulation of evils "the removal of which Christianity [ought to] appeal." Removal would come through prayer, sympathy, and moral and religious influence.[55]

The American Unitarian Association, the *Inquirer* remarked, had at last rebuked the "monster," slavery. Its previous "silence and inaction" had justifiably brought it the "censure of friends on both sides of the Atlantic." The newspaper complained that it was fast losing its respect for a church which "pertinaciously refused" to act publicly against "a system which [was] essentially impure and anti-Christian." It worried about the future testimony of the association. Would it now be silent forever?[56]

The *Christian Register* replied. The *Inquirer* faced disappointment if it looked forward to the AUA as an effective "assailant" of slavery. Public sentiment would not sustain the AUA if it functioned as an antislavery society. The *Inquirer* answered that slavery was a question on which all religious bodies, certainly Unitarians, were to give their opinion and that "silence or inactivity" practically sanctioned slavery.[57]

The debate that the British address had stimulated enabled May to keep the question before the members of the American Unitarian Association. Together with his abolitionist colleagues, May called a special meeting during the spring of 1845, "to consider [their] clerical duties and responsibilities in relation to American slavery." Not only was the British address on their minds, but the memory of George Simmon's expulsion from Mobile was still fresh. The meeting lasted three days and was boycotted by most conservatives. Out of it came a proposal to draft and to circulate a "Unitarian Protest against Slavery." James Freeman Clarke wrote the protest and 173 Unitarian ministers eventually signed it. Again, prominent leaders of the denomination held back their signatures.[58]

That the protest was partly inspired by the Simmons affair was clear in the references to "violent and lawless men" who prevented Southern ministers from preaching on slavery. It courteously divided slaveholders into good and bad: the former were those who under anti-emancipation laws involuntarily held slaves, the latter were those who for commercial gain or "personal convenience" held them. Therefore, it pronounced the system "unchristian and inhuman," but left it to God to decide the "guilt or innocence of individual Slaveholders." As the system was linked to the North politically, commercially, and socially, Northern silence upheld slavery. American Unitarians had to speak against it, for slavery "grossly violated" their three great principles—"individual liberty, perfect righteousness, and human brotherhood." Slavery degraded man, the "image of God, into a thing"; destroyed the heart of their nation; and impaired the virtue of their people. The protest dictated no course of action.[59]

The protest was favorably received by the British Unitarians and nearly all of their periodicals published it. Armstrong called it "noble" and grieved that several honored names were not on it. The *Christian Reformer* called it "powerful and dignified," and congratulated its countrymen who provoked it. The journal believed this happy result justified British interference. Hincks, in an editorial in the *Inquirer*, called it "admirable" and expressed his impatience with those who had not signed it.[60] Praise of the protest even came from the venerable Thomas Clarkson, who told a Unitarian layman that he thought the document was "the most beautiful and Christian address" that he had ever seen.[61]

The genuine excitement with which Armstrong embraced the protest could be seen at an antislavery meeting held in Bristol in November 1845. It had been called to receive a deputation from the British and Foreign Anti-Slavery Society and about 1,200 persons attended. Armstrong gave a long, rambling address and suggested one way to increase antislavery sentiment in America was for denominations in Great Britain to convey messages to their kindred churches in America. He recounted that the step had been taken by his beloved Unitarians with the "very best and happiest result," and he held up the protest and read portions from it. A very proud Armstrong then asked, "May we not, then say to the brethren of other denominations around—'Go and do ye likewise?'" It was a personal triumph for Armstrong, for himself and for his denomination. Here before more than a thousand people, he had accomplished a twofold task: he had issued a clarion call to aid the slave and he had focused attention on a good work of the Unitarians. Before a meeting that received him with the "livelist demonstrations of satisfaction," he had for a moment ceased to be perceived as a "theological negro."[62]

Notes

1. Edith Hurwitz, *Politics and the Public Conscience: Slave Emancipation and the Abolitionist Movement in Britain* (London: George Allen & Unwin, 1973), pp. 22, 31. For the quotation from Buxton, see p. 31; *Substance of the Debate in the House of Commons, on the 15th May, 1823, on a Motion for the Mitigation and Gradual Abolition of Slavery Throughout the British Dominions* (London: J. Hatchard & Son, 1823), pp. 70–73, 84–85, 163, 169, 181, 193–94; for a full account of Cooper's experience, see my "Teaching the Means of Freedom to West Indian Slaves, or, Failure as the Raw Material for Antislavery Propaganda," in *Harvard Library Bulletin* 39 (October 1981): 403–19; John Towill Rutt, "Mr. Rutt on Negro-Slavery," *Monthly Repository* 18 (May 1823): 285; "West Indian," *The Rev. Mr. Cooper and His Calumnies against Jamaica, Particularly His Late Pamphlet in Reply to Facts Verified on Oath* (Jamaica: publisher not known, 1825), pp. 5, 10; Howard Temperley, *British Antislavery 1833–1870* (London: Longman Group Ltd., 1972), p. 11.

2. Russell Lant Carpenter, *Memoirs of the Life of the Rev. Lant Carpenter, LL.D., with Selections from His Correspondence* (Bristol: Philp and Evans, 1842), pp. 270–73. See also pp. 151–52.

3. Hurwitz, *Politics and Public Conscience*, pp. 32–33, 48, 53; C. Duncan Rice, *The Rise and Fall of Black Slavery* (New York: Harper and Row, 1975), pp. 256–57; David Brion Davis, "The Emergence of Immediatism in British and American Antislavery Thought," *Mississippi Valley Historical Review* 49 (September 1962): 229.

4. "Analysis of the Report of a Committee of the House of Commons on the Extinction of Slavery, with Notes by the Editor," *Anti-Slavery Reporter* 5 (31 December 1832): 315–16, 365–66; *Report from Select Committee on the Extinction of Slavery Throughout the British Dominions: with the Minutes of Evidence, Appendix and Index* (n.p.: Ordered by the House of Commons, to be printed, 11 August 1832), pp. 136–37, 139–40; "Abstract of the Report of the Lords' Committees on the Condition and Treatment of the Colonial Slaves, and of the Evidence Taken by Them on That Subject; with Notes by the Editor," *Anti-Slavery Reporter* 5 (February 1833): 476, 557–59.

5. Robert Hibbert, Jun., *Hints to the Young Jamaica Sugar Planter* (London: T. & G. Underwood, 1825), p. 7; *The Debates in Parliament—Session 1833—on the Resolutions and Bill for the Abolition of Slavery in the British Colonies, with a Copy of the Act of Parliament* (London: 162, Piccadilly, 1834), pp. 123–24, 207–8.

6. Carpenter, *Memoirs*, pp. 374–75. Cf. Lant Carpenter, *A Discourse on Christian Patriotism: Delivered to the Society of Protestant Dissenters in Hanover Square, Newcastle-Upon-Tyne on the Sunday after the Coronation of Her Majesty; Printed at Their Request, and Dedicated, by Permission, to Her Royal Highness the Duchess of Kent* (London: Longman, et al., 1838), pp. 46–47.

7. R. L. Carpenter, *Memoirs*, p. 373; William B. Carpenter, *Nature and Man: Essays Scientific and Philosophical* (New York: D. Appleton and Co., 1889), pp. 9–10; John Bishop Estlin, "Observations on the Present State of Slavery in the Island of Saint Vincent," *Christian Reformer*, N.S., 1 (February 1834): 117–20, 124–27; William James, "Memoir of John Bishop Estlin, Esq., F.L.S., F.R.C.S.," *Christian Reformer* 11 (August 1835): 469.

8. Edwin Chapman, "Abolition of West Indian Slavery," *Unitarian Magazine and Chronicle* 1 (1834): 257–59, 262; John Relly Beard, *Extinction of Slavery. A Discourse in Commemoration of the Extinction of Slavery in the British Colonies, On the 1st of August, 1838* (London: Smallfield and Son, 1838), pp. 7–8, 9–10, 14–15.

9. R. L. Carpenter, *Memoirs*, p. 375; Samuel J. May, *Emancipation in the British W. Indies, August 1, 1834. An Address, Delivered in the First Presbyterian Church in Syracuse, on the First of August, 1845* (Syracuse: J. Barber, 1845), p. 3; George Ware Briggs, "First of August," *Monthly Religious Magazine* 4 (September 1847): 413;

William E. Channing, *An Address Delivered at Lenox, on the First of August, 1842, the Anniversary of Emancipation, in the British West Indies* (Lenox, Massachusetts: J. G. Stanly, 1842).

10. James Mott, *Three Months in Great Britain* (Philadelphia: J. Miller M'Kim, 1841), p. 44; Wendell Phillips Garrison and Francis Jackson Garrison, *William Lloyd Garrison 1805–1879. The Story of His Life Told by His Children*, vol. 3 (New York: The Century Co., 1885–1889), p. 171.

11. Robert Henderson, *A Memoir of the Late Rev. George Armstrong . . .* (London: Edward T. Whitfield, 1859), p. 81.

12. Douglas C. Stange, *Patterns of Antislavery among American Unitarians 1831–1860* (Rutherford, N.J.: Fairleigh Dickinson University Press, 1977), p. 31. See also chapter 3: "Antislavery as Philosophy: The Prudent Party—1831–1842," ibid., pp. 74–99; Anne Holt, "William Ellery Channing (1780–1842)," *Hibbert Journal* 41 (October 1942): 47–48; John Hamilton Thom, ed., *The Life of the Rev. Joseph Blanco White, Written by Himself; with Portions of His Correspondence*, vol. 2 (London: John Chapman, 1845), pp. 193, 207, 252, 346–47. White was a supporter of the Liverpool Anti-Slavery Society and had published in Spanish a sermon against the slave trade. See ibid., pp. 174–75, 467, and Jose Maria Blanco y Crespo, *Bosquejo del Comercio de esclavos y reflexiones sobre estre trafico considerado moral, politica y christianamente* (London: Ellerton and Henderson, 1814); Anna Letitia LeBreton, ed., *Correspondence of William Ellery Channing, D.D., and Lucy Aiken, From 1826 to 1842* (Boston: Roberts Brothers, 1874), pp. 190–94, 344; William Henry Channing, ed., *Memoir of William Ellery Channing, with Extracts from His Correspondence and Manuscripts*, vol. 3 (London: John Chapman, 1848), pp. 142–46; sample British editions of Channing's anti-slavery works were *Slavery* (London: Rowland Hunter, 1836), *Slavery* (Glasgow: J. Hedderwick & Son, 1836), and *Address on Occasion of the Anniversary of the Emancipation of the Slaves in the British West India Islands, etc.* (Glasgow: J. Hedderwick & Son, 1842); "E. H. H.," "Review of *Slavery* by W. E. Channing (London: R. Hunter, 1836)," *Christian Reformer* 3 (April 1836): 260. See also "Review of *Slavery* by William Ellery Channing (Glasgow: Hedderwick, 1836)," *Christian Teacher* 2 (1836): 605.

13. *The Eighteenth Annual Report of the British and Foreign Unitarian Association; the Proceedings of the Annual Meeting Held in the Chapel in Essex Street, Strand, June 7, 1843* (London: Richard and John E. Taylor, 1843), p. 43.

14. [Edwin Chapman], "Liberia," *Unitarian Magazine and Chronicle* 1 (1834): 18, 21; William Turner, Jr., "American Colonization Society," *Monthly Repository*, N.S., 7 (March 1833): 156, 158; Russell Lant Carpenter, "Free Blacks and Slaves," *Christian Reformer* 9 (August 1853): 484. This article was also published as a pamphlet; John Bishop Estlin, *A Brief Notice of American Slavery, and the Abolition Movement*, 2nd ed., rev. (London: William Tweedie, 1853), p. 25; James Haughton, "The American Colonization Society," *Irish Friend* 4 (1 May 1841): 66.

15. Davis, "Emergence of Immediatism," p. 229.

16. L. Baker Short, *Pioneers of Scottish Unitarianism* [n.p.: 1963], pp. 86, 89, 90, 93.

17. John A. Crozier, *The Life of the Rev. Henry Montgomery, LL.D., Dunmurry, Belfast; with Selections from His Speeches and Writings*, London: E. T. Whitfield, 1875): 387.

18. Mott, *Three Months in Great Britain*, p. 50.

19. Garrison, *William Lloyd Garrison*, 3: 171.

20. [George Harris], "Review of *Slavery* by William E. Channing, (London: Hunter, 1836)," *Christian Pioneer* 10 (1836): 192, 193.

21. [George Harris], "Review of *Extinction of Slavery: A Discourse* by J. R. Beard (London: Smallfield & Son, 1838)," *Christian Pioneer* 12 (December 1838): 460–61.

22. See the form letter by Harris to "My Dear Sir," Newcastle-upon-Tyne, 30 May 1849, and Prospectus for the *Christian Pilot*, Harris Papers, Unitarian Collection, John

Rylands University Library of Manchester. For a sampler of his writings, see George Harris, *Tracts and Sermons in Vindication of Christian Liberty, Righteousness, and Truth Published on Various Occasions* (Glasgow: James Hedderwick & Son, 1836).

23. [George Harris], "Slavery in America," *Christian Pioneer* 18 (January 1844): 19; Kenneth R. M. Short "English Baptists and American Slavery," *Baptist Quarterly* 20 (April 1964): 243–62; Thomas F. Harwood, "British Evangelical Abolitionism and American Churches in the 1830's," *Journal of Southern History* 18 (August 1962): 287–306; Phillips quoted by Shepperson, "The Free Church and American Slavery," *Scottish Historical Review* 30 (October 1951): 130.

24. Maria Weston Chapman, ed., *Harriet Martineau's Autobiography*, vol. 1 (Boston: James R. Osgood & Co., 1877), p. 120.

25. Martineau quoted by Short, *Founding of the BFUA*, pp. 24, 25. See also p. 17.

26. Martineau quoted by Stephen Bloore, "Miss Martineau Speaks Out," *New England Quarterly* 9 (September 1936): 409, 410, 414.

27. C. Duncan Rice, "The Anti-Slavery Mission of George Thompson to the United States, 1834–1835," *Journal of American Studies* 2 (April 1968): 29; Harriet Martineau, "The Martyr Age of the United States," *London and Westminster Review* 32 (December 1838): 1–59; James Martineau to Orville Dewey, Liverpool, 2 December 1844, James Drummond, *Life and Letters of James Martineau, LL.D., S.T.D., Etc.*, vol. 1 (New York: Dodd, Mead & Co., 1902), p. 175; Harriet Martineau, "Introduction," *Right and Wrong Amongst the Abolitionists of the United States*, by John Collins (Glasgow: George Gallie, 1841), p. 5.

28. "E. T." "To the Abolitionists of America," *Christian Teacher and Chronicle* 3 (1837): 731–32; James Freeman Clarke, "Miss Martineau's Society in America," *Western Messenger* 4 (December 1837): 260. See also George E. Ellis to Lant Carpenter, London, 20 March 1839, Lant Carpenter Papers, Manchester College Library, Oxford. Cited hereafter as OMC; Harriet Martineau, "Miss Martineau's Opinion of the American Clergy," *Christian Register*, 8 July 1837, p. 106; Garrison, *William Lloyd Garrison*, 2: 57.

29. Channing quoted by Douglas H. Maynard, "The World's Anti-Slavery Convention of 1840," *Mississippi Valley Historical Review* 47 (December 1960): 553; Betty Fladeland, *Men and Brothers: Anglo-American Antislavery Cooperation* (Urbana, Ill.: University of Illinois Press, 1972), pp. 265–66; J. L. Hammond and Barbara Hammond, *James Stansfeld: A Victorian Champion of Sex Equality* (London: Longmans, Green and Co., 1932), p. 286; Samuel Haughton, *Memoir of James Haughton. With Extracts from His Private and Published Letters* (Dublin: E. Ponsonby, 1877), p. 51.

30. Henry Solly, *"These Eighty Years" or, the Story of an Unfinished Life*, vol. 1 (London: Simpkin, Marshall & Co., 1893), pp. 328–29; William James to Maria Weston Chapman, Bristol, 1 November 1843, Clare Taylor, *British and American Abolitionists. An Episode in Transatlantic Understanding* (Edinburgh: Edinburgh University Press, 1974), p. 204; James Haughton to the editor, Dublin, 17 October 1840, *Irish Friend* 3 (2 November 1840): 99; Samuel Haughton, "American Colonization Society," p. 48; Frederick B. Tolles, *Slavery and "The Woman Question": Lucretia Mott's Diary of Her Visit to Great Britain to Attend the World's Anti-Slavery Convention of 1840*, Supplement No. 23 to the *Journal of the Friends Historical Society* (Haverford: Friends' Historical Association, 1952), pp. 15, 27, 31–32, 57, 59, 64, 68–69, 73–74. Harriet Martineau to Lucretia Mott, Tynemouth, 24 June 1840, Tolles, *Slavery and the Woman Question*, p. 79. American Unitarians who attended the Convention were Lydia Maria Child (1802–80) and her husband, David (1794–1874); George Bradburn (1806–80); Francis Jackson (1789–1861); Ellis Gray Loring (1802–58); and Samuel J. May. See Clare Taylor, "Some American Reformers and Their Influence on Reform Movements in Great Britain from 1830 to 1860" (Ph.D. diss., University of Edinburgh, 1960), pp. 178–84.

31. R. A. Armstrong, *Henry William Crosskey*, p. 127; James Haughton, "A Voice form

Erin," *Liberty Bell* (Boston: Massachusetts Anti-Slavery Fair, 1842), p. 61; George Armstrong, *A Discourse Delivered in Lewin's Mead Chapel, Bristol, on the Morning of November 6th, 1842, Being the Sunday next after the Intelligence Had Arrived of the Death of Dr. Channing* (London: J. Green, 1842), p. 28.

32. Tolles, *Slavery and the Woman Question,* pp. 5, 67. C. Duncan Rice, "The Scots Abolitionists, 1833–1861" (unpublished manuscript, 1975), p. 122.

33. John Collins to William Lloyd Garrison, London, 27 December 1840, Collins to Garrison, Glasgow, 3 April 1841, Taylor, *British & American Abolitionists,* pp. 134, 142. Garrison was raised a Baptist, but adopted a liberal theology as an adult. The theology as he described it was close to that of the Quakers. See William Lloyd Garrison to Elizabeth Pease, Boston, 1 June 1841, ibid., pp. 152–53; Howard Temperley, "Antislavery," *Pressure from Without in Early Victorian England,* Patricia Hollis, ed. (London: Edward Arnold, 1974), p. 49.

34. Herbert McLachlan, *The Unitarian Movement in the Religious Life of England* (London: George Allen & Unwin, 1934), pp. 212–15; "Sugar and Slavery," *Inquirer,* 1 August 1846, p. 481; Leslie Stephen and Sidney Lee, eds., *Dictionary of National Biography* (Oxford: Oxford University Press, 1921–22), 9: 892; for American antislavery news see *Inquirer,* 11 March 1843, 18 March 1843, 1 April 1843, etc. The newspaper also regularly gave news of the British and Foreign Anti-Slavery Society, and reprinted articles from the *Anti-Slavery Reporter.* See, e.g., 9 December 1843, 27 January 1844, 16 March 1844, 23 March 1844, et al.

35. "Conduct of American Slave-Holders," *Inquirer,* 18 January 1845, p. 33; "The Annexation of Texas," *Inquirer,* 18 January 1845, p. 34; "Texas Annexation," *Inquirer,* 29 March 1845, p. 193.

36. "The Slave Trade," *Inquirer,* 8 November 1845, 706–7.

37. James Haughton, "The Sugar Duties Question," *Irish Friend* 4 (1 June 1841): 85; "Slavery and Sugar," *Inquirer,* 7 March 1846, p. 146. See also "Sugar and Slavery," *Inquirer,* 1 August 1846, p. 481.

38. "Anti-Slavery Convention," *Inquirer,* 17 June 1843, p. 370; Fladeland, *Men and Brothers,* pp. 284–85; Phillips quoted by John White Chadwick, "Samuel May of Leicester," *New England Magazine* 20 (April 1899): 211.

39. Chadwick, "Samuel May of Leicester," p. 211; Samuel May, Jr. to George Armstrong, Geneva, 19 October 1843, *Inquirer,* 11 January 1845, pp. 27–28.

40. George Armstrong to Samuel May, Clifton, Bristol, 14 September 1843, Taylor, *British & American Abolitionists,* p. 197.

41. "Address of the Irish Unitarian Christian Society to Their Brethren in America," *Inquirer,* 23 September 1843, p. 604. *Cf.* also *Christian Register,* 2 September 1843; *Monthly Miscellany of Religion and Letters* 9 (September 1843), pp. 184–85.

42. "Address of the Irish," p. 604.

43. "The Address from the Unitarians of Ireland on Slavery," *Christian Register,* 30 September 1843; *Inquirer,* 11 November 1843, p. 708; "Veritas" to the editor, n.p., n.d., *Inquirer,* 4 November 1843, p. 692; James Haughton to the editor, Dublin, 9 November 1843, *Inquirer,* 25 November 1843, pp. 704–41.

44. Samuel May, Jr., to George Armstrong, Geneva, [9] October 1843, *Inquirer,* 11 January 1845, pp. 27–28.

45. George Armstrong to Samuel May, Jr., Clifton, Bristol, 30 October 1843, Taylor, *British & American Abolitionists,* p. 203.

46. "An Address from the Undersigned Unitarian Ministers of Great Britain and Ireland to Their Ministerial Brethren of the Unitarian Churches in the United States of North America." [broadside dated] 1 December 1843 (Bristol: Philp and Evans, 1843). A copy amended and corrected by George Armstrong is in the George Armstrong Papers, OMC.

47. William James to Samuel May, Jr., n.p., 30 November 1843, May Papers, Boston Public Library. Cited hereafter as MB; Russell Lant Carpenter, ed., *Memoirs of the Life and Work of Philip Pearsall Carpenter, . . . Chiefly Derived from His Letters,* 2nd ed. (London: C. Kegan Paul & Co., 1880), pp. 63–64; James Martineau to Orville Dewey, Liverpool, 3 October 1844, Drummond, *Life and Letters of James Martineau,* pp. 172–73. In the letter Martineau expressed his mixed feelings that Dewey approved of Martineau's not signing the document. Martineau confessed that his refusal to sign had gained him the "obloquy" of his fellow British Unitarians.

48. Martineau in a letter to William James, quoted by J. Estlin Carpenter, *James Martineau: Theologian and Teacher: A Study of his Life & Thought* (London: Philip Green, 1905), p. 256.

49. [George Harris], "Slavery in America," *Christian Pioneer* 18 (January 1844), p. 18; "Address of English Unitarians," *Christian Examiner* 36 (March 1844): 295; George Armstrong, "Address on Slavery to the Unitarian Ministers of the United States," *Inquirer,* 10 August 1844, p. 501.

50. Stange, *Patterns,* pp. 191–92; Samuel J. May, *Some Recollections of Our Antislavery Conflict* (Miami, Fla.: Mnemosyne Publishing Co., 1969 [1st ed., 1869]), p. 338; "Letter of the English Unitarian Ministers on Slavery," *Christian Register,* 20 April 1844, p. 62.

51. "Reply of the American Unitarian Ministers to the Address on Slavery," *Inquirer,* 9 November 1844, pp. 714–15.

52. J. B. Estlin to Samuel May, Jr., Bristol, 29 October 1844, Taylor, *British & American Abolitionists,* p. 231.

53. "The American Unitarians and Slavery," *Inquirer,* 21 December 1844, pp. 812–13; Stange, *Patterns,* pp. 399–401; Charles Richard Denton, "American Unitarians, 1830–1865: A Study of Religious Opinion on War, Slavery, and the Union" (Ph.D. diss., Michigan State University, 1969), pp. 101–2.

54. "American Unitarians and Slavery," p. 812; George Armstrong to the editor, Bristol, 15 January 1845, *Inquirer,* 25 January 1845, p. 52; James Haughton, "Slavery," *Inquirer,* 18 January 1845, p. 36.

55. "[Nineteenth Annual Meeting of the] British and Foreign Unitarian Association," *Inquirer,* 11 June 1844, pp. 347–350; Stange, *Patterns,* 194–98; Samuel May, Jr., to Maria Weston Chapman, Leicester, 23 July 1844, Weston Papers, MB; "The American Unitarians and Slavery," *Inquirer,* 27 July 1844, pp. 465–66.

56. "The American Unitarians and Slavery," *Inquirer,* 27 July 1844, pp. 465–66.

57. "London Inquirer—American Unitarian Association—Slavery," *Christian Register,* 4 September 1844, p. 142; "American Unitarians and Slavery," *Inquirer,* 9 November 1844, pp. 705–6; "The London Inquirer and the Letter on Slavery," *Christian Register,* 14 December 1844, p. 198.

58. Stange, *Patterns,* pp. 198–202.

59. [James Freeman Clarke], *American Slavery. A Protest Against American Slavery, by One Hundred and Seventy-Three Unitarian Ministers* (Boston: B. H. Greene, 1845), pp. 4–13; "America. Declaration Against Slavery. . . ." *Inquirer,* 1 November 1845, pp. 690–91.

60. George Armstrong to the editor, Bristol, 30 October 1845, *Inquirer* 1 November 1845, pp. 693–94; "America. Declaration Against Slavery," *Christian Reformer* 2 (January 1846): 58–59; "American Slavery," *Inquirer,* 1 November 1845, p. 690.

61. For Clarkson's remark, see "British and Foreign Unitarian Association [Twenty-Eighth Annual Meeting]," *Inquirer,* 21 May 1853, p. 330. See also George Armstrong to Thomas Clarkson, Bristol, 3 January 1846, Clarkson Papers, British Library.

62. "Anti-Slavery Meeting at Bristol," *Unitarian* 1 (January 1846): 27–31.

3

"Every Unitarian . . . An Abolitionist":
The Tactics of Radicalism—1846–47

Ignoring the Irish

William Lloyd Garrison declared that the Unitarian protest would "fall like a thunderbolt upon the guilty South," and the success of Samuel May and his American and British abolitionist friends in obtaining the protest was no mean achievement. Had not James Martineau called the American Unitarian Association "the most conservative body of Unitarians in the world"?[1] The Unitarian abolitionists were inspired with their success in securing the Unitarian protest and were determined to increase their efforts in the second half of the 1840s. To achieve their goal to make *every* Unitarian a bona fide abolitionist the Unitarian Garrisonians grew more radical and uncompromising. They utilized tactics and proposed actions that their coreligionists found very illiberal and offensive. They greeted the end of the decade fully aware that instead of every Unitarian an abolitionist, probably fewer claimed the name then, than during the early 1830s. Moreover, the year 1850 brought them the catastrophic news of the Slavocracy's shattering victory—the Fugitive Slave Law.

In the mid-1840s, Orville Dewey (1794–1882), an anti-abolitionist minister of the Church of the Messiah, New York City, and New South Society, Boston, was writing that the abolitionist movement was "dangerous to the peace of the country [and] to the union of the States"; that the abolitionists had impeded the progress of emancipation; and that the subject of slavery had to be treated with the "utmost Christian

72

seriousness and moderation." He served the American Unitarian Association as its president between 1845 and 1847. He had visited England and was held in high esteem by many British Unitarian divines. His judgment of the British interference was terse: "We say plainly we do not like the tone of *English* criticism upon us."[2]

Samples of that dissonant tone have already been quoted and the cacophony became shrill in its condemnation and immediatism: the slaveholder, proclaimed James Haughton, was "not fit to live," and the abolitionists, announced George Harris, demanded the "instant destruction" of the slave system.[3] To make every Christian an abolitionist was a formidable undertaking. Haughton for his part desired to begin by securing an answer to the Irish address. For whatever reason, the American Unitarians had chosen to respond to the British Address, but had ignored the Irish. Now, Haughton undertook a campaign to correct that sin of omission, and succeeded in making the Irish, and indeed himself, unforgettable.

Haughton, a Dublin corn and flour merchant, was one of the most interesting of the British radical abolitionists. His pen, not infrequently filled with poison, produced antislavery letters, articles, and pamphlets in great profusion. He grew up in an antislavery household of ex-Quakers, and joined the Unitarians in 1834. He threw himself into the vegetarian, peace, temperance, and antislavery movements. He subscribed to the Hibernian Temperance Society, the Loyal National Repeal Association, and was one of the founders of the Hibernian Anti-Slavery Society. He boycotted slave-produced cotton and rice and campaigned against the use of tobacco. He lobbied in Parliament to end the apprenticeship in the West Indies, actively opposed capital punishment, promoted education and sanitary reform, and pleaded with Irish immigrants in America to "love liberty" for themselves and "the colored man." For several years he met twice a week with other like-minded friends to plot strategies in the great world war against injustice. So comprehensive were their reform interests that a newspaper editor christened them the "Anti-everything-arians."[4]

Haughton could hardly have been satisfied with the Americans' reception of the Irish address. When the *Christian Register* published it, complaints flowed in that said that the Irish ought to look at home first. But Haughton was determined to look also to America and he pushed through a resolution at the annual meeting of the Irish Unitarian Christian Society in 1845 that regretted their being ignored and renewed their antislavery appeal to their American brethren.[5] To those who asked what the Irish Unitarian Christian Society had to do with slavery, he answered that it was their duty as a Christian society "to labor for its overthrow." Moreover, American Unitarians were not much advanced on the question of slavery. He remarked that one of their "pro-slavery" clergymen, Francis Parkman (1788–1852) of New North Church, Boston, was visiting England. Parkman to the year of his death, when he served the AUA as its president, had successfully blocked any radical antislavery statements by that organization. Haughton now supposed that Parkman would "strive to bamboozle" them.[6]

The Irish resolution was dispatched to America accompanied by a letter signed by the officers of the Irish Unitarian Christian Society. The letter was entitled the "Address of the Irish Unitarian Christian Society to Their Brethren in America," but ought to have been designated the "Second" Irish Address. It severely scolded the Americans:

> Surely your action as a body, on the momentous subject [of slavery], is far from consistent with the high and holy vocation of Unitarian Christianity. [There is] amongst you, an . . . unchristian inclination to discourage the labours of those who demand, and who are striving to obtain, equal civil rights for all alike, be their colour what it may. . . . We are anxious that Unitarians everywhere should be foremost in the ranks of those who are working for [slavery's] overthrow. Every Unitarian should be known as an abolitionist.[7]

Haughton sent the address along with a personal letter attacking the leadership of the AUA. Hincks accommodated him by publishing both. Although the *Christian Register* regretted the severe tone of the address, it too published it.[8]

Over a year passed with no answer from America and when an American abolitionist informed Haughton that no reply was forthcoming, he forwarded this information to the *Inquirer*. It was proof, he declared, that their denomination shared in the "common disgrace [of] the American churches" and a "more powerful public opinion, loudly expressed," was required.[9] At the annual meeting of the Irish Unitarian Christian Society in May 1847, Haughton easily obtained passage of a censorious resolution. It deplored the "want of courtesy" shown the two addresses sent to Ezra Stiles Gannett (1801–71), then president of the AUA and minister of Federal Street Church, Boston. In

a speech in support of his resolution, Haughton called upon
the society to make American slaveholders and their "pal-
liators" realize that they were viewed "as the greatest impeders
of the progress of Christianity and of Freedom, . . . upon the
face of the earth." The resolution was forwarded to Gannett.[10]
It piqued him immensely. He was openly hostile to the
abolitionists anyway, but the resolution embarrassed him before his many English friends and made him even more hostile.
He attempted to vindicate his conduct. The two Irish addresses, he declared, had not been ignored, they had been published in the Unitarian papers; only one had been sent to him,
the other to May.[11]

Actually, May had presented the Second Irish Address to the
annual meeting of the AUA in May 1846, but the committee
formed to answer it did not reach a consensus until August
1847. Their answer was courteous and subdued, revealing the
pessimism of the period. America was at war with Mexico and
slavery appeared to be advancing. But it was somewhat cheered
by the advance in public opinion on antislavery and by the
awakening of "some divisions of the Christian Church" towards
slavery. It joined the Irish in the wish that "ever Unitarian may
soon be known as an unwavering advocate of universal Freedom."[12]

"Amicus" Meets His Nemesis

To determine if a Unitarian was an abolitionist, Haughton
suggested that one ought simply to ask. When Francis Parkman
arrived in Dublin, in 1845, Haughton proceeded to practice
what he preached. He left the following note at Parkman's
lodgings:

I called at your Hotel hoping to see you. If you are an
Abolitionist it will afford me the sincerest pleasure to see you
at my home, and treat you with hospitable attention. *But I
have heard from America that you are a pro-slavery man,* or that
you lend your influence to the oppressor. If this be true, I
could not acknowledge you as a Christian minister. . . . The
first question I ask every American, . . . is, "Are you an
Abolitionist?" and I regulate my conduct according to his
reply.[13]

Parkman answered that he was not an abolitionist and disapproved of some of their measures, but as a "true lover of liberty" he accepted Haughton's invitation. In a "free and friendly conversation" with his host, Parkman defended his position with citations from Channing and Daniel Webster, declaring the former preached antislavery moderation, and the latter the danger of antislavery to the Union. Moreover, he told Haughton that preaching antislavery reform would disturb his parishioners and lesson his influence. Haughton marked Parkman as an "extenuator of slavery" if not "an absolute pro-slavery man," and called upon British Unitarians to refuse welcome to him and to all Americans who rejected "*immediate abolition.*"[14]

The incident began an exchange of correspondence in the *Inquirer* between Haughton and an anti-abolitionist known only by his pseudonym, "Amicus." The letters of Amicus provide a clear representation of the opposition to Haughton and the Garrisonians. Amicus judged Haughton's condemnation of ministers such as Dewey and Parkman to be in the same "Pharisaic spirit" as that practiced by the "Evangelical opponents of Unitarianism." Emancipation for the British colonies, he declared, required patient labor and compensation to the slaveholders, and emancipation for America required the same. American clergymen could best determine their own action without outside interference.[15]

Haughton ridiculed his critic. He suggested that Amicus was an "odd name [for] . . . a defender of slavery." There was no halfway position between pro-slavery and abolitionism. He who was not an abolitionist, that is, one who did not insist on "*immediate and unqualified freedom,*" had to be a pro-slavery man. Amicus replied by quoting an old saying that the Church of Rome was infallible and the Church of England was always right. Now, he added, another church had sprung up that aspired to perfectionism—Unitarianism, the "air-ianism of the unit Haughton." He reaffirmed that emancipation would be a slow process in the United States, as it had been in the British West Indies.[16]

The next issue of the *Inquirer* carried the Unitarian protest of 1845 and Haughton drew attention to the absence of Dewey, Gannet, and Parkman among its signers as evidence of their being "pro-slavery men." He recommended that the British help to create a "healthy public sentiment" against slavery. The Americans, he declared, were "so intimately connected" with them by language, institutions, and blood that it was no imper-

tinence for them to seek the removal of slavery. Amicus attempted to rebut Haughton's letter and predicted that
emancipation might only come through a separation of the
slave and non-slaveholding states.[17]

The exchange continued with Hincks at one point adding a
postscript. It revealed the editor's weariness with the acrimonious debate. He confessed his sympathy with the views of
Haughton, particularly the view that granting respectability to
the slaveholder directly supported slavery. But he continued to
publish letters from both sides.[18] Amicus protested the partisan
intrusion by Hincks. Furthermore, in his letter Amicus alluded
to slaves who had refused emancipation as evidence that they
had suffered no ill usage. Hincks felt forced again to intrude:
"The case of slaves refusing emancipation [had] often been put
forward," he declared, and it was "indeed a good proof how
deeply their condition degrade[d] them."[19]

Before the correspondence ended, Haughton and Amicus
had exchanged a total of fourteen letters, a debate of sufficient
magnitude to try any editor's patience. However, Amicus
rather than Hincks concluded that the readers of the *Inquirer*
had probably begun "to feel weary" of the exchange.[20] Had the
decision been left to Haughton, the correspondence would
have continued until slavery in America had been crushed by
the sheer weight of their argumentation.[21] Amicus argued in
his remaining letters that it was vain to rail against the slaveholders because slavery was "authorised and protected by law."
Haughton's replies continued his vitriolic criticism and stub-
bornly maintained that to rail against slaveholders was not un-
productive. British public opinion exerted "great force" on
America. The true test for ascertaining where an American
stood on the subject of slavery, Haughton concluded in his last
response to Amicus, was to ask: "Are you an ABOLITIONIST?
If he [could] not say yes, from his heart, to this inquiry, he [was]
rotten to the core."[22] The correspondence had ended where it
had begun.

A Unitarian Author and Her Critic

Having Amicus no longer to debate, Haughton in July 1846,
challenged an invisible and unsuspecting "opponent"
thousands of miles away. In the one-sided fight that ensued, he
resembled a blundering Don Quixote jousting with a windmill,

with not even chivalrous grace to lessen the odium of his crude attack. His opponent was a woman he had never met. She was a Unitarian, whose membership he could not prove. She was a Southern resident, whose sympathies for slavery he could not demonstrate. She was an adversary, who did not fight back.

Her name was Mary Palmer Dana (1810–83), a South Carolinian author of verse, whom history and literature have forgotten. She had written a volume called *Letters to Relatives and Friends* in which she proclaimed her personal discovery of a Christianity unfettered by orthodox dogma. Some enterprising Unitarians, always on the watch for another intellectual celebrity to add to their denomination's rolls, claimed her before she claimed them. To think Unitarian was to them to become Unitarian. Haughton, however, could not welcome her. He could not rejoice in the "accession of a supporter of slavery to [their] ranks." Better the Unitarians remained a small community for ages than "to acquire popularity by an acknowledgement of Christian fellowship with man-stealers."[23]

The muddled logic by which Haughton deduced that Dana was a "man-stealer" impaired the image of a Unitarian as a rational and intellectual believer. She lived in a slave state, did she not? he asked. "She must, therefore," he reasoned,

> be an upholder of that system which is at war with all that is great, and noble, and godlike, in man's nature. . . . It seems to me clear, that Mrs. Dana, in order to prove the sincerity of her religious convictions, was bound . . . to give utterance to generous sentiments on behalf of the poor oppressed Negro. Failing in this particular, I should say her accession to the ranks of Unitarianism was not a circumstance in which we should take pride.

Haughton sent his diatribe to the *Irish Unitarian Magazine,* a monthly published in Belfast. Probably out of impatience, and in order to insure a "more extended circulation," he submitted it simultaneously to the *Inquirer*. The editors of the two publications exhibited a total lack of journalistic discretion in publishing this slander. Haughton introduced himself to Dana by sending her a copy of the *Inquirer* that contained his tirade.[24]

Dana never responded. Others did. Letters, some under pseudonyms, complained that Haughton's remarks were "uncharitable" and "un-Christian." More than one of the writers reasoned, in grand Haughtonian logic, that a Unitarian abolitionist who lived in Dublin must be a supporter of popery or horse racing or gambling. The editor of the *Christian Register* judged that Haughton had united the "extremes of illiberality, uncharitableness and ill-temper." On his part, Haughton rejoiced in the belief that many Unitarians agreed with him, but produced no witnesses, unless he counted the *National Anti-Slavery Standard*, published in New York City. That paper cast Dana into its pit of iniquity, a column listing "Pro-Slavery" persons.[25]

Haughton's most distinguished critic to come forward publicly was the Reverend John Scott Porter (1801–80) of the First Presbyterian Church (Unitarian) of Belfast. He was an important figure in Irish Unitarianism and Haughton could ill afford to lose his possible aid. Porter confessed his partisanship for the antislavery movement, but had to condemn Haughton's denunciation of Dana as a "jumble of absurd reasoning," a "grievous wrong," and detrimental to the antislavery cause.[26]

Haughton defended his action in an attempt to show that in their elation over Dana's joining the ranks of Unitarians, his fellow sectarians were forgetting Christianity "in an attempt to exalt Unitarianism." He proceeded to proclaim three dogmatic statements of Haughtonian perfectionism. First of all, Christianity could not possibly exist among slaveholders. Second, slavery could not be named as coequal to any other sin. Third, if anyone—Scott Porter, for example—wanted "to prove to the world" that he was a determined foe of slavery and "a true friend of the coloured race," he ought to join the American Anti-Slavery Society. The password to Haughton's home and abolitionist fraternity had been amended. "Yes" no longer sufficed as an answer to the challenge, "Are you an Abolitionist?" One now had to respond: "Yes, in the style of the American Anti-Slavery Society."[27]

During the great debate between Amicus and Haughton, one anonymous writer had suggested that to oppose the abolitionists in Great Britain was to go against the "advocates of a popular cause." He denied that he chose anonymity to avoid embarrassment, but most assuredly the great use of pseudonyms and initials by anti-abolitionist writers in the Unitarian press illustrated the authors' fear of wading into the waves of popular opinion. Unlike American abolitionists who suffered from mob action, ostracism, and general unpopularity during the early years of their antislavery agitation, the British abolitionists operated in a supportive climate. Therefore, when a Dublin resident set out specifically to refute Haughton in his attack on Dana, and then generally to protest his abolitionism, he hid behind the pseudonym "Philanthropos."

For his refutation of Haughton's conduct toward Dana he wrote a letter to the *Inquirer* that called for moderation, as well as sympathy for the slaveholder. All the letter gained him was an editorial by Hincks defending Haughton.[28] For his protestation of Haughton's abolitionism, he published an essay in 1847 entitled, *Slavery Not Immoral.* The essay gained him a blistering reply from his adversary.

In his essay, Philanthropos denied thte abolitionist contention that slavery was immoral and ought to be immediately abolished. He favored gradual emancipation with education as a prerequisite to the slaves' freedom. The slaveholders controlled their slaves as parents controlled their children, employers their apprentices, husbands their wives. The idea of "equal and absolute independence [was] an absurdity." He declared that the New Testament recognized slavery in four ways: by its silence, by its depiction of slaveholders as members of the Christian Church, by its instruction in the master-slave relationship, and finally by its recognition of Philemon's claim to his slave. If the apostles had not pronounced slavery a moral evil, he concluded, then slavery was not immoral.[29]

On the cover of his response, *Slavery Immoral,* Haughton quoted Shakespeare: "The devil can cite Scripture for his purpose." Because Christianity inculcated the great principle of human brotherhood and slavery was completely opposed to that principle, Haughton deduced that slavery was opposed to Christianity and, therefore, immoral. He ridiculed as "preposterous" his opponent's demand that the education of slaves precede their emancipation, for no slaveholding nation had ever provided for the education of its slaves. He deplored citing apprenticeships or the "sacred relation of husband and father" as analogies to justify slavery. He declared that slavery equaled in weight all other crimes taken together. Certainly, if society condemned fellowship with adulterers, thieves, murderers, and "sheep-stealers", it ought to condemn it with "man-stealers."[30]

The torrent of words that had flowed from the Dana-Haughton episode dried up following the pamphlet exchange between Philanthropos and Haughton. In gaining publicity for his cause, Haughton's effort was a success. But it was dubious publicity at best, and if Porter's reaction was any indication, it may have been damaging publicity at worst. Haughton wanted no "fellowship" with "man-stealer" Mary Palmer Dana. Ironically, if he had only waited a short time, she would have granted him his wish without a fight. Her Unitarianism was as weak as his abolitionism was strong. Within the year she became an Episcopalian.[31]

Alliance and League

The Haughton-Dana affair had consumed columns in the Unitarian press. It was an important illustration of just how doctrinaire a Garrisonian Unitarian had become. Haughton called for subscription to the principles of the American Anti-Slavery Society to prove the authenticity of a person's abolitionism. With the establishment of the Anti-Slavery League in Great Britain, when Garrison visited the country in 1846, local support and commitment to the American Anti-Slavery Society was made possible.

Some British Garrisonians had felt the lack of a national organization to proclaim their views. The American antislavery movement had suffered many divisions, but the major chasm existed between two parties. On the one side stood the American Anti-Slavery Society, or Garrisonians, with headquarters in Boston, which welcomed the participation of women, opposed voting under what it thought to be a pro-slavery Constitution, and dabbled in a number of reforms, many of them extraneous to anti-slavery. On the other side stood the American and Foreign Anti-Slavery Society led by Arthur and Lewis Tappan, two archenemies of Garrison and the American Anti-Slavery Society. Its headquarters were in New York City. It opposed the Garrisonian tactics of agitation and vilification. It also opposed the participation of women, supported political action, and concentrated on antislavery reform. The split between the two parties occurred in 1840 and the tension between them was apparent at the World's Anti-Slavery Convention in London that year. The British and Foreign Anti-Slavery Society, founded in 1839, and headed principally by wealthy and conservative Quakers, took the side of the AFASS. This is where the division stood in the middle of the 1840s. When the Anti-Slavery League was formed as a national organization for the Garrisonians, Unitarians were found at the center of its activities.[32]

Several Unitarians, for example, were included in the earliest conversations held to discuss an organization for Garrisonians.

During the first week in August 1846, Haughton, Estlin, Solly, and Thomas Madge (1786–1870) met with Garrisonian luminaries and proposed a public meeting to found a league. Madge, the minister of Essex Street Chapel, London, eventually became convinced that the Garrisonians were "intolerant bigots" and fell by the wayside, but at the proposed meeting at the Crown and Anchor Tavern, August 10, Haughton and Solly, plus Dr. Hutton of London, Francis Bishop, and layman William Shaen (1820–87) took part in chartering the Anti-Slavery League. Garrison called their meeting a "real old-fashioned, old-organized, American anti-slavery meeting," such as England had never seen before. He told Estlin, who had not been able to attend, that he thought the new league could not "fail to make a deep impression on the public mind, on both sides of the Atlantic."[33]

Some British Garrisonians, including Estlin, were not so sanguine about the league's prospects. Before it was even launched, he had privately declared his doubts. The first article of the league's constitution insisted that slaveholding was a sin that "ought immediately to be abandoned." Estlin had maintained that many "rich and generous people" would not "give a farthing" to an abolition society advocating "immediate, unconditional, unrequited emancipation." The league's second article opened its membership to all persons sympathetic to its principles without regard to their nationality, race, religion, or politics (but unhappily not sex—women were to be segregated in separate "Ladies Associations"). Estlin had said that Unitarians would unite with others in any philanthropic purpose, but he had warned that they were treated "with coolness . . . by nearly all other sects." The league's third article stated its object to be the overthrow of slavery in every land, particularly in the United States, by "exclusively moral and peaceful" means. Estlin had argued that Garrison's strong language was taken as "*unchristian*," anything but moral, and certainly not peaceful.[34] When the league set sail, Estlin warned Garrison to avoid the flotsam of English reform that came into its path, disestablishment, republicanism, Chartism, universal suffrage, etc., and to set its bearings toward antislavery exclusively. He suggested that the league enlist wealthy and influential persons who could do the most for the cause, rather than the working and middle classes. It was not England's "kitchens and workshops that needed Anti-Slavery agitation for America's sake," he told May, "but [her] *drawing-rooms,* the salons of the wealthy, and the

libraries of the learned." The people Garrison had most
pleased would forget about American slavery just as soon as he
returned to the United States. Care for their own welfare
would crowd from their minds any interest in the black slaves
across the sea.[35] Estlin proved to be right; he knew his home
waters well, but Garrison was a captain who seldom heeded
advice. The voyage of the Anti-Slavery League was short.

The fault for this lay with an inferior ship and a stubborn
captain, not the crew. The many Unitarians who helped to
launch it worked very hard to keep it afloat. Hincks offered to
help Garrison, both privately and publicly in his capacity as
editor of the *Inquirer*. In a major editorial he endorsed the
league and excellently summarized the Garrisonians' position.
He confessed that their doctrine of treating the slaveholder and
his apologist as civilization's outlaws was harsh. He himself had
at first "strongly rebelled against it," but now he yielded to a
"reluctant but a sincere and full assent" to it. To those who
maintained that some of "their best friends" were slaveholders,
or apologists for slaveholders, he answered that to grant
slaveholders respectability was to retard emancipation efforts.
To those who objected to interfering with an independent nation's "domestic institution," he answered it was a duty of the
British to express their support for the downtrodden the
"world over." To those who objected to the language of the
Garrisonians, he answered that it was impossible to speak too
strongly of slavery's "abominations." He concluded: "We believe that duty demands that we give our earnest support to the
Anti-Slavery League in its endeavours to arouse, concentrate,
and direct public opinion in this country."[36] The editorial by
Hincks accompanied a complete report of the foundation
meeting of the league that carried nearly verbatim the speeches
of Haughton, Garrison, Douglass, Solly, and others.[37]

The Unitarians aided the League in many ways. Hincks
served as an agent for it by collecting memberships and donations through the *Inquirer,* and generously reporting its activities. When the general press boycotted a harangue by
Garrison upon British institutions, Hincks published its full
text.[38] Estlin offered to the visiting American Garrisonians his
"elegant residence" as their home and his phaeton as their taxi.
He helped to found, along with William James, George Armstrong, and others, the Bristol auxiliary of the league. His relative antislavery moderation discomforted Garrison somewhat,
but Estlin's opulence and generosity, and his position as the

"main spoke in the anti-slavery wheel" in the West of England, stifled any criticism that Garrison harbored.[39] Francis Bishop prepared the way for Garrison's triumphant visit to Exeter, and he was the principal founder and leader of the League's auxiliary in that city. His work pleased Garrison greatly, and even more so, when he named his daughter, Caroline Garrison Bishop.[40] William Rathbone provided Garrison his name and residence as a postal address, and he and Richard Rathbone (1788–1860) entertained the Garrison entourage when it visited Liverpool.[41] Philip Carpenter was one of the "highly influential inhabitants" of Warrington who enrolled in the League's activities there. Joseph Lupton and Charles Wicksteed, both ardent admirers of Garrison, led the organization in Leeds. Dr. John Bowring, M.P. chaired the League's first annual meeting. Unitarians were greatly represented in the "List of Donations and Subscriptions" to the League; Estlin, incidentally, providing the second largest personal donation. Sam May in America solicited members for the League there, and signed up himself, his wife, and two eldest children.[42]

Obviously, not all Unitarians opened their homes and purses to Garrison or subscribed to the League. In the spring of 1846, James Martineau had written to Mary Carpenter that he believed that the "disgraceful divisions" of the abolitionists had led to indifference in Liverpool toward antislavery. When the League was established, he did not join it. "Amicus" reopened his correspondence to the *Inquirer* to assail the "bigotry," "folly and rashness" of the league, which only excited "disgust" for the abolitionists. Another correspondent complained of the league's meddling in American affairs. Why not a league to oppose serfdom in Russia or polygamy in Turkey? he asked.[43]

Obviously, it was not only Unitarians who opened their homes and purses to Garrison or subscribed to the League. The league had some strength in Scotland, and in the land of John Knox, Unitarians were few. And in England the league's meetings were often mainly attended by Quakers. Garrison commented appreciably on the support by the considerable number of Friends of the "affluent class." But where he was received with "most warmth," Mary Carpenter wrote, was where the Unitarians had zealously come forward. And of all the religious groups who supported him in Britain, Garrison seemed to appreciate them the most. He felt greatly indebted to Bishop, James, Solly, Philip Carpenter, Harris, and other Unitarian ministers. "Religiously," he explained, the Unitarians in England were "regarded as little better than infidels," but he found them "to be much better than their revilers and persecutors."[44]

Garrison's charisma had captivated many of the Unitarians who had met him at the World's Anti-Slavery Convention in 1840, and during his visit to England in 1846 he excited more followers. "The moral grandeur of his character . . . profoundly impressed" Henry William Crosskey. Mary Carpenter was enthusiastic about his visit, and counted it a "great privilege to be reckoned among his friends."[45] Still, it was not Garrison's charismatic personality alone that won him devoted Unitarian workers for the League. Enormous credit has to go to his coworker Samuel May, Jr. The prodigious correspondence with British Unitarians that May initiated during his own visit to England in 1843—at one point he was writing to twenty of their ministers—kept his coreligionists informed, in great detail, of the progress of the antislavery cause in America. His letters were a solid, trusted source of information. British Unitarians called upon him many times to verify reports and to explain events.[46] When Estlin wrote his important pamphlet, *A Brief Notice of American Slavery, and the Abolition Movement,* May served as his "research assistant."[47]

The familial unity of the Bristol Unitarians eased Garrison's task in securing their aid. Conversions of certain individuals often brought with them their friends and families. In her study of transatlantic abolitionism, Clare Taylor has acknowledged this important phenomenon and has prepared family trees for the Westons of America and the Wighams of Britain to illustrate it. The familial and social relationships of the British Unitarians are equally revealing. This can be illustrated by focusing on Lant Carpenter. All of his children were interested in the reform—knowledge of the wrongs of the slave, said Mary Carpenter, was "implanted in [their] hearts from childhood"— and three were partial to the Garrisonians: Mary, Philip, and Anna (1808–70). Carpenter had taught and influenced James and Harriet Martineau, with opposite results. His congregation, Lewin's Mead Chapel, had among its laity Dr. Bowring, Dr. Estlin, and Estlin's daughter, Mary (1820–1902); and among its ministers, George Armstrong and William James, all prominent Garrisonians. Armstrong's wife, Frances, matched her husband's loyalty to the cause. James was greatly admired by both Francis Bishop and Henry Solly. Solly was a close friend of the Carpenters and considered Dr. Carpenter one of the "excellent of the earth." Solly married the sister of William Shaen and Francis Bishop married Solly's sister.[48] In the fashion of the present-day feminist movement for hyphenated names, Bishop's daughter might have called herself Caroline Garrison Solly-Bishop. Her name would have excellently symbolized the complexity and intimacy of the Unitarian-Garrisonian connection.

No family of people worked harder than the Unitarians in support of the Boston Bazaar, a prime source of income for the American Anti-Slavery Society. Every year during the Christmas season, Maria Weston Chapman and her sisters and friends managed a fair that relied heavily upon and appreciated immensely gifts from Great Britain. It was "the English, Scotch, and Irish donations to the Fair," declared Samuel May, that made it a financial success and produced much of its "eclat."[49] The solicitation and preparation of gifts and the feverish activity connected with their packing and shipping were wonderful social events for the British abolitionists, particularly for the women, and Mary Estlin, Mary Carpenter, Frances Armstrong, and Anna Carpenter worked tirelessly for the bazaar. As many as 600 to 700 items were shipped from Bristol alone, everything from drawings by Mary Carpenter to patchwork quilts and knitted socks made by the children of her Ragged School.[50] The philanthropy of her ragged scholars was most affecting: "Many a time did the girls freely work long hours beyond school-time to finish their neat patchwork quilts; and barefooted children who had been taught to knit, brought stockings made in secret to escape the eyes of drunken parents, and begged to be allowed to send them to the poor slaves." The some 300 people in Bristol who worked on the shipment of articles to the Boston Bazaar enabled the fair, in the late 1840s, to gross proceeds of $3,000 to $4,000 a year.[51]

Although the league encouraged its membership, particularly its Ladies' Associations, to support the Boston Bazaar, shipments to the fair were not dependent upon the existence of the league. They had gone on before it was founded and they continued long after it failed. The action that gained the league its greatest notoriety was its attack upon the Evangelical Alliance. The latter organization, an ancestor of today's ecumenical movement, was holding an international meeting in London. Although purporting to have a worldwide membership of individual Christians, most of its members in fact were British and American. At its meeting a motion was made to exclude slaveholders from membership in the alliance. Delegates from America's Southern states angrily stated their opposition and an ugly debate ensued. Eventually, the meeting erased from its minutes the whole discussion on slavery.[52]

The league immediately attacked the alliance. It held large rallies in Bristol, Manchester (where 4,000 people attended), and London. All three meetings voted to censure the alliance. Unitarians voted for the censure with alacrity. The alliance, which refused to exclude slaveholders, had summarily excluded them as infidels.[53]

The uproar over the alliance pleased Armstrong immensely. "Americans [would] see," he explained to Catherine Clarkson, "how much in *earnest* Englishmen [were] in this matter—and that the door of civilized society [would] speedily be closed against all partakers or defenders of the horrid crime of holding men in slavery." The league's attack upon the alliance gave it a great deal of publicity and it seemed to show a certain vitality. It estimated the attendance at its meetings throughout England and Scotland to hear Garrison, Douglass, and Thompson at around 60,000 persons. It had good press coverage by the *Patriot, Nonconformist,* and *Inquirer* newspapers, and itself distributed about 25,000 tracts. Letters of encouragement came from antislavery organizations in America, Ireland, and Switzerland.[54]

But storm clouds crowded its horizon. Estlin was displeased over Garrison's attacks on British institutions. Hincks was also bothered by them, and he now judged Garrison's language as "repulsive to English tastes." Both men lamented that no "distinguished names" had come forward to back the league. Estlin thought that Thompson was "unfit" to be its president and exerted no "moral influence." Frances Armstrong found so much anti-Garrisonian feeling among the Ladies' Anti-Slavery Committee in Bristol that she could not induce it to break its ties with the British and Foreign Anti-Slavery Society and join the league. Francis Bishop discovered that the orthodox were branding Garrison as an infidel.[55]

These criticisms and anxieties showed that the league was cracking apart and that, despite their overall loyalty and hard work, the Unitarians themselves might have innocently hastened its destruction. Garrison, for example, had an unfortunate experience at a meeting in Exeter Hall that showed that Unitarian support could be a liability. In enumerating various denominations as Christian groups, he happened to mention the Unitarians. His audience's reaction was immediately hostile, and must have been terribly embarrassing to the Unitarians present. Cries of "No, No!" went up and the uproar "continued for some moments" until the chairman intervened to restore order. Garrison felt compelled to apologize to the crowd: "I said nothing," he told them, "endorsing [the Unitarians'] Christian character." It was an extraordinary scene and an extraordinary statement. Unitarians had been publicly repudiated as Christians by the crowd, and as his dedicated disciples by Garrison. The audience did not want to join with the Unitarians. Time demonstrated that they did not want to join the league. Garrison and Douglass shortly returned to America. In May 1847, Dr. Bowring chaired the first annual meeting of the debt-ridden and moribund League. That meeting was also its last.[56]

Notes

1. Garrison quoted by Charles Richard Denton, "American Unitarians, 1830–1865: A Study of Religious Opinion on War, Slavery, and the Union" (Ph.D. diss., Michigan State University, 1969), p. 88. See also p. 10; James Martineau to Charles Wicksteed, n.p., 23 April 1857, James Drummond, *The Life and Letters of James Martineau, LL.D., S.T.D., Etc.* (New York: Dodd, Mead & Co., 1902), 1: 320.

2. Orville Dewey, "On American Morals and Manners," *Christian Examiner* 36 (March 1844): 263, 265, 267, 268. For information on Dewey, see Samuel A. Eliot, ed., *Heralds of a Liberal Faith* (Boston: American Unitarian Association, 1910), 3: 84–89; Allen Johnson and Dumas Malone, eds., *Dictionary of American Biography* (New York: Charles Scribner's Sons, 1928–1958), 5: 222, cited hereafter as *DAB;* Orville Dewey, *Autobiography and Letters,* Mary E. Dewey, ed. (Boston: Roberts Brothers, 1833).

3. James Haughton, "Address on Slavery," *Christian Pioneer* 18 (April 1844): 185; George Harris, "Review of *American Morals and Manners* by Rev. Dr. Dewey," *Christian Pioneer* 18 (October 1844): 478.

4. Samuel Haughton, *Memoir of James Haughton. With Extracts from His Private and Published Letters* (Dublin: E. Ponsonby, 1877), pp. 17, 20, 23–27, 30–32, 37, 44, 47; James Haughton to the Pennsylvania Anti-Slavery Society, Dublin, 16 May 1843, Sidney Howard Gay Papers, Columbia University; Haughton to Samuel May, Jr., Dublin, 28 May 1846, May Papers, Boston Public Library, cited hereafter as MB; Haughton to Irishmen in America, Dublin, n.d., *Daniel O'Connell Upon American Slavery: With Other Irish Testimonies* (New York: American Anti-Slavery Society, 1860), pp. 41–42.

5. "The Address from the Unitarians of Ireland on Slavery," *Christian Register,* 30 September 1843, cited hereafter as *CR;* "Letter by 'B' on Irish Address" [title supplied], *CR,* 21 October 1843; "Fifteenth Annual Report of the Irish Unitarian Christian Society," *Inquirer,* 30 August 1845, p. 554.

6. James Haughton to the editor, Dublin, 15 August 1845, *Inquirer,* 30 August 1845, p. 547. On Parkman, see Eliot, *Heralds,* 1: 111–18, and Samuel May, Jr., "American Unitarians," Notes submitted to Mr. Estlin, in 1853 for an article in the *Anti-Slavery Advocate,* May Papers, MB.

7. "Address of the Irish Unitarian Christian Society to their Brethren in America," *Inquirer*, 14 February 1846, p. 109.

8. James Haughton to the editor, Dublin, 6 February 1846, *Inquirer*, 28 February 1846, p. 132; "Address of the Irish Unitarian Christian Society . . . ," *CR*, 21 March 1846, p. 46.

9. James Haughton to the editor, Dublin, 23 March 1847, *Inquirer*, 17 April 1847, pp. 243–44; James Haughton to Samuel May, Jr., Dublin, 29 March 1847, May Papers, MB.

10. "Irish Unitarian Christian Society," *Inquirer*, 22 May 1847, pp. 332–33. For information on Gannett, see Eliot, *Heralds*, 3: 138–47, *DAB*, 7: 122–123, and William Channing Gannett, *Ezra Stiles Gannett, Unitarian Minister in Boston, 1824–1871* (Boston: Roberts Brothers, 1875).

11. Ezra Stiles Gannett to the editor, n.p., n.d., *CR*, 24 July 1847. Gannett wrote elsewhere that he tried unsuccessfully to correct misrepresentations "connected with [his] name in the English Unitarian Anti-Slavery papers[?]" and eventually gave up. Thereafter, he preferred "silence to controversy." See W. C. Gannett, *Ezra Stiles Gannett*, pp. 285, 295.

12. "A Response to the Address of the Irish Unitarian Christian Society, from their Brethren in America," *CR*, 30 October 1847, p. 173.

13. [Francis Parkman], "Courtesy and Charity of Abolitionism," *CR*, 18 October 1845, p. 166.

14. Ibid., p. 166; James Haughton to the editor, Dublin, 3 October 1844, *Inquirer*, 18 October 1845, p. 658. Haughton wrote to Garrison and remarked that he found Parkman a "pleasant intelligent man, but just as much fitted to be a Christian teacher, as I am to be a Doctor of Divinity; and 'I guess,' the surplice would hang rather awkwardly on my shoulders." See Haughton to the editor, Dublin, 30 October 1845, *Liberator*, 28 November 1845.

15. "Amicus" to the editor, n.p., 18 September 1845, *Inquirer*, 27 September 1845, p. 612.

16. James Haughton to the editor, Dublin, 3 October 1844, *Inquirer*, 18 October 1845, pp. 658–59; "Amicus" to the editor, n.p., 22 October 1845, *Inquirer*, 1 November 1845, pp. 691–92.

17. James Haughton to the editor, Dublin, 8 November 1845, *Inquirer*, 22 November 1845, pp. 738–39; "Amicus" to the editor, 27 November 1845, *Inquirer*, 6 December 1845, p. 775.

18. "Amicus" to the editor, n.p., 6 February 1846, *Inquirer*, 21 February 1846, pp. 115–16.

19. "Amicus" to the editor, n.p., 28 February 1846, *Inquirer*, 7 March 1846, p. 147.

20. "Amicus" to the editor, n.p., 18 April 1846, *Inquirer*, 9 May 1846, p. 292.

21. Haughton, sensing that Hincks was bored with his letters, asked abolitionist friends also to write and two complied. See James Haughton to Samuel May, Jr., Dublin, 28 May 1846, May Papers, MB; Samuel May, Jr., to the editor, Leicester, Massachusetts, 31 March 1846, *Inquirer*, 23 May 1846, pp. 322–23; Ralph Varian to the editor, n.p., n.d., *Inquirer*, 30 May 1846, p. 339.

22. "Amicus" to the editor, n.p., 18 April 1845, *Inquirer*, 9 May 1846, p. 291. See also "Amicus" to the editor, n.p., 9 March 1846, *Inquirer*, 14 March 1846, p. 164 and "Amicus" to the editor, n.p., 23 March 1846, *Inquirer*, 4 April 1846, p. 212. James Haughton to the editor, Dublin, 3 April 1846, *Inquirer*, 11 April 1846, pp. 228–29; Haughton to the editor, Dublin, 30 May 1846, *Inquirer*, 30 May, 1846, pp. 338–39; Haughton to the editor, Dublin, 4 July 1846, *Inquirer*, 25 July 1846, pp. 468–69.

23. Oscar Fay Adams, *A Dictionary of American Authors* (Boston: Houghton Mifflin

Co., 1904), p. 342; Mary Dana, *Letters Addressed to Relatives and Friends, Chiefly in Reply to Arguments in Support of the Doctrine of the Trinity* (Boston: James Munroe Co., 1845); James Haughton to the editor, Dublin, 19 July 1846, *Inquirer*, 15 August 1846, p. 515.

24. Haughton to editor, *Inquirer*, 15 August 1846, p. 515; James Haughton, "American Slavery—Mrs. Dana's Letters," *Irish Unitarian Magazine* 1 (September 1846): 268–71; James Haughton to the editor, Dublin, 26 September, 1846, *Inquirer*, 3 October 1846, p. 627.

25. Emanuel Warwood to the editor, Brades Steel Works, 10 September 1846, *Inquirer*, 19 September 1846, p. 597; "Mr. Haughton and Mrs. Dana," *CR*, 14 November 1846, 182; "A Friend to Freedom" to the editor, 18 August 1846, *Inquirer*, 22 August 1846, p. 532; J. Scott Porter, "Mr. Haughton's Attack on Mrs. Dana," *Irish Unitarian Magazine* (November, 1846), p. 335; "Mrs. Dana and Mr. Haughton," *CR*, 12 September 1846, p. 146; James Haughton to the editor, Dublin, 13 November 1846, *Inquirer*, 24 November 1846, p. 756; "Mrs. Dana and Mr. Haughton," *National Anti-Slavery Standard*, 1 October 1846, p. 69.

26. Leslie Stephen and Sidney Lee, eds., *The Dictionary of National Biography* (Oxford: Oxford University Press, 1921–1922), 16: 185–86; Porter, "Mr. Haughton's Attack," p. 337.

27. James Haughton, "Mrs. Dana, Mr. Haughton, and the Rev. John Scott Porter," *Irish Unitarian Magazine* 2 (January 1847): 3–6; Haughton to editor, *Inquirer*, 24 November 1846, p. 756.

28. "Philanthropos" to the editor, n.p., 18 January 1847, *Inquirer*, 23 January 1847, p. 52; "Mr. Haughton and Mrs. Dana," *Inquirer*, 23 January 1847, pp. 50–51.

29. Philanthropos, *Slavery Not Immoral: A Letter to James Haughton, Esq., Dublin* (Dublin: James McGlashan, 1847), pp. 9–12, 17–18, 24–25, 30.

30. James Haughton, *Slavery Immoral; Being a Reply to a Letter in Which an Attempt is Made to Prove that Slavery is Not Immoral* (Dublin: James McGlashan, 1847), pp. 8–12, 20, 22.

31. Adams, *Dictionary of American Authors*, p. 342.

32. One of the best discussions of the American antislavery division is Aileen S. Kraditor, *Means and Ends in American Abolitionism: Garrison and His Critics on Strategy and Tactics, 1834–1850* (New York: Pantheon Books, 1969). On British antislavery divisions, Howard Temperley has done a masterly job of sorting out the various factions and has provided excellent diagrams to illustrate changes of titles and relationship. See his article "Anti-Slavery," in *Pressure from Without in Early Victorian England*, Patricia Hollis, ed. (London: Edward Arnold, 1974), pp. 32, 48–49. See also Howard Temperley, *British Antislavery 1833–1870* (London: Longman Group Ltd., 1972), pp. 215–16.

33. "New Anti-Slavery Society," *Inquirer*, 8 August 1846, p. 506; "Anti-Slavery League," *Inquirer*, 15 August 1846, p. 520; Raymond V. Holt, *The Unitarian Contribution to Social Progress in England*, 2nd rev. ed. (London: Lindsey Press, 1952), p. 137; William Lloyd Garrison to R. D. Webb, London, 19 August 1846, Clare Taylor, *British and American Abolitionists. An Episode in Transatlantic Understanding* (Edinburgh: Edinburgh University Press, 1974), p. 276; William Lloyd Garrison to John B. Estlin, London, 19 August 1846, Walter M. Merrill, ed., *The Letters of William Lloyd Garrison* (Cambridge: Belknap Press of Harvard University Press, 1973), 3: 382.

34. Richard D. Webb, a Dublin Quaker, predicted the league would not get either "much money or much confidence." See R. D. Webb to Maria Weston Chapman, Dublin, 26 February 1846, Taylor, *British and American Abolitionists*, p. 253; John B. Estlin to R. D. Webb, Bristol, 13 November 1845, ibid., p. 242; Estlin to Maria Weston Chapman, Bristol, 28 February 1846, ibid., p. 257. For the constitution of the league, see "Anti-Slavery League," *The Unitarian* 1 (September 1846): 378–79.

35. John B. Estlin to William Lloyd Garrison, Bristol, 17 October 1846, Taylor, *British and American Abolitionists,* pp. 292–93. Estlin to Samuel May, Jr., Bristol, 1 October 1846, ibid., pp. 290–92; Estlin to May, Bristol, 2 November 1846, ibid., p. 296.

36. William Lloyd Garrison to Richard D. Webb, Birmingham, 5 September 1846, *Letters of Garrison,* 3: 397; "American Slavery," *Inquirer,* 22 August 1846, pp. 529–30.

37. "The Anti-Slavery League," *Inquirer,* 22 August 1846, pp. 539–41.

38. "The Anti-Slavery Cause," *Inquirer,* 5 September 1846, p. 561; "American Slavery," ibid., pp. 569–72.

39. William Lloyd Garrison to Henry C. Wright, Bristol, 26 August 1846, *Letters of Garrison,* 3: 387–88; "Anti-Slavery Meetings in Bristol," *Inquirer,* 12 September 1846, p. 588; J. B. Estlin to Samuel May, Jr., Bristol, 1 September 1846, Taylor, *British and American Abolitionists,* p. 281.

40. Letters of Garrison, 3: p. 388; William Lloyd Garrison to Richard D. Webb, Birmingham, 5 September 1846, ibid., p. 396; Garrison to Samuel J. May, Boston, 19 December 1846, ibid., p. 462; Francis Bishop to Garrison, Exeter, 3 December 1846, Garrison Papers, MB; "Exeter—American Slavery," *Inquirer,* 5 September 1846, p. 572.

41. William Lloyd Garrison to Helen E. Garrison, Sheffield, 10 September 1846, *Letters of Garrison,* 3: p. 404; "Mr. Garrison's departure from England," *Inquirer,* 14 November 1846, p. 722.

42. "Anti-Slavery League. Warrington," *Inquirer,* 24 November 1846, p. 764; Russell Lant Carpenter, *Memoirs of the Life and Work of Philip Pearsall Carpenter, B.A. London, Ph.D. New York, Chiefly Derived from His Letters* (London: C. Kegan Paul & Co., 1880), p. 98; "The Anti-Slavery League [in Leeds], and American Slavery," *Inquirer,* 30 January 1847, p. 77; Charles Hargrove, *In Memoriam: Joseph Lupton, Who Died Suddenly, Unwarned Not Unready, January 17th, 1894. A Sermon Preached at Mill Hill Chapel, Leeds* (Leeds: Samuel Moxon & Son, 1894), p. 18; "[The First General Meeting of the] Anti-Slavery League," *Inquirer,* 22 May 1847, pp. 330–31; *The First Report, Adopted at the General Meeting of the Anti-Slavery League, at Finsburg Chapel, May 19th, 1847* (London: A. Munro, 1847) pp. 3, 18–19; Samuel May to J. B. Estlin, Boston, 4 December 1846, Taylor, p. 303.

43. James Martineau to Mary Carpenter, Liverpool, 18 May 1846, Martineau Papers, Manchester College Library, Oxford. Garrison desired to see Martineau, but the latter was not in Liverpool during his visit there. Friends told Garrison that Martineau was "considerably prejudiced against the true anti-slavery band in "England]." See Garrison to Samuel J. May, Boston, 19 December 1846, *Letters of Garrison,* 3: 462; "Amicus" to the editor, n.p., 5 September 1846, *Inquirer,* 12 September 1846, p. 580; "Amicus" to the editor, n.p., 3 October 1846, *Inquirer,* 24 October 1846, p. 675; "C.F.T." to the editor, Liverpool, 26 November 1846, *Inquirer,* 12 December 1846, pp. 786–87.

44. Temperley, *British Antislavery,* 218–20; "The Anti-Slavery League, and American Slavery," *Inquirer,* 30 January 1847, p. 77; William Lloyd Garrison to Henry C. Wright, Bristol, 26 August 1846, *Letters of Garrison,* 3: 387; Mary Carpenter to Maria Weston Chapman, Bristol, 31 October 1846, Weston Papers, MB; William Lloyd Garrison to Samuel J. May, Boston, 19 December 1846, *Letters of Garrison,* 3: 462.

45. Richard Acland Armstrong, *Henry William Crosskey, LL.D., F.G.S., His Life and Work* (Birmingham: Cornish Brothers, 1895), p. 128; Mary Carpenter to Maria Weston Chapman, Bristol, 17 October 1846, Weston Papers, MB.

46. Samuel May, Jr., "Memo of English Correspondence," n.p., n.d.,; George Armstrong to Samuel May, Jr., Clifton Vale, Bristol, 3 November 1845; Frances Armstrong to May, Clifton Vale, Bristol, 16 February 1846; Joseph Hutton to May, London, 30 April 1849; May Papers, MB.

47. [John B. Estlin], *A Brief Notice of American Slavery, and the Abolition Movement* (Bristol: H. C. Evans, 1846); John B. Estlin to Samuel May, Jr., Bristol, 2 March 1845, May Papers, MB.

48. Taylor, *British and American Abolitionists,* pp. 3, 546–47; Mary Carpenter to Maria Weston Chapman, Bristol, 9 March 1845, Weston Papers, MB; J. Estlin Carpenter, *The Life and Work of Mary Carpenter,* 2nd ed. (London: Macmillan, 1881), p. 70; Christopher James Thomas, *Some Account of the Rise and Progress of the Ancient Society of Protestant Dissenters, Worshipping in Lewin's Mead, Bristol* (Bristol: Stephens and Eyre, 1891), pp. 1–2, 28; Henry Solly, *"These Eighty Years" or, the Story of an Unfinished Life,* (London: Simpkin, Marshall and Co., 1893), 1: 236–38, 328–29; "Obituary. The Rev. Henry Solly," *Inquirer,* 7 March 1903, p. 151. What Lant Carpenter's antislavery influence would have been had he lived beyond 1840 is wonderful to speculate upon.

49. Samuel May to Mary Carpenter, Leicester, 29 December 1845, Taylor, *British and American Abolitionists,* p. 246.

50. George Armstrong to Catherine Clarkson, Clifton Vale, Bristol, 5 September 1846, Clarkson Papers, Huntington Library; William James to Samuel May, Jr., Bristol, 21 October 1844, May Papers, MB; J. B. Estlin to Samuel May, Jr., Bristol, 29 October 1844, Taylor, *British and American Abolitionists,* pp. 230–31; Estlin to R. D. Webb, Bristol, 13 November 1845, 242; J. E. Carpenter, *Life and Work,* pp. 70, 94.

51. J. E. Carpenter, *Life and Works,* p. 94; Mary Carpenter to the Reverend A. A. Livermore, Bristol, 30 October 1846, ibid., p. 76; Samuel May, Jr., to J. B. Estlin, Boston, 8 January 1849, Taylor, *British and American Abolitionists,* p. 333.

52. *First Report, Anti-Slavery League, 1847,* p. 24; Temperley, *British Antislavery,* pp. 217–18; "The Anti-Slavery League and the Evangelical Alliance," *Inquirer,* 10 October 1846, pp. 666–67.

53. "Anti-Slavery League," *Inquirer,* 10 October 1846, pp. 666–67; "Anti-Slavery Meeting at Manchester," *Inquirer,* 10 October 1846, p. 667; "The Evangelical Alliance, and Slavery," *Inquirer,* 19 September 1846, pp. 593–94; "The Anti-Slavery League," *Inquirer,* 19 September 1846, pp. 603–5; C. Duncan Rice, "The Scots Abolitionists" (unpublished manuscript, 1975), p. 169.

54. George Armstrong to Catherine Clarkson, Clifton Vale, Bristol, 5 September 1846, Clarkson Papers, Huntington Library; *First Report, Anti-Slavery League, 1847,* pp. 8–10.

55. See note 35 above; [William Hincks], "Mr. Garrison's Departure from England," *Inquirer,* 14 November 1846, pp. 722–23; J. B. Estlin to Samuel May, Jr., Bristol, 1 September 1846, Taylor, 281; Estlin to May, Bristol, 2 November 1846, ibid., p. 296; Frances Armstrong to May, Clifton Vale, 16 February 1846, May Papers, MB. The letter is also in ibid., pp. 251–52; Armstrong to William Lloyd Garrison, Clifton Vale, Bristol, 3 September 1846, ibid., p. 283; "Minutes of the Bristol and Clifton Ladies Anti-Slavery Society," entry for 10 August 1846, Estlin Papers, Dr. William's Library, London; J. B. Estlin to Samuel May, Jr., Bristol, 18 May 1847, May Papers, MB; Francis Bishop to William Lloyd Garrison, Exeter, 3 December 1846, Garrison Papers, MB.

56. "The Anti-Slavery League," *Inquirer,* 19 September 1846, p. 604; *First Report, Anti-Slavery League,* p. 3; Temperley, *British Antislavery,* p. 219.

4

Some Unitarians as Abolitionists: The Rejection of Radicalism—1847–50

R(egrets) over a S(laveholding) V(ice)-P(resident): The Boston Invitation

The dogmatic abolitionist enthusiasm, some would say fanaticism, of a person such as James Haughton was so dedicated to purifying Unitarianism of the slightest taint of slavery that it had driven him to accuse a woman he had never met, and about whom he knew almost nothing, of being a "man-stealer." It seemed that Haughton was so intent on attacking a Unitarian slaveholder that, if one had not existed, he probably would have invented one. No sarcasm is intended; the observation is simply a comment on the historical evidence of the Haughton-Dana affair. It is necessary to make it in order to demonstrate the immense degree of explosive rage that must have .consumed Haughton, Armstrong, and Garrisonian abolitionists like them, when they heard that among the Board of Vice-Presidents of the American Unitarian Association was a slaveholder from Charleston, South Carolina—a Unitarian physician who owned one hundred and twenty slaves. His name was Joshua B. Whitridge (1789–1865), a native of Rhode Island, who had practiced medicine in Charleston for some thirty years. Whitridge had been elected, probably as a token Southerner, as one of the fifteen honorary vice-presidents of the AUA in May 1846. Members of the nominating committee and the AUA who knew he was a slaveholder kept the information to themselves and the election proceeded without comment from Samuel May and his friends. Time passed and May himself did not discover the "mistake" until he read a reference to Whitridge's slaveholding in the *Liberator*. It was Haughton who, having read the same reference, brought the bona fide "man-stealer" to the attention of the Unitarians in Great Britain, in the spring of 1847.[1]

At the same time that attention was being drawn to the existence of a slaveholding officer of the AUA, an invitation was received from Francis Parkman, Ezra Stiles Gannett, George E. Ellis (1814–94), and about a dozen other American Unitarian ministers. This so-called Boston Invitation encouraged Unitarian friends in the United Kingdom to attend the annual May meetings of the AUA. "Come over and help us," it said, "we can assure to you the heartiest reception."[2] George Armstrong and several British Unitarians immediately set out to "help" their American brethren, but not in a way the Americans had expected. At the half-yearly meeting of the Western Unitarian Christian Union, in Gloucester, on April 29, Armstrong presented a reply to the Boston Invitation that "met with the entire sympathy" of his colleagues. It condemned the AUA for honoring a slaveholder with an office in the association, a calamitous action that affected "seriously" their denomination's position in the world. Armstrong was asked to serve with Estlin, James, and two others, to draft a formal reply to the Boston Invitation.[3]

Armstrong's next opportunity to act was at the May anniversary meeting of the British and Foreign Unitarian Association. He prepared for the meeting by calling his friends to arms. He implored the Reverend Edmund Kell (1799–1874) to attend in order to deal honorably with the Boston Invitation and "to save [them] from being sunk to the level of the Evangelical Alliance." Help them to bear their testimony, he asked Kell, "in the cause of God's coloured children!" He knew that a good degree of help would be needed; the record of the BFUA in speaking out against slavery was not spectacular. The last time slavery had been mentioned at an annual meeting of the BFUA was in 1845: Henry Solly had been ruled out of order for proposing an antislavery resolution in protest of the Simmons Affair.[4]

The Twenty-second Annual Meeting of the BFUA opened at the New Gravel-Pit Chapel, Hackney, in London, May 1847. The abolitionist storm broke when the association's Secretary, Edward Tagart (1804–58), included a reference to the Boston Invitation in his annual report. Armstrong objected. To accept the report would give the Invitation an official sanction. Thomas Madge proposed deleting the Invitation from the report and his proposal was seconded by a distinguished layman, Henry Crabb Robinson (1775–1867). Robinson declared that the Invitation came from some ministers, who as "defenders and apologizers for slavery" had "disgraced and polluted" Unitarian pulpits. Dr. Bowring rejoiced that the BFUA showed such "extreme sensitivity" about being possibly tainted by the "unholy thing which so dishonoured" their American brethren. The Americans ought to be told that their invitations would be rejected until they had detached themselves from the "stigma" of slavery. Whatever pity the British Unitarians felt toward slaveholders, they considered "slaveholding as disentitling men to the great rights of Christianity." Both the comments by Robinson and Bowring were enthusiastically applauded.

Armstrong then reported, amid jeers and cheers, that eight of the fifteen ministers who had signed the Invitation had not signed the Unitarian protest against slavery, and one of them, Dr. Parkman, was considered by some American Unitarians as "one of the most pro-slavery men in all the north." Two ministers, including an American, testified that, although Parkman was certainly an anti-abolitionist, he was no pro-slavery man. Madge interjected to proclaim, amid great laughter and confusion, that some of the most "intolerant bigots" he ever met were abolitionists. Sheer pandemonium ensued when several people tried to speak at one time.

The confusion turned to cheering when John Relly Beard stood to offer his wisdom. American slavery, he said, was an extremely difficult question. He could be an antislavery man and still forgive the way some of their American brethren handled the question. He did not have to ostracize a slaveholder to tell him that slaveholding was wrong. It was a call for moderation by one of their most respected ministers. Armstrong, thrown on the defensive, declared that, "if he stood alone" in the association, he would protest the Invitation. The tension peaked when Robinson called for a vote on the motion to delete the Invitation. The vote was taken: fifteen favored it, and those who opposed it were so numerous they were not counted. The annual report with the Invitation was then passed. The debate showed, Haughton later wrote to May, that they too had their Drs. Gannetts, Deweys, and Parkmans, who would, as much as possible, extinguish antislavery fervor.[5] It also illustrated the minority status of the Garrisonians; not every Unitarian was, or would become, an abolitionist.

In an open letter to Edward Tagart, Estlin defended the conduct of the abolitionists at the meeting. The British Uni-

tarians seemed to be in the dark as to the *"religious* aspect" of
the slavery question. American churches were the main support of slavery. They refused to give Bibles to blacks. They sold
women and children to build theological seminaries and buy
communion plates. They defended slavery from the Scriptures.
They dispensed with moral sanctions, including marriage vows,
among the slaves. They were responsible for the continuance of
slavery. If the churches condemned, instead of encouraging it,
it would cease "immediately."[6]

The responsibility fell most heavily upon America's largest
religious bodies such as the Presbyterians, Methodists, and
Baptists, but the Unitarians were, proportionately, as "an-
swerable as other sects, for the encouragement they afford[ed]
. . . slavery." Some of the Unitarian ministers preferred to
denounce *"slavery in the abstract,"* but it could not be treated as
an *"abstraction."* It was a "positive sin" and slaveholders and
their apologists were "sinners." The English denominations
had a right to remonstrate upon this sinfulness, in answer to
any official communications from their sister churches in
America. Estlin attacked Dewey, the president of the AUA, for
his racism in recommending the removal of American blacks
"from the soil of their birth . . . to distant territories." He
attacked Dr. Whitridge for owning slaves. He declared that the
abolitionists would maintain their zeal in promoting the "Gospel Truth." While "cherishing their Unitarianism," they were
not "forgetful of their Christianity." Removed as they were
from the "prejudices" and "temptations" that beset American
Unitarians, they discerned their brethren's duty more clearly
than the Americans did themselves. America was no longer a
distant land; it was only two weeks away. Her slavery was not a
"remote evil," it shed a "baneful influence" upon the unity of the
two nations. Estlin was not suggesting what particular antislavery course his colleagues ought to follow. His object was to show
that they had "this work to do," and that the leadership of the
BFUA ought not be surprised if the abolitionists would not
allow the question to be passed over unnoticed in any future
official business with the AUA.[7]

In the months that followed several letters in the *Inquirer*
rebutted Estlin's remarks. One was by "Amicus," a lengthy epis-
tle that filled columns in three issues of the paper. All the letters
contained similar arguments: Christian duty required one to
maintain contact with sinners in order to reform and to en-
lighten them; the struggle in America over slavery was volatile
and outside interference could ignite a domestic war there;

unnecessary provocation and irritation precluded the possibility of persuading and convincing; to criticize without having to share in the consequences of one's criticism was cowardly and unjust; and the principle of "no communion with slaveholders" was "totally inconsistent" with the principles of Unitarian Christianity.[8]

Two of the more important responses to the BFUA debate and Estlin's defense of it came from Edward Tagart himself, and from the new editor of the *Inquirer*, Dr. Thomas Sadler (1822–91). In his letter, Tagart felt that the introduction of the slavery issue into the anniversary meetings of the BFUA was clearly not in accord with the original purposes of the association. Reagitation of the subject at future meetings could damage the association. The BFUA was formed to disseminate knowledge of the principles of Unitarian Christianity. The Unitarian abolitionists, he declared, were "impatient of belonging to a small and peculiar sect." They were "desirous of seeing Unitarian Christianity go forth conquering and to conquer." As a consequence, they had assumed the "bold attitude and character of a mighty deliverer," who wanted to strike the shackles from the American slaves immediately. However, he thought, the end of slavery would be "determined by . . . Providence."[9]

But shouldn't those principles be applied?

In his editorial in the *Inquirer*, Sadler accepted the idea that slavery was an "affair of humanity" and not just a national question. But Sadler, the minister of Rosslyn Hill Chapel, London, and a friend of James Martineau, advised moderation. Denunciation did more to harm, than to help, the slave. They ought to invite to their firesides men such as Dewey and Parkman, even the slaveholder himself, to talk over what Christians could do for their "coloured brother." The *Inquirer* might still have been as Gannett labelled it, an "English Unitarian Antislavery paper," but it was no longer a Garrisonian organ. Hincks would be missed.[10]

Letters supporting Estlin's position did not exactly crowd the pages of the *Inquirer*. In printing an abolitionist's contribution, Sadler expressed his disfavor over any ongoing discussion of slavery. It is known that he declined to print a letter by James Haughton and probably refused others. However, he did print one by Samuel May, Jr., which carried important news: a new constitution adopted by the AUA had abolished the entire board of honorary vice-presidents. The association no longer had a slaveholding officer. Perhaps the British Unitarians had achieved some good by their agitation. Moreover, they could not help but be pleased with the resolution passed by the AUA: "We believe slaveholding to be in direct opposition to the law and will of God, and entirely incompatible with the precepts and spirit of Christianity."[11]

Notes of No Thank You: The Irish and British Unitarians Reply

If American conservatives imagined that they could avoid the bark or bite of the British abolitionist bulldog by unceremoniously disposing of a slaveholding vice-president and by passing an antislavery resolution they were sadly mistaken. For their part, American abolitionists appreciated the watchdog vigilance of their British coworkers. The American Unitarians needed to be looked after, May once told Estlin, by "all who love[d] true Unitarianism at home and abroad." Not surprisingly, the first sentinel—one is prompted to say "hound of heaven"—to evoke an institutional response to the issues of 1847 was George Harris. At the annual meeting of his Newcastle and North of England Unitarian Tract and Missionary Society, he secured a resolution that beseeched the AUA to be steadfast and persistent in its opposition to slavery. In his covering letter to Gannett, Harris expressed his opposition to barring intercourse with slaveholders. Such action was contrary to the injuction of Christ Jesus "to seek and to save those who were lost." But Harris's concern for slaveholders was secondary to his regard for the American abolitionists. If his resolution in any way strengthened, he wrote, "those who in the spirit of Christ" labored for the freedom of the enslaved blacks and equality for the free blacks, his hopes would be fulfilled.[12] Such resolutions might be looked upon as a burden by people such as Dewey, Parkman, and Gannett, but they were important to the morale of reformers such as Samuel May.

Almost concurrently with the annual meeting of Harris's Tract and Missionary Society, a group of Irish Unitarians met at the First Presbyterian Congregation in Belfast to consider the Boston Invitation. The presence of the Reverend Dr. Henry Montgomery (1788–1865) dominated the meeting.[13] He had been one of the founders of the Remonstrant Synod of Ulster, in 1829, and of the Irish Unitarian Christian Society, in 1830. He had been a leader in the fight for Catholic Emancipation, believing that no one ought to be debarred from their civil rights because of their religious persuasion. He applied his belief in equal rights to race.[14]

Montgomery read the Boston Invitation, and proceeded to expound on American slavery. "There was nothing more atrocious," he taught, than slavery, or the idea that a man could deny the "light of divine knowledge from entering the minds of [his] fellow-creatures." Slavery, he explained, was "doubly frightful" to contemplate in a country "whose boasted declaration was, 'that all men are born free and equal.'" He thought that they all could agree on the principle of "no union with slave-holders." As a Unitarian body, they ought to "hold *no kind of religious intercourse with slave-holders, or with advocates of slavery.*" He testified that he would personally "*refuse to sit in any Christian body*" that harbored a slaveholding vice-president.[15]

Scott Porter, in whose church the meeting was held, praised the views of Montgomery as being "*those of every member present.*" He felt that something ought to be done to stir their American brethren into action. Nothing done thus far seemed to produce "any effect on them." He then accused the Unitarian Church of the United States of a "great sin, which though not slaveholding, was yet equally as bad." Porter accused them of racism. In none of the American Unitarian churches, he charged, was a "black man . . . permitted to sit with his white brother." He exclaimed:

> Oh! there was something horrible in this, and . . . if attention were properly called to the subject, such an atrocious violation of right would [not] be permitted to continue.—He must say, there was some pretext for the expression all violent as it was, that there was throughout the whole of the United States a *hatred to the coloured population,* when he reflected, that even by *those who professed to be the friends of the slave,* such a cruel exclusion was practiced.[16]

Upon what evidence Porter based his accusation is not known, for information regarding the participation of Negroes in Unitarian congregational life is sparse. There were Negro slaves in nearly every Unitarian congregation in the South. The Archdale Street Unitarian Church in Charleston, South Carolina, had in particular a large number. They took communion after their masters were discharged. The presence of these Negroes in Southern Unitarian congregations was at the discretion of their masters and could be a privilege withdrawn at any time. In the case of the Charleston congregation, the number of "colored communicants" declined. Ironically, the other Unitarian congregation that had a number of Negro members to match those of Archdale Street was abolitionist Theodore Parker's (1810–60) Twenty-Eighth Congregational Society in Boston. Here many fugitives from slavery, as well as some of Boston's most distinguished Negro citizens, attended. Of course, the freedom and responsibility they enjoyed in Parker's congregation were denied Negroes not only in Southern Unitarian congregations—Negroes were not welcomed, for example, into full church membership in the Washington Unitarian Church until 1950—but in Northern Unitarian churches as well. West Church in Boston had a Negro pew in a gallery above the organ. In the First Parish in Brookline, Massachusetts, the Negro pew was in a balcony above the choir loft, in the rear of the church. Here sat "'Black Suzy,' a well-known servant . . . and other dark-skinned outcasts," out of sight and out of mind of the church's white parishioners. Brattle Square Church, Boston, had its own Negro, Darby Vassall, an ex-slave whom it supported in his late years. The church's minister caused the "discomfort of some fastidious pewholders" when he brought Vassall down from the "negro-loft above the organ" to sit beside the pulpit.[17]

In any event, the American Unitarians were not likely to respond to Porter's accusation. The Unitarians in the Northern states could avoid slavery as not being a "local" concern, but racism was another matter. Perhaps they thought, like Porter, that the Negro pew was "one of the most *gentle* exclusions" practiced on the poor blacks, and not worth preaching about. Given the "spirit that animate[d] churches professing to be Christian," he confessed, "the coloured people need not regret their being excluded."[18]

The "religion of Jesus," explained Porter, required them to contemplate slavery, and the more they did, the less astounded they would be by the strong language of the abolitionists. Porter had clearly moved to a more radical antislavery position than that which he had held several months before when he had condemned Haughton's attack on Dana. It was time, he taught, that the principle of "No Union with Slave-holders" ought to

be honestly adopted, and faithfully acted on, by the Unitarians of these lands. . . . We may have, occasionally, to regret the use of violent and intemperate language on the part of some who advocate it, but we must learn to *regret infinitely more* the fiendish and inhuman acts that are daily perpetrated, under this frightful system on our helpless fellow-creatures. . . . Let us, in the name of the God of justice and mercy labour without ceasing for the total overthrow of this gigantic iniquity.[19]

Porter worked on a committee to prepare an answer to the Boston Invitation and to circulate it for signatures. He distributed the committee's statement as a printed circular in the middle of March 1848, and by early April forty of the Irish ministers, or about two-thirds of the ministerial roll, had signed it. Porter informed Haughton that one of the nonsigners agreed with the statement, but thought it injudicious to send it. The others did not reply.[20] Most assuredly Haughton must have wanted to add his name, but it was a clerical address and itself exclusionary.

In their statement, the Irish Unitarian ministers thanked the Americans for their invitation. Regretfully, they could send no one, but they wished they could in order to speak on a "subject . . . near to [their] hearts: the Wrongs of the Coloured Population in the United States." They praised the work of the individual antislavery reformers and asked all to labor with even more "energy and perseverance." They then spoke of a topic "not identical with that of slavery, yet relative to it." They spoke of Americans denying black citizens their "equal Rights and Privileges . . . as Members of the Church of Christ." Unlike previous addresses, the most distinguished members of their denomination all signed it. The *Christian Register* published it without comment.[21]

The soiree of the annual meeting of the Irish Unitarian Christian Society was almost a victory party for Haughton and his friends. Bishop, who was present as an honored guest, talked about cooperation with men "of all creeds and every party . . . in the promotion of moral reforms." He talked about "converting the sinful" and striving for the "moral and spiritual regeneration of the world." Then someone made the toast: "To the Unitarians of America, may they ever be foremost in advocating the physical and mental rights of the oppressed." Haughton responded to it. He congratulated their Society for the noble action against slavery it had taken the past several years. These were toasts by the converted in behalf of those to be converted.[22]

The success of the Irish assuredly buoyed the spirits of George Armstrong in Bristol. His committee from the Western

Unitarian Christian Union had decided not to confine their work to the union, but to solicit signatures from ministerial and lay members throughout the denomination. In this way the "Brethren in a Common Faith in England and Scotland" would have a reply to complement that of their Irish coworkers. Along with a printed copy of the reply, Armstrong sent to all the Unitarian clergy a form letter signed by James and himself. It requested the signatures of ministers and "as many as possible of the *adult male members*" of each congregation. To emphasize that only males could sign the reply was a curious action for the two Garrisonians to take. Probably it was the committee's decision that the exclusion of women would irritate the fewest clergymen. But the mention of a sexual qualification at all revealed that the nascent women's-right movement, which American Garrisonians supported, had made it impossible to assume that women would have neither the desire nor the expectation of signing their names. It also recognized pragmatically that, much as the Garrisonians might welcome the participation of women in their meetings, the AUA did not. The Boston Invitation was an invitation to men, to be accepted or rejected by men.[23]

The reply, antedating as it did the abolition by the AUA of its board of vice-presidents, focused on the problem of the association's slaveholding officer. It maintained that, whatever charitable feelings might privately be held for a slaveholder, public cooperation with him in religious matters was another matter. Therefore, they asked for "unequivocal guarantees" that no such appointment would occur again. After all, they conceded: "Next to our own,—nay, rather as part of our own,—your reputation is dear to us."[24] The reply instructed the Americans in the sinfulness and the stigma of a slaveholder. Its central message was clear: for the AUA to honor a slaveholder was to damage the reputation of Unitarianism. This situation needed correction immediately. The reply illustrated an intense concern over the Americans beclouding or besmirching the status of the British Unitarians as impeccable moral leaders and dedicated liberal reformers.[25]

Whether because of the impropriety of sending a remonstrance on a grievance already corrected, or because they disagreed with the "instruction" on a slaveholder's sinfulness, many ministers and laymen refused to sign the reply. Armstrong complained to Estlin: "I have had pretty much the same proportion of results [as] you. My *very* enlightened people hold back. The more unpretending and simple-minded yield to generous impulses—and *do* the needful thing." He also grumbled to his friend over the discouraging response from his fellow clergymen: "Metaphysics from Dr. Martineau,—feebleness from Mr. Tayler,—brevity and blunder from Mr. Bache,—blessedness from Mr. Wallace,—politeness not without a mixture of good sense, though withal of misimpression from Mr. Higginson—constitute pretty nearly the character of the replies which have come from adverse pastors." The Evangelical Alliance, he observed bitterly, "might have included them with great advantage." Such were the results of the sixty or so letters he had sent out.[26]

The abolitionists' greatest disappointment was the failure to secure James Martineau's endorsement. He had refused to sign the British address, in 1843, believing that he had "no right to offer *advice,* where he could give no test of the willingness which he felt to do and suffer in so good a cause." Harriet Martineau had told William James that her brother was averse to working "in association or concert with any kind of purpose." It was "his mission to work alone." Still, he may have declined to sign not so much out of any qualms about associational activity, but rather because that associational activity involved the abolitionists. He had confided in Estlin that, were he an American, he probably would not join the abolitionists, for their "methods of action" appeared to him "ill-defined and questionable." His ideal was the moderate antislavery course of Channing. Such was his thinking on the British address in 1843; now, four years later, his argument for refusing to sign the reply to the Boston Invitation showed little change.[27]

In August, he wrote to James to explain his refusal. He could not satisfy himself that their "means were irreproachable." And he could not concur with the "expression of sentiments" in the document. Haughton believed that the primary reason of those who refused to sign was their willingness "to find excuses for the Slaveholder on the ground that he [was] the victim of circumstances." Martineau was no different, for he told James:

> I cannot but shrink from the denunciation of Slaveholding as a private immorality. It is the misfortune of the individual; the *crime* of the State. . . . The main duty of the American citizen of the South, appears to me to consist not in manumission on his estate, but in moving the Legislature to a reform

in the constitution of property. I am far from being satisfied that individual emancipation has any tendency to diminish the aggregate guilt and evil of Slavery; there is so much reason to believe that it may even prolong the system, as to render the indiscriminate condemnation of Slaveholders altogether unjust.[28]

Martineau admitted that, if he were to inherit some slaves, he was not so sure that he might not consider it a "criminal evasion of responsibility to manumit them." To be a slaveholder was not "proof of indifference to the wrong of Slavery." It only proved that one was against private manumission, an opinion that could be the result of "thoughtful conscientiousness." Such were his views on the condemnation of individual slaveholders, but he also opposed the raison d'être of the reply:

> I must confess that the plan of scrutinizing not the public acts and aims of an Association, but the personal composition of its Committees and the private concerns of its members, before rendering a reply to a friendly invitation in which it is a sort of partner, appears to me a somewhat farfetched scrupulosity. . . . Nor can the soft words mingled in your reply, remove the impression of eager severity which it leaves. Upon my own perverse heart, were I among its Transatlantic receivers, I fear it would operate only to hush and harden. May you have to deal with more charitable souls!

Martineau told James that this was his "honest" and "reluctant" feeling on the matter. He differed as to their means, but honored their "aims."[29]

The British Garrisonians poured out their lamentations to their American comrades. The majority of their friends, wrote Estlin to Maria Weston Chapman, disagreed with their efforts. But he thought their course was right and believed that others "after time and reflection" would join them. Haughton was more pessimistic. He deeply regretted, he wrote to May, that the Unitarians "in general, [took] so low a position on all great moral questions." They were "little, if at all, in advance of others in this respect." Mary Carpenter implored Chapman not to "think harshly of her three brothers" for not signing the reply. Let each one, she advised, give public testimony to the cause in his or her own way. The publication of the reply in the *Inquirer* showed few Unitarian ministers had publicly chosen to testify in this way. Only sixty ministers had come forward.[30]

The reply, which had been engrossed at Bristol, carried four columns of signatures and formed a roll more than twenty feet long. The amazing length of the document was due to the approximately 15,000 names of laymen who had signed it and had recorded their occupations. Historians have provided evidence that the working classes shunned, even opposed, the antislavery movement. The names of the green grocers, drysalters, wire workers, coal heavers, bakers, etc., who signed the reply demonstrate that at least some members of the Unitarian working class wanted to aid the cause. Perhaps, in part, the aversion of artisans to the movement was because few opportunities such as this were provided them. Mary Carpenter, the Unitarian reformer who best knew the English working classes, thought that they were of a right mind on the subject. The Americans often alleged, she wrote, that it was "not disinterested love of the oppressed, but a certain jealousy of the Sister country which [made] the English so indignant against slavery." She was sure that there was no truth to this allegation as far as the "labouring classes" were concerned. There was in the British mind, she testified, "a strong feeling of sympathy for the oppressed." When she told her ragged children, for example, about the American fight for independence, they always sided with the Americans![31]

George E. Ellis, writing in the *Christian Register,* derided the "respectable" laborers who were so bold to accuse him and his American brethren of not doing their duty on the issue of slavery. He discredited the abolitionists and their methods. He marveled that the English could spare time away from their own domestic reforms to remonstrate against American deficiencies. He warned Americans who planned trips to England to expect neither tea nor muffins. None of Ellis's points was new and his article would have probably been ignored had he not been so abusive. His "sneers at the humble occupations of several of the signers," ranted Samuel May, were "so peculiarly appropriate to an Unitarian minister!!" The *Liberator* condemned Ellis to its "Refuge of Oppression" column, and judged him a *"hater of God and man."* This condemnation distressed Dr. Hutton, but he agreed that Ellis was wrong to ridicule the common folk who had signed the reply. "The time [was] coming, let us hope," he told May, "when the voice of such men will be better heard and more influential in Europe, as well as America, than it [had] heretofore been!"[32]

It was James Freeman Clarke who anwered the reply for the AUA. He and his colleagues appreciated it, but he acknowledged that many Americans believed the British knew too little of their institution of slavery to advise them wisely. However, he personally thought that their perspective from afar might actually aid them in viewing it sagaciously. He explained how carelessly the AUA had chosen its vice-presidents. He indicated that Dr. Whitridge had been appointed in recognition of the kindness he had shown a Massachusetts official who had been harassed while on a mission in Charleston. In the end, his appointment lasted only one year. Clarke promised to display the reply in a Boston bookstore where it could be seen by all. The *Inquirer* remarked laconically "that the whole affair was much ado about nothing."[33]

The Incidental Inquirer *on Antislavery*

With the problem of a slaveholding vice-president solved, the British Unitarian abolitionists were temporarily without an immediate issue upon which to direct their energies. One magnificent opportunity escaped their vigilance. A slaveholding Unitarian minister from New Orleans, Theodore Clapp (1792–1866), visited England in 1847. He preached in Edward Tagart's pulpit and dined with the London minister's family and friends. This delightful scene of a British Unitarian minister welcoming a "man-stealer" not only to his fireside, but into his pulpit, was the kind of portrait that Haughton would have relished to vandalize. Fortunately for Tagart and his American guest, the latter's presence in England had not been preannounced, and the abolitionist watchdogs had been inattentive or asleep. Few of them had known of his slaveholding, and Clapp's trip had been so unobtrusive that he escaped without their noticing him. His only impact was his influence upon Tagart, whom some abolitionists accused of having been too much swayed by Clapp's pro-slavery testimony.[34]

Having missed the opportunity of Clapp's visit, and with no pressing communications from America, the abolitionists let the annual meeting of the BFUA, in 1848, pass without slavery's being mentioned. Gannett, Parkham, and Dewey, particularly the last, continued to bear the brunt of the abolitionist attacks. Dewey, for example, had preached in Washington, D.C., that there was nothing "of Abolitionism . . . in the Gospel Record." Dr. Hutton maintained that all persons had different boiling points as far as reforms were concerned, and Dewey's statement made the good doctor reach his quickly. He argued in a long rebuttal to Dewey that the Gospel indeed "preached Abolitionism most distinctly."

Dewey was something of a problem for the British Unitarian ministers. They admired his homiletical and literary gifts, his "noble talents," but were deeply grieved that he did not even partially measure up to the abolitionist standard. It was a grief that consumed his friends as well. James Martineau conceded to Estlin: that it was "plain that the 'silent system,' and refusal of all action on the part of the ministers of Dewey's class, [was] utterly disgraceful; and all their smooth excuses for their skulking ways [were] a downright betrayal of 'the Son of Man with a kiss.'" Given the general opposition to Dewey, it was remarkable that Hincks would praise him and Gannett at the BFUA's annual meeting of 1849. He spoke after a minister had thrown doubt upon Dewey's rightful place among the denomination's leaders. One reason for Hincks's praise was that he had just returned from a year in the United States and had heard Dewey's eloquence first hand.[35]

Hincks, of course, was no longer editor of the *Inquirer* and there was talk that his antislavery opinions, certainly his reforming zeal, had contributed to his resignation. Estlin had warned that Hincks might have to surrender control of the *Inquirer* because "wealthy and influential" Unitarians refused to support his work. Haughton told May that many Unitarians counseled Hincks to take a different course, but he had remained firm, had acted nobly on slavery, and deserved praise. On 22 May 1847, Hincks resigned. Haughton regretted his departure. Hincks had given the paper, he explained, much "right feeling" on slavery.[36]

The abolitionists were not happy with Dr. Sadler, Hincks's successor. They disagreed with his previous call for moderation in antislavery reform, and his next antislavery editorial was ambivalent. In it he condemned the Mexican-American War and in so doing was in complete agreement with the abolitionists. But he went on to expound on the moral responsibility of slaveholders. He differentiated between the slaveowners in the original slave states and those slaveholders who desired to settle with their slaves in the conquered Mexican territories. The former ought not to be condemned for they were not wholly responsible for their predicament, whereas the latter were to be judged with severity.[37]

The editorial dismayed Haughton and he complained to

Sadler that it fell below the "noble and generous" stand on human liberty that had characterized the *Inquirer* under Hincks. Slaveholders ought to be labeled for what they were— "men-stealers, women-whippers, cradle-plunderers." Sadler answered that it hardly became the English, only recently slaveholders themselves, to speak harshly of American slaveholders. To exert any influence, they had to be temperate. They had best reserve, he advised, their "strongest blame" for their own misdeeds.[38]

Happily for the abolitionists, Sadler lasted as editor only about six months. In the beginning of 1849, following a period during which the editorial responsibilities were shared, John Lalor (1814–56), a former Roman Catholic and successful newspaperman, became editor. But ill health forced his resignation in 1850.[39] Most abolitionists probably longed to have Hincks return, that is, until they heard his praise for Gannett and Dewey at the BFUA meeting and read his impressions of America in the *Inquirer*. Regretfully, they found that their co-worker had undergone a transformation in his thinking during his year-long visit to the States.

In two missives to the *Inquirer* he related that his "abhorrence of slavery" remained unaltered. "Slavery was essential injustice," and the English had every right to express their feelings on it. But he had changed his views as to how one might aid the cause.[40] He no longer considered himself a follower of Garrison. He thought the man's political notions were extravagant and his denunciations against those who disagreed with him were unjust. The Garrisonians, he explained, diluted and handicapped their antislavery efforts by mixing them with other obnoxious causes. English antislavery reformers were wrong to identify themselves only with the Garrisonians. It could lead them "into injustice towards [some] most estimable individuals."[41]

Lalor offered a commentary on Hincks's letters and on slavery—"the greatest political question now agitated in the world." Slavery would only be gotten rid of by "organized and powerful agitation." He called the abolitionists "true champions of humanity" who had only adopted "injudicious" modes of action. "Every American . . . ought to be an Abolitionist" and publicly testify in speech and action against slavery.[42] Hincks replied that he too defended agitation, but it had to be "respectable," have a "reasonable and possibly attainable object, and be pursued only by legitimate means."[43]

Naturally, Haughton had to answer the "new" Hincks. He deeply regretted that his coworker had fallen under the spell of those in America who had "neither hearts nor souls," a phrase that Lalor probably printed with mixed feelings. Shortly after, Lalor announced a new policy for the *Inquirer:* American Slavery thereafter would be dealt with "incidentally." He regretted that he could not publish the several letters on the topic sent by his readers. He had published the letters of Hincks and the rebuttals because Hincks was a former editor of the newspaper,

> but it would be mere folly and Quixotism to go on day after day, and week after week, preaching and declaiming against distant abuses, over which he and his readers [had] comparatively little power, whilst there [was] a crowd of social evils which they might remove, surrounding them at home.[44]

In the euphoria surrounding the foundation of the Anti-Slavery League, the Garrisonians hoped that every Unitarian would become an abolitionist. The league's demise, the trifling support shown for Armstrong's reply to the Boston Invitation, the defection of coworkers such as Hincks, and the loss of the *Inquirer* as their journal dampened their hopes. The debate over the Boston Invitation illustrated clearly their minority status in their denomination, particularly within the BFUA. To obtain the desired reply to the Boston Invitation, Armstrong had to circumvent the association to solicit help. Most of that help came from the provincial centers of the West Country and from the few congregations in Scotland: Aberdeen, Glasgow, and Edinburgh. The London churches continued to express little interest. But most depressing was the conspicuous absence of names of persons who had previously helped the Garrisonians: the Carpenters, Harris, Hincks, Kell, and Crosskey.[45] Apparently, the major task of the Garrisonians was not to have every Unitarian an abolitionist, but to keep their own numbers and enthusiasm intact.

Their reverses could have been related to Garrison's zeal in espousing controversial English causes during his lecture tour in 1846. If Estlin as his friend became disturbed by his conduct, how much more so were Unitarians disturbed who were not his friends. Moreover, the attack upon slavery, a popular cause in Great Britain, had also been transformed into an unpopular attack upon American Unitarian ministers and laity. This disturbed the Unitarians' love of personal freedom and responsibility, their commitment, Solly called it, to the "intense 'individuality of the individual.'"[46] They were prone to be long-suffering and forgiving of the slaveholder and his so-called apologist despite their abhorrence of the slave system. The issues of the AUA having a slaveholder as an officer, or American Unitarian ministers not meeting Garrisonian standards of abolitionism, were simply not universally appealing or alarming. More significant issues or crises than those were needed for British Unitarians to reach, to use Dr. Hutton's phrase, their reform boiling points.

In 1850, the needed crisis arrived. It was an event in America that fanned the dying embers of abolitionist zeal and ignited much of the deadwood of the denomination's indifference. To lessen the sectional animosities in the United States, Congress had passed the Compromise of 1850. As part of the compromise, a more stringent Fugitive Slave Law was enacted to aid the South in stopping the flow of fugitive slaves to the North. Overnight thousands of fugitives and free blacks in the North became the possible victims of slave catchers. Two fugitives, William and Ellen Craft, were nominally members of Theodore Parker's congregation. Their Unitarian friends shared the Crafts' fear that they might be seized and returned to slavery, and, therefore, they placed them on a ship bound for England. When they arrived in Liverpool, they were met by Francis Bishop and his wife and taken to the Estlins. "Oh! shame, shame upon us," lamented Sam May, "that Americans, whose fathers fought against Great Britain, in order to be FREE," had to send the Crafts there to obtain their freedom.[47]

Notes

1. James Haughton to the editor, Dublin, 23 March 1847, *Inquirer,* 17 April 1847, pp. 243–44; "Unitarians and Slavery," *Inquirer,* 8 May 1847, p. 307.

2. George E. Ellis, "Correspondence Between English and American Unitarians on Slavery," *Christian Register,* 11 December 1847, p. 198; "Correspondence Between Unitarians in America, and Unitarians in England and Scotland," ibid., p. 196. Hereafter the *Christian Register* will be cited as *CR.*

3. George Armstrong to Samuel May, Jr., Clifton, Bristol, 3 May 1847; "Reply of the Western Unitarian Christian Union, to the friends of Unitarian Christianity in Boston" [titled supplied], n.p.: 29 April 1847; May Papers, Boston Public Library, hereafter cited as MB.

4. George Armstrong to Edmund Kell, Clifton [Bristol], 21 May 1847, [Robert Henderson], "Memoir of the Late Rev. George Armstrong, of Bristol," *Christian Reformer* 14

(August 1858): 458; "[The Twentieth Annual Meeting of the] British and Foreign Unitarian Association," *Inquirer*, 17 May 1845, p. 315.

5. "[The Twenty-Second Annual Meeting of the] British and Foreign Unitarian Association," *Inquirer*, 29 May 1847, pp. 344–45. James Haughton to Samuel May, Jr., Dublin, 30 August 1847, May Papers, MB.

6. J. B. Estlin, "On the Present Position of English Unitarians, in Reference to the American Slavery Question," *Inquirer*, 12 June 1847, p. 372.

7. Ibid., pp. 372–73.

8. "A Voice from the Avon" to the editor, n.p., n.d., *Inquirer*, 26 June 1847, pp. 409–10; James Gifford to the editor, Myrtle Cottage, Jersey, n.d., *Inquirer*, 24 July 1847, p. 475; "M.S." to the editor, London, 24 June 1847, *Inquirer*, 3 July 1847, pp. 423–24; "Amicus" to the editor, 16 September 1847, *Inquirer*, 16 October 1847, pp. 666–67, 23 October 1847, pp. 681–82, 30 October 1847, pp. 697–98.

9. Edward Tagart, "Unitarians and American Slavery," *Inquirer*, 3 July 1847, p. 423. For more on Tagart, see *A Memoir of the Late Edward Tagart, Who Died 12th October, 1858* (n.p.: n.d.).

10. [Thomas Sadler], "English Unitarians, American Unitarians, and Slavery," *Inquirer*, 3 July 1847, p. 417; Leslie Stephen and Sidney Lee, eds., *Dictionary of National Biography*, (Oxford: Oxford University Press, 1921–1922), 17: 601; William C. Gannett, *Ezra Stiles Gannett, Unitarian Minister of Boston, 1824–1871* (Boston: Roberts Brothers, 1875), p. 295.

11. Francis Bishop to the editor, Exeter, n.d., July 1847, *Inquirer*, 17 July 1847, pp. 458–59. See Sadler's editorial postscript, pp. 458–59; George Armstrong to the editor, n.p., n.d., *Inquirer*, 24 July 1847, pp. 475–76. See May's letter, pp. 475–76. James Haughton to Samuel May, Jr., Dublin, 30 August 1847, May Papers, MB.

12. Samuel May, Jr., to J. B. Estlin, Leicester, 30 March 1846, May Papers, MB; Ezra Stiles Gannett to the editor, Boston, 6 September [1847], *CR*, 11 September 1847, p. 146.

13. "Unitarian Meeting—Slavery," *Irish Unitarian Magazine* 2 (September 1847): 298.

14. J. Estlin Carpenter, *James Martineau, Theologian & Teacher: A Study of His Life & Thought* (London: Philip Green, 1905), pp. 70–72; John Crozier, *The Life of the Rev. Henry Montgomery, LL.D., Dumurry, Belfast; with Selections from His Speeches and Writings* (London: E. T. Whitfield, 1875), 1: 166, 386–87.

15. "Anti-Slavery Meeting at Belfast," *Irish Unitarian Magazine* 2 (September 1847): 278; "Unitarian Meeting—Slavery," pp. 298–99.

16. "Anti-Slavery Meeting at Belfast," p. 278; "Unitarian Meeting—Slavery," p. 229.

17. Dexter Clapp, "Letter on the Religious Condition of Slaves," *Monthly Religious Magazine* 3 (May 1846): 207; Clarence Godhes, "Some Notes on the Unitarian Church in the Ante-Bellum South: A Contribution to the History of Southern Liberalism," *American Studies in Honor of William Kenneth Boyd*, David Kelly Jackson, ed. (Durham, N.C.: Duke University Press, 1940), p. 341; Henry Steele Commager, *Theodore Parker: Yankee Crusader* (Boston: Beacon Press, 1967 [1st ed., 1936]), pp. 201, 214–15; Laurence C. Staples, *Washington Unitarianism: A Rich Heritage* (Washington, D. C., 1970), p. 112; Katherine Gibbs Allen, ed., *Sketches of Some Historic Churches of Greater Boston* (Boston: Beacon Press, 1918), p. 86; [William Henry Lyon], *The First Parish in Brookline: An Historical Sketch* (Brookline, Mass.: The Riverdale Press, 1898), p. 26; Andrew P. Peabody, *Memoir of Rev. Samuel Kirkland Lothrop, D.D., LL. D.* [reprinted from the *Proceedings of the Massachusetts Historical Society*] (Cambridge, Mass.: John Wilson and Son, 1887), pp. 12–13. See also "'American Slavery and Colour,'" *Liberator*, 22 January 1858.

18. "Anti-Slavery Meeting at Belfast," p. 279.

19. Ibid.

20. John Scott Porter to James Haughton, n.p., 4 April 1848, May Papers, MB.

21. Ezra Stiles Gannett to the editor, Boston, 1 May 1848, *CR*, 6 May 1848, pp. 74–75.

22. "Anniversary of the Irish Unitarian Christian Society," *CR*, 29 July 1848, p. 121.

23. George Armstrong and William James to the Rev._____. n.p., 1 August 1847, [printed circular]. May Papers, MB.

24. "Reply to the Invitation of "The Friends of Unitarian Christianity in Boston to Their Brethren in a Common Faith in England and Scotland" (n.p.: n.d.) [printed circular], May Papers, MB.

25. Ibid.

26. George Armstrong to J. B. Estlin, Clifton, [Bristol], 26 August 1847, May Papers, MB. Besides Martineau, the ministers mentioned by Armstrong were John James Tayler (1797–1869), cominister for a time with Martineau; Samuel Bache (1806–78), a successor of Dr. Priestley at Birmingham; Robert Wallace (1791–1850), of Trim Street Chapel, Bath; and Edward Higginson (1803–80) of the Unitarian Chapel in Wakefield, Yorkshire. See George Carter, *Unitarian Biographical Dictionary, Being Short Notices of the Lives of Noteworthy Unitarians, and Kindred Thinkers, Brought down to the Year 1900* (London: Unitarian Christian Publishing Office, 1902), pp. 11, 63–64, 117, 124.

27. William James to Samuel May, Jr., Bristol, 26 June 1844, May Papers, MB; James Martineau to J.B. Estlin, Liverpool, 24 November 1845, Estlin Papers, Dr. Williams's Library, London.

28. James Martineau to William James, Liverpool, 18 August 1847, James Haughton to Samuel May, Jr., Dublin, 30 August 1847, May Papers, MB.

29. James Martineau to William James, Liverpool, 18 August 1847, May Papers, MB.

30. John Bishop Estlin to [Maria Weston Chapman], Bristol, 2 September 1847, Weston Papers, MB; James Haughton to Samuel May, Jr., Dublin, 30 August 1847, May Papers, MB; Mary Carpenter to Maria Weston Chapman, Bristol, 31 October 1847, Weston Papers, MB; "Answer to the Invitation of the Boston Unitarian Ministers," *Inquirer*, 20 November 1847, pp. 748–49.

31. "Answer to the Boston Invitation", *Inquirer*, 20 November 1847, p. 749; "Correspondence on Slavery", *CR*, p. 11 December 1847, 198; C. Duncan Rice, "Abolitionists and abolitionism in Aberdeen: A Test Case for the Nineteenth-Century Anti-Slavery Movement," *Northern Scotland* 1 (December 1972): 68; Mary Carpenter to Maria Weston Chapman, Bristol, 31 October 1847, Weston Papers, MB.

32. "Correspondence on Slavery", *CR*, p. 11 December 1847, 198; Samuel May, Jr., to J. B. Estlin, Boston, 15 December 1847, May Papers, MB; *Liberator*, 31 December 1847; Joseph Hutton to Samuel May, Jr., King's Cross, [London], 28 March 1848, May Papers, MB; Charles Richard Denton, "American Unitarians, 1830–1865: A Study of Religious Opinion on War, Slavery, and the Union" (Ph.D. diss., Michigan State University, 1969), pp. 106–7. Ellis was probably also perturbed, as were some of his colleagues, over laymen being so bold as to reply to what was essentially a clerical invitation. Russell Lant Carpenter declared that the American ministers who "objected to [the reply] intimated that they did not want a refusal from persons whom they had never invited." See Russell Lant Carpenter, "American Slavery," *Christian Reformer* 7 (December 1851): 736.

33. "Answer to the Invitation from the Boston Unitarian Ministers," *Inquirer*, 1 January 1848, p. 8.

34. Theodore Clapp, *Autobiographical Sketches and Recollections, During a Thirty-Five Years' Residence in New Orleans* (Boston: Phillips, Sampson, & Co., 1857), pp. 317–21;

Henry Wilder Foote, "Theodore Clapp," *The Proceedings of the Unitarian Historical Society* 3, part 2 (1934): 30–31; Samuel May, Jr., to J. B. Estlin, Boston, 30 September 1847, May Papers, MB.

35. "[The Twenty-Third Annual Meeting of the] British and Foreign Association," *Inquirer*, 22 April 1848, pp. 267–70; Joseph Hutton to the editor, King's Cross, [London], 29 September 1847, *Inquirer*, 29 September 1847, p. 632; George Armstrong to Samuel May, Jr., Clifton, Bristol, 3 May 1847, May Papers, MB; James Martineau to J. B. Estlin, Liverpool, 24 November 1845, Estlin Papers, Dr. Williams's Library; "[The Twenty-Fourth Annual Meeting of the] British and Foreign Association," *Inquirer*, 2 June 1849, p. 344.

36. J. B. Estlin to Samuel May, Jr., Bristol, 18 May 1847, James Haughton to Samuel May, Jr., Dublin, 29 March 1847, May Papers, MB; Herbert McLachlan, *The Unitarian Movement in the Religious Life of England* (London: George Allen & Unwin, Ltd., 1934), pp. 214–15; James Haughton to Samuel May, Jr., Dublin, 30 August 1847, May Papers, MB.

37. [Thomas Sadler], "The Mexican Treaty and Slavery," *Inquirer*, 28 August 1847, p. 545.

38. James Haughton to the editor, Dublin, 14 September 1847, *Inquirer*, 25 September 1847, p. 616; [Thomas Sadler], "Slavery in America," ibid., p. 609.

39. McLachlan, *Unitarian Movement*, pp. 215–16.

40. William Hincks to the editor, n.p., *Inquirer*, 20 January 1849, p. 41.

41. William Hincks to the editor, n.p., n.d., *Inquirer*, 3 February 1849, p. 73.

42. [John Lalor], "American Slavery and Its Opponents," *Inquirer*, 3 February 1849, pp. 65–67.

43. William Hincks to the editor, n.p., n.d., *Inquirer*, 10 February 1849, p. 90.

44. James Haughton to the editor, Dublin, 8 February 1849, *Inquirer*, 17 February 1849, pp. 105–6; "An American Citizen" to the editor, Stoke Newington, 5 February 1849, *Inquirer*, 17 February 1849, p. 105; [John Lalor], "American Slavery and Its Apologists," *Inquirer*, 17 February 1849, p. 98; James Haughton to the editor, Dublin, 15 March 1849, *Inquirer*, 24 March 1849, p. 195.

45. "Answer to the Invitation of the Boston Unitarian Ministers," *Inquirer*, 20 November 1847, p. 749.

46. Henry Solly, *"These Eighty Years" or, The Story of an Unfinished Life* (London: Simpkin, Marshall, & Co., 1893), 1: 279.

47. Samuel May, Jr., to J. B. Estlin, Boston, 6 November [1850], William Craft, *Running a Thousand Miles for Freedom; or, the Escape of William and Ellen Craft from Slavery* (London: William Tweedie, 1860), p. 91. See also p. 108.

Protection From American Slavery

—— 5 ——

"Reform America, or It Will Corrupt Us": Confronting America's Reign of Terror—1851–52.

"The Steam Is Up": Britain Boils over America's "Melancholy Disgrace"

Almost one month after President Fillmore had signed the *1850*
Fugitive Slave Bill into law, the Western Unitarian Christian
Union held its tenth half-yearly meeting. Brooke Herford
(1830–1903), a student at the Unitarian college and later one of
the leading lights of both American and British Unitarianism,
reported on his work as a summer missionary in Cornwall. His
experience there had convinced him that to attack orthodox
doctrine was "*perfectly* useless." He found that the orthodox in
places such as Cornwall were accustomed to think and to speak
of Unitarians "as infidels, and therefore would not argue *at all*."
Unitarians had to make them feel, by "joining them in every
Christian work," that they were "really Christians like themselves," and then they would listen to their arguments. It would
no longer be a case as it was now "between *Christianity* and
Infidelity, which [needed] no discussion, but between two forms
of Christianity." Therefore, Herford had endeavored to mix in
a "friendly way" with the members of other sects, and to join

115

them in reform activity.[1] At the same meeting George Armstrong spoke on the crushing hindrances to the spread of their denomination and on ways to improve their religious life. The whole world was arrayed against them. Until recently, every loyal and religious person in the British Isles considered it a duty to condemn their doctrines, to vilify their principles, and to oppose their progress. This *"ignorance* and *prejudice"* toward them was still prevalent everywhere. Armstrong instructed his listeners to be bold, to be united, to be worshipful, and to possess the courage "to fill that place in the Church to which a gracious Providence" had called them.[2]

The message of the conference was clear. Unitarians remained theological and social outcasts who needed to prove their Christian status by their leadership and fervor "in every Christian work." The emotional commitment of the Unitarian abolitionists intensified in the surge of antislavery activity actuated by the Fugitive Slave Law controversy, and then in reaction to the wide dissemination in Great Britain of Harriet Beecher Stowe's sensational novel, *Uncle Tom's Cabin.* Thus the first half of the decade was a period in which the British Unitarian antislavery reformers achieved their highest level of activity. However, after the mid-1850s a turnabout occurred; antislavery enthusiasm in Great Britain generally diminished and Unitarian interest accordingly decreased. There were several reasons for this decline. Of great importance was the increasingly complex political nature of the antislavery struggle in the United States. In face of the Kansas-Nebraska Act, the Brooks-Sumner Affair, the 1856 presidential election, the Dred Scott Decision, and John Brown's raid on Harper's Ferry, antislavery reformers in Great Britain felt more and more helpless to influence Americans morally to end slavery.[3] Unitarians experienced their own special difficulties. Their antislavery activity was seriously hampered by the deaths of Estlin in 1855 and of Armstrong in 1857. Moreover, they were plagued by the orthodox attack upon the alleged infidel opinions of Garrison. Ironically, their attempt to be accepted as "ordinary" Christians through their participation in a popular reform movement in part failed when their association with Garrison and his Christian anarchist followers highlighted their own reputation as "infidels." Lastly, many Unitarians believed that America had become so universally corrupt that her redemption and reform were necessary before she corrupted Great Britain. This belief gradually evolved into the idea that America was so morally corrupt that only her isolation or quarantine could stifle her sins of slavery and racial prejudice.

The Fugitive Slave Law, which opened the decade of the 1850s, raised from England "a cry more indignant [and] more widely extended" than had been raised since the time of her own triumph over slavery. It was the most "melancholy disgrace" of their age, preached the Reverend Charles Wicksteed (1810–85).[4] Most Unitarians agreed that the law encouraged the South to reclaim the thousand or so fugitive slaves who fled to the North each year; that under the law no free Negro was safe from possible seizure as a slave; that it denied him the right to a jury trial or court hearing to prove his freedom; and that it prescribed severe penalties for those who aided him. They knew that Daniel Webster and Samuel A. Eliot, two Unitarian laymen, had assisted the bill's passage in Congress; that another Unitarian layman, President Millard Fillmore, had signed it into law; that Edward Everett and Jared Sparks, presidents of Harvard College and Harvard Divinity School respectively, supported its enforcement; and that Orville Dewey and Ezra Stiles Gannett, sometime presidents of the American Unitarian Association, wanted it obeyed. They were proud that Canada was a refuge for fugitive slaves, and saw several of the most famous fugitives, Shadrach, Anthony Burns, and Jerry McHenry, seek freedom there, as William Wells Brown and the Crafts sought safety in England.[5] They perceived the explosive nature of the law as antislavery propaganda and its direct bearing on their work as British abolitionists.

Francis Bishop, the Unitarian missionary to the poor in Liverpool, knew firsthand the law's relevance to Britain. He turned his little mission into an "English terminus for escaped slaves." He boarded fugitives and their children in his home, and solicited funds and jobs for them.[6] Liverpool's direct links with America gave Bishop abundant opportunities to serve fugitives. He lamented, however, that Liverpool Unitarians generally were not enthusiastic about his work.[7] In Bristol, another port city with strong American ties, Estlin also harbored American fugitives and sought financial aid for them.[8] Eliza Lee Follen (1787–1860), the widow of Garrisonian disciple Dr. Charles Follen (1796–1840), was yet another Unitarian who assisted the fugitives. She was vacationing in England and evangelizing among the wealthy and influential Unitarians who were lukewarm to the cause.[9]

Despair over the implications of the Fugitive Slave Law engulfed Great Britain. Northern compliance with the law bitterly disturbed Mary Carpenter. A writer in the *Christian Reformer* saw the law join the free and slave states into a "United States of Slavery." Russell Carpenter felt that it was beneficial that the North could no longer pretend to be separated from the slave system. The new pervasiveness of slavery, he thought, posed dangers for Great Britain. Mary Estlin and the women of the Bristol and Clifton Ladies' Anti-Slavery Society perceived American slavery, revivified under the law, as an international plague. Its "poison" so polluted "the moral atmosphere of America," they warned, that British visitors there, trained to hate slavery, could not sufficiently protect themselves from contamination.[10] Could the pestilence of slavery leap the Atlantic and infect Britain? It was a distinct possibility.

The *Inquirer* offered no apologies for its constant attention to the Fugitive Slave Law.[11] It called the law a "shameless defiance" of civilized opinion, and predicted that moral men and women would resist it.[12] However, when Theodore Parker advised forceful resistance, the paper condemned him. Through the law, American slavery had become the "Goddess, Queen, or Patron of a nation of Republicans," but the *Inquirer* insisted that to resist violently was neither wise, right, nor Christian.[13]

Those Unitarians disturbed over the law cared little about Theodore Parker and his plea for violent resistance; they were more concerned about the American ministers who advocated no resistance. Such conduct embittered and embarrassed British Unitarians. It was one thing for a Unitarian minister in Maine to tell Russell Carpenter privately that President Fillmore had acted quite rightly, but it was another thing for Dewey, Gannett, and other conservative Unitarian leaders to preach compliance publicly. British Unitarians were perturbed over Gannett's statements that the "perpetuity of the Union" depended upon the law's enforcement, and that the minister's mission on slavery was silence. They were appalled at Dewey's alleged statement that he would rather return his mother to slavery than sacrifice the Union. His excuse, substituting "brother" for "mother," did not mollify their rage.[14] They were further distressed over the praise of the *Christian Register* by the *Times* of London as the only American religious paper that was not opposed to the Fugitive Slave Law, "now that it [was] the *law of America!*"[15]

The response to these declarations was anger. The message that their mission on slavery was silence came from the very pulpit where Channing once preached. How could they possibly entrust the cause of the slave to his kind of Christianity? Susan C. Cabot (1794–1861), visiting England with her sister, Eliza Follen, was puzzled that Gannett could be silent on slavery and yet "rant and rave" on all other things. This kind of criticism hounded Gannett in 1853. Expecting him to appear in London, Armstrong wrote to Sam May that some ministers were already asking what Channing's successor had "really said or done (or *not* done)" in regard to slavery. Could May oblige him *"with Chapter & verse?"*[16] Some Unitarians in Great Britain were not convinced of Gannett's guilt. There were "murmurs of dissent" at a Unitarian meeting when Philip Carpenter condemned his conduct. The lack of united opposition to him was partially due to the difficulty of separating those views he privately shared from those he publicly proclaimed.[17]

But there were no ambiguities to provide excuses for the rhetoric of Orville Dewey. He would return his brother to slavery to preserve the Union, indeed, he was prepared to urge on slaves their positive duty not to seek escape. "Personal rights," he was prepared to tell a fugitive, "ought to be sacrificed to the general good. You yourself ought to see this, and to be willing to suffer for a while—one for the many. If I were in your situation I should take this ground." To this William Craft replied, would the good Doctor Dewey like to take my place as a slave, seeing I am unwilling to return to bondage? He himself might accept "suffering awhile—one for many."[18]

Dewey's intransigent racism (he even declared that there were "impassible barriers between the races") outraged the Unitarians in England. "I am shocked at our friend Dewey's doctrine and position," James Martineau confided to Mary Carpenter. An American correspondent informed Russell Carpenter that, if fugitives could or would not be helped in the Northern states, the only thing to do was to turn them over to Great Britain. Their American brethren, wrote Dr. Estlin in the *Inquirer*, needed to be sent "a fresh remonstrance."[19]

The Excluded Reject Exclusion: Debating Inhospitality as an Antislavery Measure

Meeting at Estlin's home in late March 1851, the Bristol and Clifton Ladies' Anti-Slavery Society raised the problem of Northern preachers' advocating compliance with the Fugitive Slave Law. The women decided to ask religious leaders to debate the issue at their spring denominational conferences. The time was auspicious, for several American ministers were sure to attend the Great Exhibition of 1851. The women asked their ministerial brethren to consider how they might bar their pulpits to American clergy who had not testified against the law. Within the next two months they sent their request to nearly 400 selected organizations and individuals, including 32 Bristol ministers, 53 antislavery societies, 64 Congregational Unions, 3 Unitarian Associations, 32 "Influential London ministers," 20 Unitarian ministers, 22 Free Church ministers, and several other groups. They ignored the Church of England clergy, probably believing that the Anglicans were not likely to admit any alien ministers into their pulpits, and were cold to the antislavery cause anyway. The women's labors were amply rewarded. In early April, a large antislavery meeting of about a thousand persons was held in Bristol that recommended their suggestion. The proposal of exclusion met with general success, and "it became virtually impossible," Howard Temperley has said, "for any minister sympathetic to slavery to enter a British pulpit." As far as the Unitarians were concerned, however, it was a dismal failure. Although widely discussed at their gatherings, it was adopted in only one instance.[20]

The proposal of exclusion received a chilly reception at the first Unitarian spring meeting. It was the Armstrong-dominated Western Unitarian Christian Union, which met in Bridgwater on April 22. Unfortunately for the Garrisonians, Armstrong could not attend, and it fell upon William James to state their case.[21] As secretary of the WUCU, James reported that the Committee of the Union recommended compliance with the proposal of exclusion. His report was vigorously opposed.

The Reverend Robert Mortimer Montgomery (dates unknown) of Mary Street Chapel, Taunton, led the opposition. He deplored the attacks upon men such as Dewey, and declared his pulpit at Taunton was always open to brother ministers from America. He reminded his hearers, perhaps thinking of the recently established Hibbert Trust, that money originally gained from the labor of the West Indian slaves sustained many of their chapels and charities. He suggested, thus directly attacking James and Armstrong, that this was the case with Lewin's Mead Chapel. Would *they* send back the money? He advised ministering to England's ills first before attending to America's afflictions. He condemned the committee's course as an "unjustifiable interference with the right of private judgment." James, recognizing that the discussion was going solidly against the committee's recommendation, expressed his disappointment, not only over the acrimonious debate, but over their inability to secure a resolution that other denominations in Britain, "particularly their brothers of the Independent Churches," passed with ease. He carried disheartening news back to Armstrong—the committee's report had not been approved. He and his fellow committee members resigned.[22]

For the Garrisonians the meeting set a poor precedent for the Unitarian gatherings to follow. The *Inquirer* explained their failure: Unitarian bodies could not pass regulations that departed totally from their reputation for individual responsibility, requiring "an investigation" into the past conduct of ministers invited to their pulpits. The crux of the issue was the attempt to secure a binding regulation "at variance with the whole of [Unitarian] church usages."[23] Few Unitarian leaders or groups wanted to apply, as a Unitarian minister in Wales exclaimed, "the worst and the most dangerous power of the Inquisition, . . . excommunication!" Because Unitarians "in all ages and countries" had been excommunicated by the orthodox, he abhorred the idea that they could use a "foul weapon" they justly condemned being used against themselves.[24] As one after another of the spring meetings began to reject the weapon of exclusion, it became clear that most Unitarians shared his abhorrence.

Several meetings took place the last week in May. At the Spicer Street Domestic Mission Chapel, in London, Francis Bishop and the presence of two fugitive slaves could not prevent the meeting from expressly condemning any policy of exclusion. Philip Carpenter's congregation in Warrington protested the Fugitive Slave Law, but passed no resolution of exclusion. At an interdenominational meeting in Bury, a Unitarian minister recorded a resolution condemning American slavery, but the gathering ignored the question of exclusion.[25] The May monthly meeting of the Unitarian Sunday Schools of Manchester, under the leadership of Dr. John Relly Beard, was exclusively devoted to the question of American slavery. Beard labeled "thoroughly unchristian," and refused to condone, any plan to exclude American ministers from their pulpits. But his group passed resolutions against the Fugitive Slave Law; pledged support for the American abolitionists and the Ladies Anti-Slavery Society of Manchester; and instructed Unitarian Sunday school teachers to inculcate in their children a love of liberty and a sympathy for the slave.[26]

The meetings in June and July followed the same pattern as

those in May. There was great support for opposition to the Fugitive Slave Law, but almost none for the doctrine of exclusion. The West Riding Tract and Village Mission Society, meeting in Halifax on June 18, condemned the new developments in America, but specified no new modes of action. The Midland Presbyterian or Unitarian Association, meeting in Chesterfield, June 18 and 19, condemned both American slavery and "Papal Aggression." At the Lancashire and Cheshire Provincial Meeting, on June 19, the Reverend John James Tayler proposed a resolution against the Fugitive Slave Law. That this conservative professor of ecclesiastical history chose to act illustrated the enormous impact that the law had made upon the English Unitarians. Following the lead of James Martineau, Tayler had refused to sign his denomination's antislavery addresses. Now he initiated antislavery action himself. Tayler felt obligated to explain his change of attitude. Those whom he had previously thought to be the slaves' friend in America had now revitalized slavery through their support of the Fugitive Slave Law. These Americans had rejected the free principles inherited from England in favor of new principles "introduced by the necessities of the Union." They had stood by and permitted America to become nationally corrupted by a law entirely inhumane and unjust. As a Christian and Englishman, Tayler had to protest. His resolution, eagerly supported by Francis Bishop and others, passed unanimously.[27]

Also in June, Unitarian congregational meetings held at the Unity Chapel, Topsham; St. Mark's Chapel, Edinburgh; George's Meeting, Exeter; Abbey Chapel, Tavistock; and Mill Hill Chapel, Leeds; all condemned the Fugitive Slave Law, but either avoided, or rejected the doctrine of "systematic exclusion."[28] Mill Hill Chapel's congregation was the most agitated, and not a little embarrassed. Many years before, they had sent an invitation to Orville Dewey to be their minister. Now they sent to him a copy of their protest. Writing on the law in the *Prospective Review,* their present minister, Charles Wicksteed, declared, "We tell the Apologists for the Fugitive Slave Bill in the North, that they are cowards. . . . Slaves make slaves."[29]

In July, the annual meeting of the Southern Unitarian Society in Wareham, Dorsetshire, strongly protested the "iniquitous" law. Edmund Kell had orchestrated the passage of the resolution, but opposed an exclusionary statement. No Englishman, he admonished, ought to set foot in America until the law had been repealed. The ubiquitous Francis Bishop was there to urge the forwarding of their resolution to their abolitionist brethren in America.[30] At approximately the same time that the Southern Unitarian Society was holding its conference, the North of England Unitarian Christian Association was meeting at George Harris's Hanover Square Chapel in Newcastle. Harris, in tandem with George Armstrong, added their protest against the "infamous" law.[31]

Among all the spring meetings there was one only that went the whole way in supporting the Bristol resolution of April. On 16 May 1851, the ministers and congregation of the Lewin's Mead Chapel met, with Estlin, Armstrong, James, and Edwin Chapman present. They resolved not to invite anyone to their pulpits who had "directly or indirectly, by speech or by silence," supported the Fugitive Slave Law, or failed to oppose it, and they recommended that the British and Foreign Unitarian Association treat this subject at its spring assembly.[32]

In two letters to the *Inquirer*, Russell Carpenter denounced the congregation's exclusionary resolution as a departure from their denomination's honored history of personal and congregational independence. He repudiated the idea that Unitarians ought to ally themselves to a popular cause in order to gain the recognition and appreciation of other Christian sects. He preferred their denomination to suffer "false reproach" as an ally of the slave system than to have it adopt a policy of "exclusiveness and denunciation." Abolitionist and Unitarian were not synonymous. Their denomination did not exclude ministers opposed to peace, temperance, and other reforms, and it ought not excommunicate those opposed to abolition. When he had visited the Southern states, clergymen had invited him to preach, and his British colleagues ought to be as generous. Supporting Carpenter's view were letters by Samuel Bache (1804–76), minister to Priestley's old congregation in Birmingham, and Charles Wicksteed. The latter considered excommunication to be "using a tyranny to get rid of a tyranny." But whereas Bache felt that the British and Foreign Unitarian Association ought not to deliberate on American slavery, Wicksteed believed it should. If it did not, he warned that perhaps he personally would have to act "in company with others who were freer to express their Christian convictions."[33]

Opposing Carpenter's view were Solly, Estlin, and Armstrong. It was a question, Solly declared, of whether their associations were Unitarian meetings for mere denominational business or Christian assemblies for universal action. As Chris-

tians they had every right to admonish and then to separate
from slaveholders and their supporters. Solly, who accepted
the policy of exclusion and felt that many of his Unitarian
brethren did likewise, remarked that they only had to view
their sisters and mothers in slavery. Then they would rejoice at
church meetings that protested against "the foulest system of
villany ever practiced in God's sight since Christ died to redeem
[them]." Armstrong believed that the discussion on the Fugitive
Slave law was "intimately related" to "Unitarian controversy,
Unitarian teaching, Unitarian missions." Carpenter's equating
their proposal of exclusion with excommunication was a red
herring; they had neither "the power nor the will" to employ
excommunication. They simply would refuse their pulpits or
homes to those who had not spoken, preached, and written for
the slave. Estlin declared that a strong antislavery protest by the
BFUA would better serve Unitarian Christianity "than the most
decided Anti-Trinitarian tracts or resolutions." However, none
of these arguments swayed the committee of the BFUA. They
had already rejected the possible discussion of slavery at the
forthcoming annual meeting, believing that it would impede
the handling of the association's official business, and would be
likely to "foment unhappy divisions in [their] body."[34]

Denominational Business and Christian Reform: The British and Foreign Unitarian Association and the London Antislavery Meeting of 1851

The "great and important objects" for which the BFUA was
chartered were to assist poor congregations, to distribute
theological books and tracts, and to protect and extend
Unitarian civil rights. Its members were concerned about its
status and strength. Never a strong organization, in the early
1850s it faced a variety of problems; expenditures exceeded
income, the condition of its poorest congregations was
"wretched," and over ten percent of its churches lacked ministers. In addition to their concern that every Unitarian have
entirely free action on controversial issues, men such as Samuel
Bache were frightened that disharmonious discussion on a
topic such as slavery could further weaken, if not completely
destroy the association. The Committee of the Western
Unitarian Christian Union had resigned over this very issue,

and when a minister such as Wicksteed suggested that there might be other Christian groups in which a Unitarian could more freely operate, the anxiety of those who feared for the survival of the BFUA only increased.[35]

Thus, many Unitarians probably breathed a sigh of relief, when Jerom Murch (1807–95) proposed, and the Garrisonians agreed, to hold a meeting separate from the regular session of the BFUA to discuss American slavery. Twelve ministers used the *Inquirer* and distributed broadsheets to advertise the special enclave. They planned to meet at Exeter Hall, the center for reform conferences, but were refused its use because of their Unitarianism. Armstrong and Estlin publicized this act of discrimination to gain Unitarian sympathy for the proposed meeting. The meeting's purpose was "to deliberate on the Duty of English Unitarianism in reference to Slavery in the United States" and to adopt suitable resolutions.[36]

On Friday, 13 June 1851, Unitarians crowded into the Freeman's Tavern for their antislavery deliberations. Dr. Joseph Hutton was in the chair, and familiar friends of the slave were there: Armstrong, Bishop, Crosskey, Solly, William Carpenter, Russell Carpenter, Thomas Cooper, and others; joined by their American coworkers, the Crafts, William Wells Brown, Maria Weston Chapman, and Susan Cabot. Estlin outlined the long and tortuous path that led to their meeting. He commended the various orthodox bodies—the Baptist Union, the Congregational Union of England and Wales, the Evangelical Alliance—which had issued exclusionary statements against those who, by "*speech* or by *silence*," had lent support to the Fugitive Slave Law. He hoped that the Unitarians would not be overshadowed by their orthodox brethren on this issue.[37]

Armstrong moved the first resolution, an attack on the notorious law that named several Unitarian ministers who opposed it. As usual, he spoke at great length. He described slavery in the South, disparaged moderation (which he defined as being "not too much in the right"), praised Channing, and condemned Dewey. Thomas Cooper then reminisced about his experiences with West Indian slavery. After a few others spoke, the resolution passed unanimously.[38]

Francis Bishop moved the second resolution, which simply proposed that the first be sent to Samuel May, Jr. As an "Orthodox Unitarian . . . of the old school," he wanted them to put into action the glorious principles of the Fatherhood of God and the Brotherhood of Man. Otherwise, their denomination was "cold, formal, and lifeless" and repelled potential converts. Russell Carpenter spoke in favor of moderation. Their remonstrances ought to be "brotherly," and ought not to specify individuals. His brother, William, expressed the same concern, but the Carpenters received little support. After the second resolution was passed, Hutton introduced William Wells Brown. The fugitive slave spoke of America's "reign of terror"; praised British abolitionist men and women, especially the women; and pleaded for the policy of exclusion. Greatly moved by the proceedings, Henry Solly declared that "he had long been at boiling point, and the steam was up." As a "lover of Unitarian doctrine," he did not want to see it, nor the associations formed to promote it, divorced from the "great wants and crying evils of the age." To do that would alienate Unitarians from affection and respect.[39]

Joseph Hutton sent a copy of the resolutions to May and to the *Christian Register*. There was no sense of triumph about the meeting or its action. The *Inquirer* was pleased, and the Garrisonian Massachusetts Anti-Slavery Society voted its appreciation.[40] But the *Christian Register* printed Hutton's letter and the resolutions with an obnoxious preface.[41] And when Samuel J. May proposed some severe resolutions against the law and its supporters at the spring meeting of the American Unitarian Association, he saw them voted down.[42] This action grieved Hutton and he blamed it on "the voluntary principle" of American church life; American ministers feared losing their pulpits and were "shepherds unrighteously subservient to the sheep."[43] Samuel May, Jr., complained to Mary Carpenter that the resolutions secured in London were not sanctioned by the BFUA and could not be publicized as the expression of the Unitarian denomination in Britain. The BFUA, said May, apparently was demoralized by the "time-serving spirit" that had long characterized the American Unitarian Association.[44] Added to the inaction of the AUA was the allegation, repeated several times in the *Inquirer,* that the *Christian Register* had censored a report on the rendition of a slave in Boston.[45] Relations between the British and American Unitarians were at a nadir. Transatlantic antagonism was intense. "Mr. Armstrong," complained an American minister, "was doing his best to separate the Unitarians of America and of England."[46] Russell Carpenter feared that the London meeting had accomplished nothing, for some of the American periodicals were suggesting that it carried the sanction of only a "small and that not the most prominent portion" of the British Unitarian ministers. Would not a moderate and charitable address, he asked, written by a prominent divine be signed by almost every Unitarian minister in England, and strengthen the antislavery cause among almost every Unitarian minister in America?[47]

The "Motley Group": The Carpenters, a Quartet of Discordant Voices

That no Garrisonian leaped to second Carpenter's proposal illustrated that he was persona non grata in their company. One reason was his frigid personality. He exhibited no open intensity of feeling over slavery. In a group of Garrisonians—reformers such as Solly who "had long been at boiling point, and the steam was up"—he was an iceberg of moderation, independence, and fastidiousness. He could not become enthusiastic about "any subject" discussed by those around him. He was a "wet blanket," explained Estlin, and the doctor, whose health was not good, dreaded his visits. Yet when some American abolitionists accused Carpenter of being a "timeserver," Estlin defended him; they simply did not comprehend his personality. It was difficult, explained Mary Estlin, to give a "correct picture" of Russell and his family with all their "virtues and peculiarities"—they were such a "motley group."[48]

Among the defects that the Garrisonians saw in Russell Carpenter, and in his sister Mary, whom they believed he had indoctrinated, was an inability to see the Garrisonians as the most important representatives of abolitionism in America and a tendency to see them as "injudicious and intolerant." Moreover, they objected to Russell's defense of indefensible ministers such as Gannett, and they loathed his regarding the antislavery movement as merely one branch of reform and not necessarily the most important of all. Still, Samuel May, Jr., saw Russell as potentially helpful to them, and the Garrisonians generally tried to sow the seeds of abolitionist truth among the Carpenters. However, "it was a hard row to hoe," confessed Susan Cabot, "in penetrating the Carpenter ground."[49]

The Carpenter ground, or "motley group," consisted of the children of the Unitarian patriarch, Lant Carpenter: Mary, William Benjamin, Philip Pearsall, Russell Lant, Anna, and Su-

[handwritten: Four most important carpenters]

san (1811–97). Little is known of the last two and their contribution to reform was apparently small. The other four
comprised a quartet of genius, imagination, creativity, and energy for social progress and reform. Each deserves a modern
full-length biography; only one, Mary, has been so honored.
With the exception of Russell, an exception as inexplicable as it
is unfortunate, they all were given a place in the *Dictionary of
National Biography*. They all inherited a moderate and tolerant
spirit from their father, the dominant person in their lives,
whose accidental, or suicidal death by drowning left an indel-
ible mark on their minds. They all devoted the major part or
the whole of their lives to religion and social reform.[50]

Mary Carpenter's fame was not as an antislavery reformer,
but as the founder of the first reformatory for girls in England.
Her pioneering work at her famous Red Lodge became the
model for similar institutions to be later established. Her social
conscience had been awakened by the squalor of the "wretched
neighborhoods" that enveloped her father's wealthy congregation. It was a visiting Unitarian minister, and one of the
founders of American social work, Joseph Tuckerman (1778–
1840), who first suggested to her to look after Bristol's ragged
children. It was another visiting American minister, ironically
Orville Dewey, who advised her to aid also the slave. She
strongly dissented from Dewey's later proclamations, but she
respected him for rekindling her antislavery interest. Despite
her ambivalent attitude toward the tactics and proscriptions of
the Garrisonians, they were in fact the group with whom she
most closely identified. She had met Garrison and many of his
lieutenants and she corresponded with them all. She also came
under the influence of Mary Estlin and Harriet Martineau. She
wholeheartedly supported the antislavery movement from the
time of Dewey's visit in 1843 to the spring of 1851, when she
practically dropped out of the movement, allegedly because the
greater claims of her "Ragged School" precluded her involvement in a foreign cause.[51]

However, perhaps the real reason for her withdrawal was her
loss of faith in America's Republican ideal of freedom. In April
1851, a fugitive slave had been returned to slavery from Boston, and the event so upset Carpenter that she wrote to May
one of her most discouraged antislavery missives. In passing
the Fugitive Slave Law, she told May, his nation had committed
an "atrocious act . . . against humanity, against itself, against
God." She was completely disgusted with America. The United

States had regained a "pre-eminence" in the annals of history (which she hoped would never be imitated); they had carried out a "daring and unblushing defiance of the laws of God, [done] with the Bible open before them." A free, educated people had done this, whose clergy told Europe "to admire and copy . . . the glorious freedom of their adored Union." Her American friends had assured her that Boston would never return a slave and now they had betrayed her trust. This letter was one of her last major demonstrations of interest in the antislavery cause. It could be argued that her contempt for America and her loss of faith in its possible redemption turned her to concentrate on events at home. She continued to send annual gifts to the Boston Bazaar, but it was her sister, Anna, who prepared them.[52]

William Benjamin Carpenter played an important role in the antislavery movement. As a scientist, he provided expert opinion to correct American racial fallacies. His physiological writings were widely circulated in the United States.[53] His reform boiling point matched that of Russell rather than Mary's or Philip.

"Eccentric" best describes Philip Pearsall Carpenter. His fame rested on his contribution to the study of mollusks. He was antitobacco, antiwine, antimeat, antifilth, antisectarian, antiwar, and antislavery, but pro-mollusca. At one point in his career he purchased fourteen tons of shells and spent nearly a quarter of a century examining, describing, naming, and classifying them. He received his B.A. from the University of London and his ministerial training at the Unitarian College then located at York. His first congregation was at Strand, and his second, and last, at Warrington. In 1858 he visited the United States, where he received an "honorary" Ph.D. from the University of the State of New York, and returned to England in 1860. Five years later, he moved to Canada, converted to the Anglican Church, and lived out his days teaching natural history, particularly conchology. He spoiled his teaching, writes his biographer in the *Dictionary of National Biography,* by performing antics that his students found memorable, but taught them little. "He was neither judicious nor profound."[54]

To those who pictured the Garrisonians as insane and irresponsible "Anti-everything-arians," it came as no surprise that brother Philip was one of that group. He was "much drawn" to Henry C. Wright, Eliza Lee Follen, Maria Weston Chapman, and "above all," William Lloyd Garrison, his "dear friend and brother." Unlike Russell, but in agreement with Mary, he judged slavery as the world's worst sin.[55] In addition to preaching antislavery sermons, participating in antislavery meetings, and procuring gifts for the Boston Bazaar, he published antislavery tracts from his own press in Warrington. His antislavery titles were augmented by such stimulating reform propaganda as "Dirt!," "Smokers! Beware!" (also printed in Welsh), "Don't Poison My Air!," "Indirect Advantages of Tetotalism [sic]," and "Rules of Health," printed in large type for the visually impaired. Neither "judicious nor profound," Philip *was* "a virtuous . . . and a labourious" reformer.[56]

Of the Carpenters, William probably made the most important contribution to the antislavery cause through his scientific attacks upon American racism (and his contribution will be discussed in chapter 7). However, as far as general antislavery propaganda was concerned, Russell was preeminent in his family and foremost among the non-Garrisonian Unitarians. He was a fine representative of the liberality, reasonableness, and tolerance traditionally attributed to the Unitarian faith, and logically one could assume he had a beneficial effect in stimulating antislavery interest in his denomination. Upon Carpenter's death, Frederick Douglass declared in a eulogy that in his own life he tried to imitate his English benefactor's "calmness," "large charity," and "justice." He knew of "no writer who took more pains to be as exactly right than Mr. Carpenter." Russell had always admired Frederick's sagacity.[57]

Russell Carpenter received his early education under his father, a man all of whose opinions "were in favour of freedom and reform." He later studied with his brother Philip at the Unitarian College in York, the ancient cathedral city in which the "little body of Unitarian students was not in great favour." His first permanent ministerial assignment was at Bridgwater and he remained there from 1842 to 1849. An ardent temperance man, he resigned his pastorate when he learned that public houses helped to endow his chapel. In August 1849, he undertook a tour of the United States. Upon his return, he served a succession of Unitarian chapels in Birkenhead, Halifax, and Bridport, where he remained the rest of his life. Throughout his ministerial career he labored against everything he believed enslaved the mind and spirit and lent his time, money, and pen to antislavery, peace, temperance, women's rights, funeral reform, disestablishment, and the prevention of cruelty to children and animals. When he died in

1892, he was "rightly esteemed" in his denomination as one of "the Fathers of the Church."[58]

A Travelogue on Slavery and Suggestions for Reform: Russell Carpenter, the Independent Abolitionist

Carpenter became an expert on slavery on his visit to America in 1849. His antislavery pronouncements thereafter usually made reference to that experience. He wanted to get at the truth of the antislavery question, and while in America, he moved with great diplomacy among Garrisonians, conservatives, and Southern slaveholders. Like so many other English travelers to America during this period, Carpenter published an account of his journey. Called "Observations on American Slavery," his essay appeared as a five-part serial in the *Christian Reformer* and then as a separate pamphlet.[59] Reviews of his essay ranged from a conservative's judgment that it was "conscientiously fair and just" to a Garrisonian's that it was "*very* offensive."[60] It may have been his essay that moved the Bristol Ladies' Anti-Slavery Society to warn that Southerners had "almost uniform success" in infecting English travelers with their prejudices.[61]

In his first installment in the *Christian Reformer,* Carpenter provided a careful and detailed explanation of the various antislavery parties. The main platform of the Garrisonians, he explained, was to dissolve the Union and to abstain from political participation. On the other hand, the Free Soil party and its supporters wanted to use the ballot box to end slavery. He discussed implementation of the Fugitive Slave Law and resistance to it.[62]

In his second installment he told of his travel to the upper South. In Baltimore, he discovered slaveholders in the city's Unitarian Church. In Washington, he interviewed Millard Fillmore and Daniel Webster. In Virginia, he saw tobacco farms and factories. "Prejudice against colour subside[d] before affection for [this] weed," he remarked, and Americans had no objection to chew what Negroes had handled. He saw slave coffles driven southward to be sold, and he admitted that the sight of slavery's "horrors" made him "more sensitive than ever to heartless oppression of every kind."[63]

In his third and fourth installments, he recalled his travel in the lower South. In South Carolina, he saw mothers and children sold at a slave auction and he became "half hysterical, half sick." He viewed the prevalence of mulattoes as evidence of "licentiousness." In Charleston, he sojourned with Dr. Samuel Gilman (1791–1858), the city's Unitarian minister and "nominally a slaveholder." To Carpenter, the importance of Gilman as a Unitarian preacher in a hostile orthodox environment and as a temperance reformer outweighed his association with slavery. He was pleased that Gilman and his wife had established a "Teetotal Society" among Charleston's slaves. After a stay of ten days, Carpenter departed, somewhat impressed by Gilman, greatly impressed by Charleston: "Nowhere did I live in a domestic atmosphere of greater kindness." He traveled on to Georgia, and then northward to Tennessee and Kentucky.[64]

In his fifth and final installment Carpenter related his travels to St. Louis, Missouri, and his long return trip to New England. When he arrived in Boston, he attended the anniversary meeting of the American Unitarian Association and spoke on slavery. It was, he declared, "a cloud that shed so much of its darkness" even in New England that his countrymen feared to come among them. In circulating among the Unitarian ministers, Carpenter found not one who was in favor of slavery. Some never spoke against it, while others, ultraradicals on antislavery, rarely stopped speaking. He encountered no Unitarian minister who approved of the Fugitive Slave Law, but some, out of respect for national authority, wanted it obeyed. His happiest and most profitable days in America were spent with the Garrisonians. He sympathized fully with their antislavery work, but had he resided in America, he would not join them, preferring to strive "for freedom freely." He ended his travelogue on slavery with recommendations to the British people on how to assist emancipation in America.[65]

In his many pamphlets, articles, and letters on slavery published after his "Observations," Carpenter often repeated his recommendations. As Christians the British people could send "earnest, candid, and mild" appeals to religious associations in the United States. If a denomination practiced discipline and excommunication, it could employ them against slaveholders and their abettors. If a denomination had faith in denunciation, it ought not here be silent. However, he cautioned his Unitarian friends: until they agreed to the doctrines of other churches in respect to discipline and denunciation, they ought not to copy them. In addition to denominational appeals, they could address individual appeals to friends and relatives, and to religious and political leaders in America.[66] They could use literature as an antislavery vehicle, or they could publish popular tracts in the manner of his brother Philip's Oberlin tracts or the Leeds Anti-Slavery Series.[67] They could support the American antislavery societies, bazaars, and newspapers.[68] They could indirectly assist the antislavery fight by helping to raise the educational, economic, and social level of blacks in Britain and in her colonies. And they could help raise the living standards of the working classes of their own country, thus enabling their pronouncements on other nation's ills to carry greater moral weight.[69]

In a sense, all of the above were moral means to fight slavery; there also was an economic measure. "If there were no cotton markets," taught Carpenter, "there would be few slave markets." But he believed that a complete boycott of American cotton could cause starvation and revolution in Great Britain in a single year. Moreover, free trade had advocates as well as free labor. He suggested that cotton production be encouraged in suitable British colonies. In the meantime, because the English "as customers of stolen goods" robbed the slave of his labor, they had an obligation to help mitigate his oppression. Sadly, there were many former British subjects who were the slaves' oppressors. Carpenter estimated that about a million Irish and a quarter of a million English had recently emigrated to the United States. Some of these settled in the South and became parties to the sin of slavery. Therefore, the Negro slaves had a twofold claim upon the British people. They imported that which had been *"robbed from them"* and they exported those who might be *"trained to rob them."* He again and again returned to this theme of Britain's direct connection with slavery, particularly as a consequence of British emigration to America. "If England refused to admit slave-booty," he testified, and if his countrymen who resided in America took a "truly British and manly position" on slavery, it would cease.[70]

Finally, there was a political or diplomatic method of opposing the slave power. Under the provision of the Negro seamen acts of several Southern states, many free blacks who came into the ports of those states were imprisoned for the duration their vessels were in port. The cost of imprisonment fell upon the ship's captain and, if not paid, the hapless black seamen could be sold into slavery.[71] Carpenter was intensely concerned about the plight of British Negro seamen under these acts. In South Carolina, in 1851, thirty-six were seized and incarcerated.

Moreover, he was offended by the laws of some Northern states that restricted the travel and residence of blacks. As long as the British permitted their black countrymen who traveled to America to be abused in this way, they recognized America's right "to degrade" those whom they had raised to political equality with themselves. They showed "a cowardly falseness to [their] own convictions." They boasted that American slaves became free men as soon as they touched British soil, but the American "braggards for independence" turned their British freemen into slaves. American air, he remarked, poisoned liberty.[72]

Carpenter did not advocate going to war to protect Britain's black subjects, but pressed for negotiations to secure their protection. He was anxious to have the English people comprehend the magnitude of the slave power's agression. War was inevitable. "As long as the slave tyranny," he taught, was "dominant in America, England [was] in constant peril either of being robbed, or engaged in a war to prevent robbery." America lusted after Cuba, the West Indies, and Canada. All America's wars of annexation were "prompted by southern ambition" to propagate slavery. As the 1850s progressed the Garrisonian call for disunion began to appeal to Carpenter. He saw the South so dominating the North that the whole of America was being corrupted. But already in 1851, he feared the despotic South's steady march. *"All the weight of [Great Britain's] national influence,"* he pleaded, ought to "be enlisted to curb, and if possible repress, the lawless and anarchical despotism, which, if allowed to develop itself, [would] prove fatal to all free and constitutional government." There seemed to be no choice. "Either we must endeavor to reform America," warned Carpenter, "or America will corrupt us."[73]

Notes

1. *Report of the Western Unitarian Christian Union, Adopted at the Tenth Half-Yearly Meeting, Held at Honiton, October 17, 1850; with A Letter to the Churches of the Union by the Rev. Geo. Armstrong, B.A.* (London: E. Whitfield, 1850), pp. 7–8.

2. Ibid., pp. 20, 22–23, 31.

3. Betty Fladeland, *Men and Brothers: Anglo-American Antislavery Cooperation* (Urbana, Ill.: University of Illinois Press, 1972), pp. 342, 349; Howard Temperley, *British Antislavery 1833–1870* (London: Longman Group Ltd., 1972), pp. 221, 224, 246.

4.　Charles Wicksteed, *The Englisman's Duty to the Free and the Enslaved American. A*

Lecture, Twice Delivered at Leeds, in January, 1853 (London: W. & F. G. Cash, 1853), pp. 8–9.

5. Douglas C. Stange, *Patterns of Antislavery among American Unitarians, 1831–1860* (Rutherford, N. J.: Fairleigh Dickinson University Press, 1977), pp. 38, 214–15; "[Twenty-first Annual Meeting of the] British and Foreign Unitarian Association," *Inquirer*, 6 June 1846, p. 363. Between 1850 and 1860, 15,000 to 20,000 blacks fled to Canada. See Fred Landon, "The Negro Migration to Canada After the Passing of the Fugitive Slave Act," *Journal of Negro History* 5 (October 1920): 22, 29.

6. Francis Bishop to the editor, Liverpool, n.d., *Inquirer*, 12 July 1851, p. 439; Bishop to the editor, Liverpool, 31 July 1851, *Inquirer*, p. 2 August 1851, p. 486; Bishop to the editor, Liverpool, 9 March 1853, *Inquirer*, 19 March 1853, p. 188; Ian Sellers, "Liverpool Nonconformity, 1786–1914" (Ph.D. diss., University of Keele, 1969), p. 232.

7. Bishop to the editor, Liverpool, 31 July 1851, *Inquirer*, 2 August 1851, p. 486; Francis Bishop to Mary Estlin, Liverpool, 4 October 1850, Weston Papers, Boston Public Library, cited hereafter as MB.

8. William Craft, *Running a Thousand Miles for Freedom; or, the Escape of William and Ellen Craft from Slavery* (London: William Tweedie, 1860), pp. 88, 109; John Bishop Estlin to_____, Bristol, December, 1853 [printed letter to thank the benefactors of the Crafts], May Papers, MB; Estlin to Samuel May, Bristol, 2 May 1851, Clare Taylor, *British and American Abolitionists. An Episode in Transatlantic Understanding* (Edinburgh: Edinburgh University Press, 1974), pp. 377–78.

9. Eliza Lee Follen to Mary Estlin, Brighton, 31 January 1852, Follen to Estlin, Kingston on the Thames, n.d., Estlin Papers, Dr. Williams's Library, London, cited hereafter as LDW; Mary Estlin to Miss Weston, Bristol, [17 September 1850], Weston Papers, MB.

10. Mary Carpenter to Samuel May, Jr., Bristol, 29 May 1851, J. Estlin Carpenter, *The Life and Work of Mary Carpenter*, 2nd ed. (London: Macmillan & Co., 1881), pp. 103–4; "Negro Life in America," *Christian Reformer* 8 (August 1852): 427; Russell Lant Carpenter, "American Slavery, No. V," *Christian Reformer* 7 (December 1851): 737; Bristol and Clifton Ladies' Anti-Slavery Society, *Statements Respecting the American Abolitionists; by Their Opponents and Their Friends; Indicating the Present Struggle Between Slavery and Freedom in the United States of America* (Dublin: Webb and Chapman, 1852), p. 5.

11. "The Slavery Question in the United States," *Inquirer*, 9 November 1850, p. 708. Several successive editors led the newspaper during the 1850s, none of them prominent in the antislavery movement. John Lalor (1814–56) and Richard Holt Hutton (1826–97) were its editors during the uproar over the Fugitive Slave Law. See Herbert McLachlan, *The Unitarian Movement in the Religious Life of England* (London: George Allen & Unwin, Ltd., 1934), pp. 215–16.

12. "The Slaveholders' Last Move," *Inquirer*, 14 September 1850, p. 577.

13. "The Slavery Crisis in America," *Inquirer*, 23 November 1850, p. 739; "Morality of Lynch Law," *Inquirer*, 7 December 1850, p. 770; "Theodore Parker's Morality," *Inquirer*, 28 December 1850, p. 821; "Fruits of the Fugitive Slave Law," *Inquirer*, 5 October 1850, p. 625.

14. Joseph Henry Allen to Russell Lant Carpenter, Bangor, 11 December 1850, Allen to Carpenter, Bangor, 16 March 1851, Joseph Henry Allen Papers, Andover-Harvard Theological Library, cited hereafter as MH-AH; William C. Gannett, *Ezra Stiles Gannett. Unitarian Minister in Boston, 1824–1871* (Boston: Roberts Brothers, 1875), p. 288. "Speech of Rev. Dr. Dewey at the Great Union Meeting in Pittsfield, Dec. 17th, 1850," *Christian Inquirer*, 18 January 1851, pp. 1–2; for an essay on the attitudes and

action of American Unitarian conservatives in regard to the Fugitive Slave Law, see Douglas C. Stange, "From Treason to Antislavery Patriotism: Unitarian Conservatives and the Fugitive Slave Law," *Harvard Library Bulletin* 25 (October 1977): 466–88.

15. John Bishop Estlin, "American Slavery and American Unitarian Ministers," *Inquirer*, 1 February 1851, p. 70.

16. S. Alfred Steinthal, *American Slavery. A Sermon, Preached at Christ Church Chapel, Bridgwater, On Sunday, May the First, 1853* (Bridgwater: J. Whitby, 1853), pp. 12–13; Susan C. Cabot to Mary Estlin, London, 12 and 13 February, n.y., Estlin Papers, LDW; George Armstrong to Samuel May, Jr., n.p., [May or June] 1853, May Papers, MB.

17. Parker Pillsbury to the editor, Manchester, 4 August 1855, *Inquirer*, 11 August 1855, p. 508.

18. "Letter from Rev. Dr. Dewey," *Christian Inquirer*, 29 February [sic, for 1 March] 1851, p. 2; Craft, Running a Thousand Miles, pp. 97–98.

19. James Martineau to Mary Carpenter, Liverpool, 16 May 1851, Martineau Papers, Manchester College, Oxford; Joseph Henry Allen to Russell Lant Carpenter, Bangor, 16 March 1851, Allen Papers, MH-AH; John Bishop Estlin to the Rev. Franklin Howorth, Bristol, 4 December 1850, *Inquirer*, 1 February 1851, p. 70.

20. Entries for 27 March 1851 and 15 May 1851, "Bristol and Clifton Auxiliary Ladies Anti-Slavery Society Minutes," Estlin Papers, LDW; John Bishop Estlin to William Lloyd Garrison, Bristol, 21 February 1851, Taylor, *British and American Abolitionists*, pp. 364–65; "American Slavery," *Inquirer*, 2 June 1851, p. 393; Temperley, *British Antislavery*, 246–47.

21. "Western Unitarian Christian Union," *Inquirer*, 3 May 1851, pp. 282–84.

22. "Western Unitarian Christian Union," *Inquirer*, 3 May 1851, pp. 282–84; "American Slavery," *Inquirer*, 21 June 1851, p. 394.

23. "Slavery and Its Supporters," *Inquirer*, 3 May 1851, pp. 273–74.

24. David Lloyd to the editor, Carmarthen, 2 June 1851, *Inquirer*, 7 June 1851, p. 358.

25. "Meetings Upon American Slavery," *Inquirer*, 31 May 1851, pp. 343–44; "American Slavery. [Meeting at] Bury, Lancashire," *Inquirer*, 7 June 1851, p. 364.

26. Ibid., p. 343.

27. Edward Higginson to William James, Wakefield, 15 July 1851, *Inquirer*, 19 July 1851, p. 454; "Midland Presbyterian or Unitarian Association," *Inquirer*, 28 June 1851, p. 412; "Provincial Meeting," *Christian Reformer* 7 (July 1851): 435–40.

28. "American Slavery," *Inquirer*, 14 June 1851, p. 380; "American Slavery," *Inquirer*, 28 June 1851, p. 472.

29. Philip Henry Wicksteed, ed., *Memorials of the Rev. Charles Wicksteed, B.A.* (London: Williams and Norgate, 1886), pp. 39–41; "What is Thought and Said of Us in the Fatherland," *Christian Register*, 26 July 1851, p. 118, [Charles Wicksteed], "The American Fugitive Slave Act," *Prospective Review; A Quarterly Journal of Theology and Literature* 7 (1851): 443.

30. *Report of the Fiftieth Anniversary of the Southern Unitarian Society, Adopted at the Annual Meeting at Wareham, Dorsetshire, July 9, 1851—the Rev. Hugh Hutton, A.M., in the Chair* (n.p.: [1851]), n.p. nos.; "Annual Meeting of the Southern Unitarian Society," *Inquirer*, 19 July 1851, pp. 459–60; Edmund Kell to Samuel May, Jr., Newport, 25 July 1851, May Papers, MB.

31. "Northern Unitarian Association and the Fugitive Slave Bill," *Inquirer*, 12 July 1851, p. 444; "Northern Unitarian Association," *Inquirer*, 19 July 1851, pp. 458–59.

32. "Anti-Slavery Meeting of the Lewin's Mead Congregation, Bristol," *Inquirer*, 24 May 1851, p. 322 [sic, should be p. 332].

33. Russell Lant Carpenter to the editor, n.p., 19 May 1851, *Inquirer*, 24 May 1851,

p. 324 [sic, should be p. 334]; Carpenter to the editor, n.p., 26 May [1851], *Inquirer,* 7 June 1851, p. 360; Samuel Bache to the editor, [Birmingham], 26 May 1851, *Inquirer,* 31 May 1851, p. 341; Charles Wicksteed to the editor, Leeds, 5 June 1851, *Inquirer,* 7 June 1851, pp. 358–59.

34. Henry Solly to the editor, n.p., n.d., *Inquirer,* 7 June 1851, p. 359. See also Henry Solly, *"These Eighty Years," or, The Story of an Unfinished Life* (London: Simpkin, Marshall, & Co., 1893), 2:118; George Armstrong to the editor, Clifton, 5 June [1851], *Inquirer,* 7 June 1851, pp. 359–60; John Bishop Estlin to the editor, Bristol, 2 June 1851, *Inquirer,* 7 June 1851, p. 358.

35. "[The Twenty-sixth] Annual Meeting of the British and Foreign Unitarian Association," *Inquirer,* 14 June 1851, p. 375.

36. Jerom Murch to the editor, Bath, 1 June 1853, *Inquirer,* 4 June 1853, p. 361; "Our Concern with Slavery," *Inquirer,* 7 June 1851, p. 353; "American Slavery," [broadsheet announcing special meeting of the Unitarians to discuss American slavery, 13 June 1851], Weston Papers, MB.

37. "American Slavery," *Inquirer,* 21 June 1851, pp. 393–94.

38. Ibid., pp. 394–95.

39. Ibid., pp. 395–97. The report in the *Inquirer* was reprinted with additions as *American Slavery. Report of a Meeting of Members of the Unitarian Body, Held at the Freemasons' Tavern. June 13th, 1851, to Deliberate on the Duty of English Unitarians in Reference to Slavery in the United States. Rev. Dr. Hutton in the Chair* (London: E. T. Whitfield, 1851). Solly's remarks are from the pamphlet, page 23.

40. "Anti-Slavery Meeting of Unitarians," *Inquirer,* 14 June 1851, p. 370; *Twentieth Annual Report, Presented to the Massachusetts Anti-Slavery Society, By Its Board of Managers, January 28, 1852* (n.p.: n.d.), pp. 48–50.

41. "English View of Our Position Respecting the Fugitive Slave Law," *Christian Register,* 9 August 1851, p. 126.

42. "The American Unitarian Association and Slavery," *Inquirer,* 28 June 1851, pp. 412–13; "Slavery Discussion at the Unitarian Ministerial Conference," *Inquirer,* 26 July 1851, pp. 476–77.

43. Joseph Hutton to Samuel May, Jr., Dublin, 3 July 1851, May Papers, MB.

44. Samuel May, Jr., to Mary Carpenter, Leicester, 15 July 1851, May Papers, MB.

45. "The Boston Christian Register and Slavery," *Inquirer,* 31 May 1851, p. 338; "The Rev. S. May and the 'Boston Christian Register,'" *Inquirer,* 20 September 1851, p. 605; Samuel May, Jr., to the editor, Boston, 9 September 1851, *Inquirer,* 27 September 1851, p. 614.

46. "Impressions of an American Minister," *Inquirer,* 19 July 1851, p. 453.

47. Russell Lant Carpenter to the editor, n.p., 30 July 1851, *Inquirer,* 2 August 1851, p. 486.

48. John Bishop Estlin to [Caroline] Weston, Bristol, 31 October 1850, Mary Estlin to Miss Weston, Bristol, 30–31 October 1850, Mary Estlin to Miss Weston, 13 February 1851, Weston Papers, MB.

49. Mary Carpenter to Maria Weston Chapman, Bristol, 19 March 1848, Mary Estlin to Miss Weston, Bristol, 13 February 1851, Weston Papers, MB; Russell Lant Carpenter to the editor, Birkenhead, 17 December 1851, *Inquirer,* 27 December 1851, p. 823; Susan Cabot to Mary Estlin, London, 12 and 13 February, n.y., Estlin Papers, LDW; Mary Estlin to Miss Weston, Bristol, 30–31 October 1850, John Bishop Estlin to [Caroline] Weston, Bristol, 31 October 1850, Weston Papers, MB.

50. Leslie Stephen and Sidney Lee, eds., *The Dictionary of National Biography* (Oxford: Oxford University Press, 1921–1922), 3:1068–70, 1071–72, 1075–77, cited hereafter as *DNB;* J. Estlin Carpenter, ed., *Personal and Social Christianity Sermons and Addresses by the*

Late Russell Lant Carpenter, B.A. With a Short Memoir by Frances E. Cooke (London: Kegan Paul, Trench, Trubner & Co., 1893), pp. 9–11; Harriet Warm Schupf, "Single Women and Social Reform in Mid-Nineteenth Century England: The Case of Mary Carpenter," *Victorian Studies* 17 (March 1974): 306–7. This brilliant essay on Mary Carpenter gives a prominent place to Lant Carpenter's formative influence upon his daughter's career as a reformer. Schupf flatly states that Dr. Carpenter committed suicide, but supplies no evidence. See page 307. Carpenter's modern biography is Jo Manton's *Mary Carpenter and the Children of the Streets* (London: Heinemann Education, 1976).

51. Ruby J. Saywell, *Mary Carpenter of Bristol*, Bristol Branch of the Historical Association Local History Pamphlets, No. 9 (Bristol: Bristol Historical Association, 1964), p. 6; J. E. Carpenter, *Mary Carpenter*, pp. 45–46, 69–71, 82, 97, 104; Schupf, "Single Women and Social Reform," p. 309.

52. J. E. Carpenter, *Mary Carpenter*, pp. 102–4, 157.

53. "American Slavery," *Inquirer*, 21 June 1851, pp. 396–97.

54. *DNB*, 3: 1071–72; Russell Lant Carpenter, ed., *Memoirs of the Life and Work of Phillip Pearsall Carpenter, B.A., London, Ph.D., New York, Chiefly Derived from His Letters* (London: C. Kegan Paul & Co., 1880), pp. 1–32, 62, 241.

55. R. L. Carpenter, *Philip Carpenter*, pp. 64, 98–99, 198; Philip P. Carpenter to William Lloyd Garrison, Warrington, 21 May 1852, Garrison Papers, MB; [Philip Pearsall Carpenter], *Words in* [*on?*] *the War: Being Lectures on "Life and Death in the Hands of God and Man"* (London: W. & F. G. Cash, 1855), pp. 4, 54; J. E. Carpenter, *Mary Carpenter*, p. 98.

56. Philip Pearsall Carpenter, *The Oberlin Tracts* (Warrington: Oberlin Press, n.d.). There were at least twenty-nine tracts in the series. They were sold in sixpenny packets for free distribution. His antismoking concern—"a trivial subject upon which to lecture"—was curious for his times, but the modernity of his reform interest is illustrated by the significant legislation recently lobbied for and passed in the United States to protect the rights of nonsmokers. In this reform, Russell joined him. See Russell Lant Carpenter, "A Lecture on Tobacco . . . Delivered before the Mayor and People of Bridport, England," Abiel Abbot Livermore, *Anti-Tobacco* (Boston: Roberts Brothers, 1888).

57. J. E. Carpenter, *Personal and Social Christianity*, p. 36.

58. Ibid., 4–5, 7, 13–14, 17–18, 21, 33. "Obituary. The Rev. Russell Lant Carpenter, B.A.," *Inquirer*, 30 January 1892, pp. 70–71.

59. John Bishop Estlin to [Caroline] Weston, Bristol, 31 October 1850, Weston Papers, MB; J. E. Carpenter, *Personal and Social Christianity*, p. 15; Russell Lant Carpenter, "American Slavery" [Parts I–V], *Christian Reformer*, (August 1851), pp. 483–94, (September 1851), pp. 537–48, (October 1851), pp. 585–97, (November 1851), pp. 650–60, (December 1851), pp. 717–37, and reprinted as *Observations on American Slavery, after a Year's Tour in the United States* (London: Edward T. Whitfield, 1852).

60. Joseph Henry Allen to Russell Lant Carpenter, Bangor, 28 August 1852, Allen Papers, MH-AH; Thomas Hincks to Mary Estlin, Exeter, 17 May 1852, MB.

61. Bristol and Clifton Ladies' Anti-Slavery Society, *Statements Respecting the American Abolitionists*, p. 5.

62. R. L. Carpenter, "American Slavery," pp. 484–92.

63. Ibid., 537–38, 542–43, 547–48.

64. R. L. Carpenter, "American Slavery," pp. 588–90, 592–94, 652, 655.

65. Ibid., pp. 484–92.

66. Russell Lant Carpenter, "Our Conflict with American Slavery," *Christian Reformer* 9 (October 1853): 646–47; R. L. Carpenter, "American Slavery," p. 736.

67. R. L. Carpenter, "Our Conflict with American Slavery," pp. 644, 645, 650. See also footnote 56 above.

68. R. L. Carpenter, "Our Conflict with American Slavery," pp. 648, 649. Carpenter and his wife were partial to the antislavery society, bazaar, and newspaper associated with Frederick Douglass, much to the consternation of the Garrisonians. See ibid., p. 649; R. L. Carpenter, "Douglass's Bondage and Freedom," *Christian Reformer* 12 (May 1856): 288–95; R. L. Carpenter to the editor, Halifax, 20 January 1857, *Anti-Slavery Advocate* 2 (February 1857): 11; R. L. Carpenter to the editor, Halifax, 12 December 1859, *Inquirer*, 17 December 1859, p. 1146.

69. R. L. Carpenter, "Our Conflict with American Slavery," pp. 648–49, 651; R. L. Carpenter, "American Slavery," p. 737.

70. Russell Lant Carpenter, "Our Concern with American Slavery," *Christian Reformer* 9 (September 1853): 556–58; R. L. Carpenter, "Our Conflict with American Slavery," pp. 643–44, 650; R. L. Carpenter, "American Slavery," p. 737; R. L. Carpenter to the editor, n.p., 19 May 1851, *Inquirer*, 24 May 1851, p. 324; R. L. Carpenter to the editor, n.p., n.d., *Inquirer*, 18 March 1854, p. 173.

71. On the question of the imprisonment of British Negro seamen, see Fladeland, *Men and Brothers*, pp. 319–21; Philip M. Hamer, "Great Britain, the United States, and the Negro Seamen Acts, 1822–1848," *Journal of Southern History* 1 (1935): 3–28; and Hamer, "British Consuls and the Negro Seamen Acts, 1850–1860," *Journal of Southern History* 1 (1935): 138–68.

72. R. L. Carpenter, "Our Conflict with American Slavery," pp. 641–42; R. L. Carpenter, "Our Concern with Slavery," pp. 554–56; [Russell Lant Carpenter], *Imprisonment and Enslavement of British Coloured Seamen; Illustrated in the Case of John Glasgow*, Leeds Anti-Slavery Series, No. 89 (Leeds: n.d.), pp. 4–6.

73. R. L. Carpenter, "Our Conflict with American Slavery," pp. 640–42; R. L. Carpenter, *Imprisonment and Enslavement of Seamen*, pp. 2–3, 15–16; R. L. Carpenter, "Our Concern with Slavery," pp. 552–53, 560; R. L. Carpenter to the editor, n.p., n.d., *Inquirer*, 18 March 1854, p. 173.

6

Abstinence from America's Curse: The Decline of Abolitionist Enthusiasm—1853–60

One Book Worth a Thousand Tears:
Beecher Stowe, Bishop, and the BFUA (Again!)

For antislavery propaganda, the years 1852 and 1853 were very important in Great Britain. Readers of all classes and religious persuasions were emotionally stirred by the provocative novel by Harriet Beecher Stowe. *Uncle Tom's Cabin* appeared in 1852 and in eight months sold over one million copies in Great Britain. Through dramatic and musical adaptations of the novel, even the illiterate could share in Uncle Tom's anguish. Queen and consort, politicians and preachers, men and women, young and old, orthodox and infidels, all found the sentimental novel to be *the* book on slavery. When Stowe revisited England in 1853, her tour was triumphant. Her hosts were the wealthy and aristocratic and even Queen Victoria would have welcomed her, had not political considerations stood in the way.[1]

One of the benefits of Stowe's visit was "The Stafford House Address," an antislavery appeal to the women of America from the women of Great Britain. Written by Lord Shaftesbury, it originated at a meeting at Stafford House, the London residence of the antislavery patron, the Duchess of Sutherland. Over a half million women signed it. Charles Wicksteed made a special effort to get women of his congregation to add their names. The address amused Dr. Estlin. It showed the laity of the "Established Church condescending to think & speak [on slavery], if not very sensibly."[2] Antislavery assistance from un-expected and traditionally unfriendly quarters was a bit curious to comprehend, but of course, the spreading antislavery fer-ment did please the Garrisonians.[3] They planned to capitalize on the excitement over *Uncle Tom's Cabin* and to convert the tears shed over it into "*pearls* of value & enduring workman-ship."[4]

The new antislavery excitement encouraged the production of antislavery propaganda by a number of Unitarians. In a review article on *Uncle Tom's Cabin*, the conservative Reverend Charles Beard (1827–88) spoke on antislavery for the first time. He generally praised Stowe's genius (she had written passages "no man could have written"), and denounced American slav-ery as "the greatest wrong . . . upon God's earth." In 1853, his father, John Relly Beard, wrote a biography of Toussaint L'Ouverture that glorified liberty for blacks, women, children, servants, and "all orders and degrees" of humanity; Estlin is-sued a revised edition of his *Brief Notice of American Slavery;* and two of the finest antislavery sermons by Unitarians were pub-lished: Alfred Steinthal's *American Slavery* and Charles Wick-steed's *The Englishman's Duty to the Free and Enslaved American.* Also in the same year, the *Inquirer* printed two lengthy antislav-ery addresses, by George Armstrong and Henry Montgomery. Some of these writings were surely inspired by Stowe's "glori-ous" book.[5]

To authenticate her description of slavery, Stowe published a volume of documentation called *A Key to Uncle Tom's Cabin.* Unitarians found especially interesting and disconcerting her quotation from the Reverend Theodore Clapp, the Unitarian minister in New Orleans, that the slaves ought to enjoy their God-appointed role in slavery. Clapp had previously referred to God as a slave dealer, but that blasphemy had not been broadcast in a best-seller. Bishop called Clapp's preaching a "wretched perversion of religion and piety."[6]

The Unitarians sadly added Clapp's statement to their an-thology of infamous quotations by Dewey and Gannett. They generally began to disbelieve that America could ever possibly redeem herself. In their two antislavery addresses, Armstrong and Montgomery had alluded to America as a nation "overrid-den by crime and tyranny" speedily sliding to disaster. At one time everything relating to America had interested Armstrong and he believed it to be providentially "the hope of the world." But Northern complicity in slavery taught him "a sad and different lesson"; he now favored disunion, that the "unholy league" be broken up. Montgomery as a youth had delighted to read about America's birth in freedom, now he was horrified by her decline in slavery. Both men agreed with Bishop's view that "the slave power" was vastly increasing its influence in America in 1853.[7]

Amid the new antislavery excitement, Bishop's words and role took on a greater importance. He had been an enthusiastic Garrisonian since 1840 and held the strategic post of a slum missionary for the Liverpool Domestic Mission.[8] What undoubtedly increased his credibility among Unitarians on the slavery issue was his visit to the Southern states in the summer and fall of 1852. He became one of that select group of English Unitarians to see slavery at firsthand and in an age without radio and television immediate observation was honored and appreciated. Only fugitive slaves exceeded in importance the observers of slavery as purveyors of slavery's horrors.

As an English observer in the South, Bishop's style contrasted sharply with that of Russell Carpenter. Whereas the latter strained to be neutral, Bishop was rabidly partisan. Where Carpenter exercised diplomacy, Bishop was blunt. Where Carpenter became "half-hysterical" over slavery, Bishop became completely hysterical. No better illustration of the difference between their styles was Bishop's breach of "*good taste* and *good manners*" at the autumn meeting of the American Unitarian Association in Baltimore, Maryland. There Bishop "lifted up his voice against slavery." He told the startled delegates:

> No Christian Church, worthy of the name, could ever prosper unless it bore a faithful testimony against [slavery's] system of unrighteousness,—least of all could a church which acknowledged in theory the brotherhood of man, and recognized the right of all, whatever the complexion of their skin, to address God as "Our Father in Heaven."

It took courage, or reckless abandon, to utter antislavery remarks in a slaveholding church, in a "slaveholding and intensely pro-slavery" city. No American minister would have been so bold, remarked Samuel May, not even one from Massachusetts. "He had bearded the dragon of slavery," said the *Anti-Slavery Advocate*, "on [its] own soil." Estlin declared that he had greatly honored their denomination, for his antislavery testimony as a visiting English minister was "almost without example."[9] Bishop's friends probably exaggerated the significance of his action, although it was true that Garrison had once been incarcerated in Baltimore, and another abolitionist, Charles Torrey, had died in the city's jail.[10] Bishop's statement at the AUA meeting was indeed stronger than Carpenter's sympathetic declaration given two years before. But more important for the cause were the graphic descriptions of slavery that he sent to his friends, and then presented to every audience that he came before upon his return home.

The most shocking of these descriptions referred to slave auctions. Bishop emphasized their licentious aspects, the intimate details of which he dared not even write to Garrison. He saw "families scattered—husbands and wives, mothers and daughters, sisters and brothers divided. [He] saw the shameless indecent exposure . . . of men and women and GIRLS." He witnessed "the foul and abominable insults [of] defenceless women by the *'chivalrous'!!!* men—[or] fiendish monsters"—who conducted the slave sales. He saw for sale a mother and her teenage daughter, "a beautiful young woman, nearly white," who belonged to a "brutal, coarse, and repulsive-looking man." He was distressed to have to ignore the pleas of the mother and daughter to have Bishop purchase them together, and was stunned to see the mother sold to a person from Alabama and the daughter sold to a man from Virginia. The parade of horrors continued to pass before him. An old woman was sold for fifteen dollars. An old man was separated from his wife, despite his cries that he could not live without her. Men, women, and children were marched to the block, their naked backs showing the scars of the lash. Bishop imagined himself in hell, surrounded by fiends. Completely hysterical, he ran to a nearby Baptist bookstore. He begged its managers to use their influence to stop such horrors, but was told that he would eventually become accustomed to them. "Never!" shouted Bishop. The scenes "were burned so deep into [his] soul that nothing [could] eradicate them."[11]

The sight of slavery affected Bishop differently from Carpenter. The scenes burned into his soul were a source of anti-slavery energy and enthusiasm. Somehow he had to convey or to transfer the heat of his compassion and commitment to those "cold" to the cause. Armstrong also believed this: "Men must be shocked, tortured, agonized," he taught, "with perpetual pictures of [slavery's] horror," until their consciences could stand it no longer. Then they would exclaim: "Away with slavery, whatever . . . the result!" Perhaps now, in 1853, in the midst of so much antislavery propaganda and enthusiasm, the Unitarians as a body would act. On April 1, the British and Foreign Anti-Slavery Society provided them with a marvelous opportunity. It recommended to Christians in the United Kingdom to utilize their spring denominational meetings to address their corresponding denominations in America on slavery. Wondrously, it included in its appeal to Christians the Unitarians. Estlin was gratified: the BFASS had paid them a compliment seldom bestowed on them by the orthodox "in considering them as a portion of the *Christian* church." The Unitarians ought to respond.[12]

The first Unitarian group to respond was George Harris's congregation in Newcastle-on-Tyne. From their pulpits, Armstrong and Steinthal beseeched their people to do likewise. The Western Unitarian Christian Union also complied, and recommended that action be taken by the British and Foreign Unitarian Association as well. Probably important to the successful course pursued by the WUCU was a terse statement by the Reverend Robert Brook Aspland (1805–69), who declared that the enforcement of the Fugitive Slave Law in Boston, the center of Unitarianism, made it obvious that their coreligionists there had not taken a "noble stand for freedom." Unlike the acrimonious meeting of two years before, the proceedings of the WUCU in 1853 "were uninterruptedly harmonious." Harmony also prevailed at the gathering of the Yorkshire West-Riding Unitarian Tract and Mission Society, where Joseph Lupton, as spokesman for an absent Wicksteed, secured an antislavery resolution with ease.[13] The BFUA was next.

The Garrisonians' master lobbyist, Armstrong, began to prepare. The BFUA had avoided a discussion of slavery in 1852, and now, under the impetus of the BFASS Appeal, Armstrong wrote to his friends to prevent a repeat performance. They had to give, he wrote to Solly, an energetic protest to their American coworkers, who were becoming deeper and deeper involved in America's "national tragedy." Writing to Kell, he urged him to rally around the "*stirring* circular" of the BFASS. They had to get the BFUA to speak out, as befitted an organization dedicated to "'civil and religious liberty' . . . abroad as well as at home, 'Foreign' as well as 'British.'" It ought to speak boldly on this "one great master question of [their] age[:] Slavery in the bosom of an English race!" He urged Kell to stir those "far and near" who might be able to help.[14]

Despite Armstrong's call to arms, the Garrisonians were out-numbered and fared poorly. Steinthal and Estlin were unable to schedule their resolution during the business session of the BFUA, thereby making it an official action of the body. Instead, they were forced to present it at the evening festivities in a response by Estlin to the annual toast, "Civil and Religious Liberty the World over." Their resolution, the first ever entertained by the BFUA on slavery, "affectionately" asked American Unitarians to testify against slavery in some way corresponding to their "social position and elevated religious principles." It passed unanimously, but a second attempt, this time by Solly and Steinthal, to give it official sanction failed by a majority. Henry Crabbe Robinson then delivered a caustic speech that compared the pulpit in which a man such as Orville Dewey preached to a devil's ground. No pulpit prospered that supported laws that tended to prop up slavery. His words were greeted by "loud and repeated cheers."[15] Although weak in votes, the Garrisonians were strong in voices.

After the meeting the familiar debate reopened between those who saw the BFUA and all Unitarian associations as strictly ecclesiastical business meetings, and those who saw them as platforms for universal Christian reform and renewal. Some in the former group condemned Robinson's diatribe in particular and Garrisonian insolence in general. Some of those in the latter group, firing the fears of ministers and laity anxious over the prosperity of the BFUA, advocated the "immediate foundation of a new association of Unitarians." Had "Uncle Tom" been a devout Unitarian, Dr. Hutton believed, the BFUA would have acted differently. Jerom Murch disagreed. He opposed the discussion of slavery at their meetings and believed disputed resolutions were effectively neutralized. Even if Uncle Tom had been a Unitarian, he confessed, he would gladly shake hands with Tom's relatives and friends "anywhere but at a business meeting of one of [their] Associations." Although the BFUA had responded "unofficially" to the BFASS appeal, Unitarian response to it throughout the country had generally been good. Almost one-third of the congregations and associations listed by the BFASS as having complied with its request were Unitarian. The meeting of the BFUA in 1853 was the high-water mark of Garrisonian activity in the denomination. Not until 1865 did the BFUA again treat American slavery. It took two cataclysmic events, the assassination of President Lincoln and the abolition of American slavery, to move it to comment, and the sponsorship by their most distinguished minister, James Martineau, to goad it to act.[16]

The Garrisonians. "True Servants of the Living God" or Infidels?

If in 1853 the Garrisonians had reached the peak of their influence in the affairs of the British Unitarians, in the first half of the 1850s the Unitarians reached the peak of their influence in the affairs of the British Garrisonians. James Haughton and his family shared command of the Hibernian Anti-Slavery Society, Mary Estlin and Frances Armstrong controlled the Bristol and Clifton Ladies' Anti-Slavery Society, and generally, even more than in the 1840s, Unitarians were the Garrisonians' primary source of support. They all identified themselves principally with the American Anti-Slavery Society and "tenderly cherished" (to use Philip Carpenter's words), Garrison, his adjutants, and his work. As Dr. Estlin's health failed, Mary Estlin assumed a more important role, and in the accession of Alfred Steinthal (1826–1902) to their ranks in 1853, the Garrisonians gained a dedicated and uncompromising colleague. For antislavery news in general, they depended upon publications and letters from American Garrisonian friends, and for Unitarian involvement with slavery, no matter how obliquely, they continued to rely on Samuel May, Jr.[17]

Steinthal was the archetypical Unitarian Garrisonian of this period. Born in Manchester of German parents, he graduated from Manchester New College in 1852, and served four Unitarian pastorates in his lifetime: Christ Church Chapel, Bridgwater; the Liverpool Domestic Mission; and Platt Chapel and Cross-Street Chapel, Manchester. Like so many of the British Unitarian Garrisonians, he was a theological conservative who lacked the "critical negations" of religious liberalism, and preached a "positive interpretation of the spirit of Christ." His identification of antislavery activity as a component of a religious life was exemplified in his calling abolitionist propaganda "theological reading." He saw the function of a Christian minister as that of a prophet, and churches and denominational assemblies as prophetic agencies. As was typical of so many of his Garrisonian coworkers, he supported a wide range of reforms: antislavery, women's rights, temperance (himself becoming a total abstainer), economic reform, child health care, and education for the working classes. His Unitarian familial links to antislavery reform lay in his being the successor of Francis Bishop at Liverpool, and the son-in-law of Franklin Howorth (1804–82), a Garrisonian minister in Bury. He thoroughly enjoyed the mutual admiration society of the Garrisonians.[18] They thought him "excellent," and he looked upon Garrison as "the most-Christlike man" he had ever known.[19] He was moved to support them after reading about the anti-abolitionist attacks described in Maria Weston Chapman's *Right and Wrong in Boston*. Moreover, he tended to sympathize with "the most radical movements."[20] He maintained with Armstrong that slavery was the "master sin of the world" and that to compromise with it was to sin. He concurred with the American Garrisonians on disunion and anti-institutional agitation, and he defended them from all attacks.[21] They ought not to be blamed, he declared, for "their noble wrath." Their "abhorrence of evil," he preached, "once fired the heart of [their] master Christ." Unitarians ought to "welcome them as true servants of the living God."[22]

Not all British Unitarians did welcome the Garrisonians, but the Garrisonians welcomed them. The Garrisonians had early dispensed with the "silly distinctions" of "Esquire, Reverend, and the honorable," and they knew no distinction of creed. They welcomed women as full participants, a fact that pleased Unitarian women and feminists such as Steinthal, Haughton, Beard, and Bishop.[23] Unitarians flourished in a group of reformers who held no distinctions of class, religion, or sex, which fought to overcome the distinction of color. They also throve on the American praise of their efforts. Their names were "household words" among the American Garrisonians; their help important and eagerly sought.[24]

When so many problems plagued their own homeland, the British Garrisonians were driven to explain their preoccupation with a foreign issue. The issue was simply the "crime above all crimes," explained Mary Carpenter, and nothing in England quite compared with it. Those who worked hard to end slavery in America, she remarked, generally worked the hardest to rectify abuses at home. Their country's domestic evils, declared Edwin Chapman, could be solved by all classes working out their own redemption. No English institutions demanded the "everlasting degradation" of a class of people as did America's "peculiar" institution. Their country's poor, taught Haughton, were rising up from poverty while America's slaves and free men, were "sinking lower and lower." There existed, said Steinthal, a great disparity between England's problems and

America's "one great" problem. England did not enslave her own people; her Established Church did not tell its members "to send Bibles to the heathen"; she never pledged her army to keep in servitude those of her citizens who were black; she did not surrender and confine men whose only crime was their love of freedom. England's "direct wrongs" did not compare with slaveholding in the "Model Republic."[25]

The Garrisonians also believed that American slavery was so persuasively an international issue, rather than a foreign issue, and so forcibly impinged upon Britain's life and future well-being, that it took on the aura of a *domestic* issue. The *Anti-Slavery Advocate* warned in an editorial entitled "American Slavery an English Question" that, unless Great Britain realized the immensity and contagiousness of "the prodigious guilt and folly of [America's] boastful freemen," her "theology," "political morality," and civic responsibility would soon be as notoriously corrupted as these were among America's "pro-slavery divines and politicians." American slavery, taught Armstrong, was "a European question; . . . a world's question; . . . a question . . . of life or death—for the religion of the Son of God, throughout . . . this suffering and sinning earth." Steinthal agreed: its "baneful blight" hampered human progress everywhere. To free the slaves in America, Edmund Kell wrote, would beneficially affect the "well-being of the whole civilized world." Steinthal at this time trusted that "noble and enlightened" England could influence America to free her slaves. It was their duty to see that England did. "True charity [began] at home, but it [was] a very false charity that stop[ped] there." He proclaimed the Wesleyan motto: their country was the world, their countrymen all mankind![26]

Many of the ways in which the Garrisonians sought to influence English and American public opinion matched the recommendations of Russell Carpenter. They believed antislavery publications to be extremely important, and in 1852, they organized the "Anglo-American Anti-Slavery Association," whose principal object was the publication of the *Anti-Slavery Advocate*. They encouraged their friends to buy and to lend copies of *Uncle Tom's Cabin*, to support the publication of tracts, to send letters to newspapers, and to write articles for popular magazines.[27] They continued to recommend that antislavery addresses be sent to American individuals, associations, and denominations, and a few such as Solly and Armstrong practiced to the last a policy of exclusion.[28] They addressed petitions to Parliament to aid British Negro seamen who were imprisoned in American jails.[29] Some of them recommended the boycott of slave grown produce. Steinthal set up a free-labor goods depot in Bridgwater and Solly commended a boycott as the most rapid and effective way to abolish slavery. Support for this idea was far from universal. Free traders objected to it, and others were troubled by their inability to differentiate accurately between free goods and "stolen goods."[30] All the British Unitarian Garrisonians generously sent merchandise and funds to the Boston Anti-Slavery Bazaar. They shipped a great variety of items, some "very saleable," some not at all, such as the "Simnel cake" from the Howorths of Bury, which was "somewhat crushed at the Custom-House." All their activities were directed towards awakening "*the national* conscience [of America] to a sense of guilt of slavery."[31]

The momentum of their activities in the 1850s, however, was somewhat retarded by the "infidel cry" that reemerged against them. It was directed primarily at Garrison, whose attacks upon the "pro-slavery" American churches began to be viewed by some as direct attacks, not upon slavery, but upon Christianity and religion. Two of the most important assaults upon him were, in 1851, by the *London Daily Advertiser,* a secular newspaper edited by a devout Calvinist; and, in 1852, by the *British Banner,* a Congregationalist publication. Probably the most publicized and damaging attack upon his movement was by the Glasgow Association for the Abolition of Slavery. In a widely distributed circular it discouraged support for the Boston Anti-Slavery Bazaar. The *Anti-Slavery Advocate* and Estlin tried to fend off these attacks. Abolitionism, explained the *Advocate,* was "an infidel movement" only to the degree that "Jesus was a blasphemer, and the apostles were 'pestilent and seditious fellows, seeking to turn the world upside down.'" While on a sojourn in Paris, Estlin published a reply to the Glasgow Association. People had to differentiate, he explained, between individual Garrisonians and the society which supported the bazaar. The American Anti-Slavery Society was "opposed to slavery and to *slavery alone.*" It did not attack Christianity.[32]

Obviously, this tide of religious bigotry did not fail to engulf the many Unitarian individuals who were Garrisonians. Their presence in the Garrisonian ranks simply authenticated the orthodox charge of infidelity. To those who had been Garrisonians for some time, the attacks were mildly irritating, but to others the charges of infidelity were frightening, especially if they were just beginning to consider aiding the Garrisonians, or had wished to gain respectability through involvement in a popular cause. Thus, the charges did affect the Garrisonians in terms of recruitment and support. Bishop found that the orthodox in Liverpool refused to work with him because they feared damaging their "religious standing." Solly found that as a Unitarian he was regarded as "a sort of theological leper, to be feared and shunned."[33] Anne Tribe, a "Calvinistic Baptist" and Garrisonian president of the women's antislavery society in Bristol, was embarrassed and disturbed by the malevolence and irrationality of the attacks against the Unitarian abolitionists. Writing about her Unitarian friends in Bristol, Tribe confided to an American abolitionist,

> I need not tell you that their Unitarianism operates strongly against them even here, many cannot act comfortably with persons whose religion they are so strongly opposed to—not from mere feelings or without much respect and affection towards them as individuals—but from the conviction that God will not bless efforts made in conjunction with persons they consider opposed to his truth.

The "promiscuous ecumenism" of the Garrisonians was ahead of its time and the sectarian attack upon their movement was unfortunate. Their welcome to all creeds, declared Steinthal, broke down barriers between people. Their opponents might "sneer at the Abolitionists as Infidel and Anti-Christian," yet he believed that they were "pioneers of the true Church"; united not in "Intellectual agreement," but in "spiritual awareness."[34] The Unitarian abolitionists never escaped the infidel cry. There were always orthodox clergymen such as the one who preached that the English abolitionists such as Clarkson and Wilberforce prevailed because they "believed in the Trinity," but the Garrisonians would achieve nothing by their "infidel howling." Garrison thought otherwise, and he privately told "infidel" Harriet Martineau, "Heresy is the only thing that will redeem mankind."[35]

Steam and Ice or Courageous Radicals and Timid Friends: Garrisonians and the British and Foreign Anti-Slavery Society

In light of the vehemence demonstrated toward the infidelity of the Garrisonians, and considering that the same net of criticism enveloped the Unitarians, it was extraordinary that the BFASS decided to send its appeal to the Unitarian churches as

Christian bodies. The BFASS had been directed primarily by orthodox Quakers who had opposed the participation of women at the World's Anti-Slavery Convention, had been appalled by Lucretia Mott's Hicksite heresy, and had aligned themselves with the American and Foreign Anti-Slavery Society. Dr. Estlin referred to the leadership of the BFASS as the "silver slippers" of the antislavery movement; men "too peaceful and sectarian . . . to *comprehend* much less to appreciate the stern uncompromising" Garrisonians. But in 1853, many of its old guard were either dead or inactive, and it became more conciliatory and catholic under its new Secretary, Louis Chamerovzow. He desired to unite the fragmented antislavery groups in Britain. Toward that end, he began for the first time to carry news of the Garrisonians in *The Anti-Slavery Reporter.* He probably was also responsible for the inclusion of the Unitarians in the BFASS Appeal. Some Unitarian Garrisonians responded to his peaceful overtures. Steinthal and Dr. Estlin, for example, joined his organization. But Garrison, Samuel May, Jr., and Irish Quaker Richard D. Webb cautioned that the conciliation of "Broad Street," as the BFASS was popularly known, might be a cul-de-sac. It was *"impossible"* to effect "fraternization," Garrison told Mary Estlin, "between straightforward, radical, courageous abolitionists, whose position [was] higher than Church or State, . . . and round-about, compromising, timid friends of emancipation," whose antislavery was "sentimental" and whose action was "spasmodic."[36]

Garrison's assertion proved (with a little help from his friends) to be correct. The first attempt at fraternization by the BFASS was to join with the Garrisonians in launching the Manchester Anti-Slavery Union in 1853. Their first project was to publish the *Anti-Slavery Watchman,* edited by Frederick William Chesson, an avowed Garrisonian and son-in-law of George Thompson. They intended the magazine to be an educational vehicle for the working classes of Lancashire and Yorkshire. Their effort was short-lived. When it was discovered that the union's recently appointed agent had called Garrison a "sceptic" and "infidel," John Relly Beard resigned his membership. Chesson, Thompson, and others followed, and the union with its *Watchman* went under. In its place arose the North of England Anti-Slavery and India Reform League, an organization exclusively Garrisonian.[37]

The following summer of 1854, Dr. Beard, as one of three honorary secretaries of the league, issued an invitation for an antislavery conference to meet in Manchester on the first of

August.[38] About 500 persons came, a great number of them women.[39] George Thompson and Parker Pillsbury, one of the most fanatical of the American Garrisonians, attended, as did Unitarians Beard, Bishop, Steinthal, Howorth, and Philip Carpenter. The meeting's distinct Garrisonian bias was revealed in the first resolution of the conference. Proposed by Bishop, it welcomed as delegates all who believed "slaveholding to be a sin, and immediate emancipation to be the right of the slave and the duty of the master." Many of the topics of the conference were introduced by Unitarians. Franklin Howorth contended that all Christians ought to recognize at once their "coloured brethren . . . fully and freely as fellow-men." Bishop used the occasion to describe once again the "horrible scenes" of slave sales in the South, and Steinthal recommended petitions to Parliament in behalf of British Negro seamen. Near the close of the meeting, Beard testified eloquently to their right to oppose American slavery and to proclaim the rights of their black "brothers." As Christians, he declared, they had to oppose the "anti-social, illiberal, narrow, and selfish doctrine" that forbade their involvement in foreign causes such as antislavery. Pillsbury, Thompson, and others, of course, contributed significantly to the conference, but the Unitarians dominated it. To a large degree it was their meeting.[40]

Steinthal considered the conference a success. England had a natural hatred of oppression, he wrote to Samuel May, but it needed an "active and enlightened Abolitionism." The *Inquirer* was not so pleased. It lambasted the conference and the "verbal invective" of some of the delegates. Such meetings were needless because English public opinion was solidly anti-slavery and needed only practical guidance. This attack mortified Steinthal and Armstrong and in letters to the editor they rejected the view that English antislavery opinion was satisfactory. Armstrong judged that there was "infinitely and disgracefully too little 'anti-slavery.'" The *Inquirer* remained unconvinced.[41]

Another attempt by Chamerovzow at cooperation was the invitation to all antislavery reformers to attend an Antislavery Conference in London in November 1854. Several Garrisonians consented to come, including a number from the Manchester conference, one-third of whom were Unitarian. The London meeting brought together under one roof distinguished members of the BFASS such as Samuel Gurney, Joseph Sturge, and Chamerovzow; and Garrisonians, Thompson and Pillsbury, along with their Unitarian friends, Solly, James, and Bishop. Before the conference, James Haughton had demanded that it seat women as delegates, and when it opened, Bishop presented the credentials of two women delegates from Manchester. The women were seated without objection as full participants, wonderful evidence of the great change in the attitude of the leaders of the BFASS. The conference encompassed two full days of deliberations, a major portion of which was devoted to an attempt by Bishop and James to secure a vote of praise for the Garrisonians of the American Anti-Slavery Society. They portrayed them as a "noble band of men and women" who had been "shunned" and "condemned as infidels." Both their attempts, and a similar one by Pillsbury in the last hours of the conference, went down to defeat. The BFASS was not about to vote appreciation of the radical American Anti-Slavery Society. Unfortunately, instead of improving the relations between the BFASS and the Garrisonians, the London conference exascerbated their differences; the great experiment of reconciliation and peace between the "timid friends of emancipation" and the "courageous abolitionists" was over.[42] The following spring Estlin and Steinthal withdrew their membership from the BFASS.[43]

The Garrisonians turned to sponsoring a variety of antislavery meetings throughout the country that featured Parker Pillsbury. His standard presentation was to define the antislavery movement as "a moral and religious movement" and to attack those ministers and churches who defended and performed *"deeds of slavery."* At most of his meetings Unitarians were prominent. In Leeds, Thomas Hincks and Joseph Lupton shared the platform with him; in Liverpool, Bishop; in Birkenhead, Russell Carpenter and Bishop once more; in Warrington, Philip Carpenter; and in Bristol, the whole entourage of Lewin's Mead. At Warrington, he applauded a resolution by Philip Carpenter that viewed "the rapid growth of the slave power as most dangerous to the liberties of mankind" and that demanded "the zealous watchfulness of the English Government."[44] Pillsbury's lecture tour was the last Garrisonian effort in Britain until the visit by Samuel J. May in 1859. During the next several years the antislavery movement was generally characterized by lethargy and decline.

The End of the Decade: Decline, Despair, and Disunion

The death of Estlin in the spring of 1855 marked the beginning of the decline. His abolitionist friends marveled that he was summoned by "the Heavenly Father" in the midst of an antislavery meeting. His death was a crushing loss. He was crucial to the work of the abolitionists, cried Steinthal; no one could replace him. His death would be harder for the Garrisonians to sustain, Samuel May callously remarked, than the possible loss of George Thompson.[45] Both the Garrisonians and the supporters of the BFASS mourned his death, and the great outpouring of eulogies and resolutions from all parties revealed how much he was loved and venerated.[46] Two years later, the loss of Estlin was compounded by the death of Armstrong. Never again would his strong and enthusiastic voice call the Garrisonian warriors to arms. And in this period of decline his strength and enthusiasm were sorely needed. The Bristol antislavery women began to meet less often each year until in 1857 they met only once. In 1858, Samuel May had to urge his British friends to continue to publish the *Advocate*.[47] Moreover, confusion and consternation beset the Garrisonian camp when Maria Weston Chapman announced that the Boston Anti-Slavery Bazaar no longer accepted merchandise, only cash. No longer could Mary Carpenter's barefooted ragamuffins knit socks for the Boston abolitionists. Chapman's arbitrary decision closed an extremely popular way to assist the cause.[48]

Another reason for the steady decline of interest in antislavery reform was the hopeless and dismal political news emerging from the United States. The *Inquirer* kept Unitarians thoroughly informed on the political contest that unfolded between the slave South and the submissive North. It vigorously opposed President Franklin Pierce's truckling to the South on the question of Kansas. Pierce, whom Armstrong called that "most wicked ruler," did not protect free-soil settlers in Kansas or stem the flow of pro-slavery ruffians into the territory. In the midst of the controversy over "Bloody Kansas," the paper and its readership were shocked by the Brooks-Sumner affair. Incensed over a speech on Kansas by Sumner in the Senate, Preston S. Brooks, a congressman from South Carolina, beat the Massachusetts senator unconscious. Sumner, a friend of many Unitarians and a leader who possessed a large following in England, became a hero.[49] The South, declared the *Inquirer*, progressively disregarded the restraints of law and its passions were driving America to Civil War.[50] In 1856, the newspaper favored the Republican presidential candidate, Colonel John C. Frémont, in an election that the paper believed to be the "most momentous" in the history of the United States, and, James Martineau maintained, involved the "destinies" of "the whole

Future of Humanity." Generally the Garrisonians, their aversion to politics notwithstanding, desired Frémont's election. At least they believed that it could do no harm.[51] Frémont's defeat showed America's refusal to elect an antislavery president, and naturally it was gloomy news. Gloomier still was the news of the Dred Scott decision, in which the Supreme Court decided that Negroes were not American citizens and had no rights that a white person had to respect. Frémont's defeat, the Brooks-Sumner affair, and the Dred Scott decision illustrated clearly that no redemption from slavery was possible through the executive, legislative, or judicial branches of the American government. These events drove abolitionist hopes in Britain to a catastrophic low. The North was in "truckling subserviency" to the South and refused to stop her steady aggression. The *Inquirer,* in 1858, recommended disunion rather than a union to uphold slavery. The machinations of the slave power had converted the newspaper to an idea of the "brave abolitionists."[52]

Of greater interest than the *Inquirer*'s shift in opinion was the appearance in a popular literary magazine of a remarkable essay by James Martineau. For the first time, he was stirred to comment publicly on the issue of American slavery. His essay, "The Slave Power of the West," appeared in the *National Review* in January 1857. The "best hopes of the world," he declared, depended upon resistance to the "Southern policy" of America. He saw constant victories by the slave principle over the free, and he lamented that "professed ministers of Christ unblushingly defend[ed slavery], . . . and bless[ed] its . . . new conquests." The Southern oligarchy controlled the entire machinery of the United States government. It had its eyes on Latin America and contemplated the formation of a "vast Slave-Empire." Southern policy threatened to promote war, to reopen the slave trade, to shatter the Union, to advance its "curse." What was England to do? He issued no call of support for the radical abolitionists; his words for the Garrisonians were harsh, his criticism of their tactics and goals, devastating. Rather, England's duty was to maintain a "negative policy of abstinence and forbearance." American slavery was a "*world*-question," and England ought to protect her "lands and peoples" from any crusade by it. He favored all schemes to check its extension.[53] Martineau's essay was a lecture in political temperance, England's goal ought to be total abstinence from intoxicating contact with America's curse.

Martineau could find in the Garrisonians, despite his aversion to their style, compatible ideas. He would have had no difficulty, for example, with Maria Weston Chapman's view that the "world's progress" was "hitched" to America and "from that hitch harm [came] to England and all the rest of the world." This thought had likewise troubled Armstrong. "Slavery was a stumbling-block to the progress and the power of the Anglo-Saxon race," he had told his beloved congregation in his farewell address. It was at work "weakening, degrading, demoralizing, and depressing the WHOLE family of man."[54] Yet England complimented America's slaveholding politicians and presidents at state dinners and other public functions. This was dangerous and unfortunate because it was vitally important to keep intact "the purity and elevation of [England's] natural sentiment" for freedom and civilization. Armstrong had complained to Lord Brougham, in 1857, that their nation was "retrograding" as an antislavery leader. England took "the utmost pains . . . to *flatter* the Americans and ignore their frightful sins against humanity; as if politics and cotton were the only things [the] English people . . . care[d] for."[55]

The political power of the "Slave Oligarchy" in the American republic had long troubled the British Garrisonians. It was "making republicanism," Webb told May, "stink in the nostrils of the English people." As early as the controversy over the Fugitive Slave Law, Steinthal had been so "downhearted and despondent" over the political dominance of slavery in America that it required all his "faith in God's justice to prevent [his] giving the whole thing up as useless."[56] He anticipated that only a bloody conclusion could come of the struggle over the control of America, and surmised that the "inevitable horror" of the struggle would be blamed on the "so-called Christian Church!"[57] He vacillated between the hope of averting such a catastrophe and the desire to hasten it along. He could not help but sometimes join "with the gruff old Dr. Johnson in the toast 'success to the next Negro-Insurrection'!" In America, Samuel May, Jr., and his coworkers had argued that disunion could prevent the pending "war of extermination." But in Great Britain, Steinthal believed that there was little support for disunion. That was in 1855. Yet a year and a half later the bold encroachments of the slave power in America "thoroughly convinced" the *Advocate* for the first time of the "wisdom" of disunion. It published on its front page Samuel May's proclamation that the Union was "the sole strength, the only preservative power, of slavery." To destroy slavery, the Union had to be forsaken.

"THERE [WAS] NO OTHER REMEDY!" May's emotional and militant language was, of course, matched by the aggressive tirades of the "fire-eaters" in the South. In the summer of 1857 Harriet Martineau perceived on America's horizon "a second great revolution."[58]

At the end of the decade antislavery sentiment in Great Britain had reached an impoverished state. In 1858, the only antislavery activity among Unitarians was Russell Carpenter's call to their churches to observe the anniversary of the First of August. The *Inquirer* wholeheartedly supported his proposal. The antislavery movement deserved the "peculiar devotion" of the Unitarians, it explained, since they "everywhere proclaim[ed] themselves the friends of freedom and human rights." Despite the *Inquirer's* blessing, the response to Carpenter's call was disappointing. Only seven congregations commemorated the event, and two of those were Carpenter's and his brother Philip's—hardly a major demonstration of the "peculiar devotion" of the Unitarians.[59]

The moribund state of antislavery activity continued into 1859. Aside from a trip to the slave South by Philip Carpenter, a convalescent tour of England by Samuel J. May, and the news of John Brown's raid on Harper's Ferry, the year inspired little antislavery discussion or action. In the winter and spring, James Haughton, the most rabid and caustic of the British Unitarian Garrisonians, was delivering abstract and technical lectures on the statistics and economics of American slavery and West Indian emancipation—indeed a great departure from his early emotional diatribes and scathing letters. As an assignment for Samuel May, in March 1859, Haughton's colleague, Richard D. Webb, measured the abolitionist boiling point of each of the British Garrisonians. He included the Unitarians from Bishop to Steinthal, and sent his conclusion to May. They were all "friendly" to the cause, he declared, but "except in a few cases, it would be too much to speak of a strong interest."[60]

Some interest, however, was stimulated by Philip Carpenter in his letters from the United States. He largely retraced the route followed by his brother nearly ten years before. Unlike Russell, he was outspoken in his criticism of American life, particularly Southern society. He complained of swearing and spitting in Southern hotels, protested against smoking aboard public conveyances, tried unsuccessfully to deliver an abolitionist lecture in St. Louis (narrowly escaping tarring and feathering in the process), boarded with black families, and generally acted as obnoxiously as possible. He attended the anniversary meeting of the American Unitarian Association and waited in vain to hear "this great meeting of the elite [make] some appeal for humanity." He succinctly expressed his opinion of America: "The Model Republic—Sovereign People! Bah! Really Old England, with all its aristocracy, . . . look[ed] highly respectable in comparison."[61]

While Carpenter toured the slaveholding South and the "slavecatching" North, the Reverend Samuel J. May of Syracuse, New York, traveled to England. His Unitarian hosts publicized him as the first minister to accept Garrison's leadership, and one of the earliest to denounce the Fugitive Slave Law. Although his congregation had financed the trip to restore his health, he turned it into a speaking tour to preach abolitionism. He spoke in Birkenhead, Hackney, Liverpool, Birmingham, Sheffield, Glasgow, and Bristol.[62] He also preached at the Unitarian District Meeting at Tenterden, lectured before the Leeds Anti-Slavery Society, and inspired an antislavery rally in a Methodist Chapel in London.[63] Generally his message contained nothing new. He called for the usual antislavery remonstrances from churches and denominations, but what was new and unusual was his severe criticism of the torpid antislavery feeling in Great Britain. He was shocked to hear in England talk of emancipation in the West Indies as being a "sad failure" because of sagging profits, declining exports, and economic stagnation. Emancipation could only be judged a failure if the emancipated slaves believed it so. There needed "to be a revival of anti-slavery zeal in England." Their country had not atoned for her "mountainous transgressions against Africa" by her Act of Emancipation in 1834. Her exoneration could only come, he declared, when she helped to deliver the last black man from bondage. It was a severe indictment of Britain's antislavery apathy and the British Unitarian Garrisonians loved it.[64]

When May returned home, the news of John Brown's raid at Harper's Ferry greeted him. To the prophets of doom for America, the news of an attempt by a fanatical abolitionist to free slaves through armed revolt came as no surprise. Neither the British Unitarians nor their American friends tried to justify Brown's means, but most lauded the man and his goal. The North had adopted him, wrote Maria Weston Chapman to her English friends, as "its Hero, Saint, and Martyr." Brown's admirers simply separated the man from the deed. The *Inquirer* pronounced his action criminal, but admired his "daring and lofty character." Success would have made him "one of the world's recognized heroes."[65] In future years, the newspaper predicted, people would observe the date of his death "as a sacred anniversary." Philip Carpenter was in America when Brown's raid occurred. As a pacifist, he differed from Brown's methods, but admired the man. Washington and other noted heroes, he observed, had fought for "their *own* freedom and their own people: [Brown] laid down his life for the oppressed of a despised race." Back in England Carpenter's sister, Mary, was deeply moved by the news of Brown's execution, and immediately began to collect aid for the "martyr's" family. His execution, she believed, was the "beginning of the end," and she wrote to the dying Theodore Parker: "Nothing but a separation of a diseased and rotten part from the comparatively sound [could] save the body."[66] The separation was but a year away.

That spring of 1860, the West Unitarian Christian Union met in Bridport. Either in response to the stirring event of John Brown's raid of the past winter, or perhaps in consideration of Samuel J. May's call for antislavery remonstrances, the WUCU issued an address. Filled with rhapsodic imagery—"a spring of heavenly promise is opening on the long and benumbing winter of American slavery"—it asked American Unitarians to use their ministerial and congregational influence against slavery. Remarkably, the autumnal convention of the American Unitarian Association assigned two abolitionists to answer it, a clear sign that abolitionism in America and in the Unitarian denomination had gained respectability. In their answer, Samuel J. May and James Freeman Clarke declared that either American slavery would be abolished "by moral or religious influences" or else by "civil and servile war." They honored the British abolitionists of the past, and praised the British addresses and admonitions, but asked for cooperation. Hundreds of thousands of English people were gaining "the comforts of life" and tens of thousands were "accumulating wealth" from the manufacture of American cotton. Were they not the receivers of stolen goods? The Americans hoped that their English friends would help to protect England and her people from the "demoralizing effects of any participation" in America's great iniquity.[67]

Notes

1. Frank J. Klingberg, "Harriet Beecher Stowe and Social Reform in England," *American Historical Review* 43 (1937–38): 544–45; Betty Fladeland, *Men and Brothers: Anglo-American Antislavery Cooperation* (Urbana, Ill.: University of Illinois Press), pp. 350–51.

2. Klingberg, "Harriet Beecher Stowe," p. 547; Fladeland, *Men and Brothers,* pp. 352–53; Charles Wicksteed, *The Englishman's Duty to the Free and Enslaved American. A Lecture Twice Delivered at Leeds, in January, 1853* (London: W. & F. G. Cash, 1853), pp. 17–19; John Bishop Estlin to Maria Weston Chapman, Bristol, ? December 1852, Clare Taylor, *British and American Abolitionists. An Episode in Transatlantic Understanding* (Edinburgh: Edinburgh University Press, 1974), p. 392.

3. Mary Estlin to Maria Weston Chapman, [Bristol], 10 January 1853, Samuel May, Jr., to John Bishop Estlin, Boston, 28 February 1853; George Thompson to [Anne Warren Weston?], n.p., 4 March 1853; Taylor, *British and American Abolitionists,* pp. 392, 393–94, 395.

4. S. F. Dawson to Mary Estlin, Teignmouth, Devon, 6 October 1852, Taylor, *British and American Abolitionists,* p. 389.

5. [Charles Beard], "Uncle Tom's Cabin." *Prospective Review* 8 (1852): 492, 493, 498–501, 503–5, 513; John R. Beard, *The Life of Toussaint L'Ouverture, The Negro Patriot of Hayti* (London: Ingram, Cooke, and Co., 1853), see especially pages 38–43, 47–52; John Bishop Estlin, *A Brief Notice of American Slavery and the Abolition Movement,* 2nd ed., rev. (London: William Tweedie, 1853), pp. 8, 43; S. Aflred Steinthal, *American Slavery. A Sermon Preached at Christ Church Chapel, Bridgwater, on Sunday, May the First, 1853* (Bridgwater; J. Whitby, 1853), pp. 11–12; Wicksteed, *Englishman's Duty,* p. 9; George Armstrong, "Slavery in America. A Call to the Church," *Inquirer,* 14 May 1853, pp. 314–15; "Working Classes' Association, Belfast. Lecture on Slavery by the Rev. Dr. Montgomery," *Inquirer,* 5 February 1853, pp. 91–92; George Armstrong, "Letter to an Englishman Recently Returned from the Slave States," *Anti-Slavery Advocate* (January 1853), p. 30, the *Advocate* cited hereafter as *ASA.*

6. Harriet Beecher Stowe, *A Key to Uncle Tom's Cabin; presenting the Original Facts and Documents upon which the Story is founded, together with corroborative Statements verifying the Truth of the Work* (London: Sampson Low, Son, and Co., 1853), p. 83; [Francis Bishop], "Key to Uncle Tom's Cabin," *Prospective Review* 9 (1853): 254–55.

7. Armstrong, "Slavery in America," p. 315; Armstrong, "Letter to an Englishman Recently Returned from the Slave States," *ASA* (February 1853), p. 38; Montgomery, *Lecture on Slavery,* p. 91; Bishop, "Key to Uncle Tom's Cabin," p. 251.

8. William Lloyd Garrison, *The Letters of William Lloyd Garrison,* Louis Ruchames, ed., (Cambridge: The Belknap Press of Harvard University Press, 1975), 4: 209, fn. 1.

9. "Testimony of an English Minister on American Slavery," *ASA* (January 1853), p. 26; Samuel May, Jr., to Richard D. Webb, Leicester, 12 April 1859, May Papers, Boston Public Library. Cited hereafter as MB; "Effect of New English Air upon Old English Abolitionism," *ASA* (April 1853), p. 50; for Estlin's remark, see "Western Unitarian Christian Union," *Inquirer,* 14 May 1853, p. 311.

10. Louis Filler, *The Crusade Against Slavery 1830–1860* (New York: Harper & Row, 1960), pp. 27, 58, 164.

11. Francis Bishop to William Lloyd Garrison, Springfield, Illinois, 22 August 1852, Garrison Papers, MB; Wicksteed, *Englishman's Duty,* pp. 11–12; "[Francis Bishop Speaks at] Warrington," *Inquirer,* 5 February 1853, p. 92; Bishop, "Key to Uncle Tom's Cabin," pp. 260–63; "Anti-Slavery Conference at Manchester," *ASA* September 1854), pp. 193–94.

12. Armstrong, "Letter to an Englishman," p. 38; *American Slavery and the British Christians. A Tract Containing Reprints of the Addresses to Christians of All Denominations, and Especially to Christian Ministers Issued by the Committee of the British and Foreign Anti-Slavery Society in April 1853 and 1854. . . .* (London: British and Foreign Anti-Slavery Society, 1854), pp. 3, 6, 14–18; Armstrong, "Slavery in America," p. 314; "Western Unitarian Christian Union," p. 310.

13. George Harris, "Statement on American Slavery at the special General Meeting of the Unitarian Congregation of Newcastle-on-Tyne," [title supplied], *Christian Register,* 11 February 1854, p. 22; Steinthal, *American Slavery,* pp. 20–22; Armstrong, "Slavery in America," p. 314; "Western Unitarian Christian Union," *Inquirer,* 14 May 1853, pp. 310–11; "Western Unitarian Christian Union," *Christian Reformer* 9 (June 1853): 398–99; "Yorkshire West-Riding Unitarian Tract and Village Mission Society," *Christian Reformer* 9 (July 1853): 454–55; "Resolutions on Slavery at Unitarian Meetings," *Inquirer,* 1 October 1853; p. 636; Alfred Steinthal to the editor, Bridgwater, 5 October 1853, *Inquirer,* 15 October 1853, p. 666.

14. George Armstrong to Henry Solly, Clifton, 16 April 1853, Robert Henderson, *A Memoir of the late Rev. George Armstrong. . . .* (London: Edward T. Whitfield, 1859), p. 275; Armstrong to Edmund Kell, Clifton, 15 April 1853, Robert Henderson, "Memoir of the Late Rev. George Armstrong, of Bristol," *Christian Reformer* 14 (August 1858): 458–59.

15. "[The Twenty-seventh] Annual Meeting of the British and Foreign Unitarian Association," *Inquirer,* 5 June 1852, pp. 359–62; "[The Twenty-eighth] Annual Meeting of the British and Foreign Unitarian Associations," *Inquirer,* 21 May 1853, pp. 327, 329–30.

16. "A North Country Layman," to the editor, n.p., n.d., *Inquirer,* 25 June 1853, p. 410; "An Old Stager" to the editor, Chichester, 24 May 1853, *Inquirer,* 4 June 1853, p. 362; Samuel Shaen to the editor, [London], 19 May 1853, *Inquirer,* 4 June 1853, p. 362; Joseph Hutton to the editor, Derby, 23 May 1853, *Inquirer,* 28 May 1853, p. 342; Jerom Murch to the editor, Bath, 1 June 1853, *Inquirer,* 4 June 1853, p. 361; BFASS, *American Slavery and British Christians,* p. 20; "[The Fortieth Annual Meeting of the] British and Foreign Unitarian Association," *Inquirer,* 10 June 1865, p. 363.

17. Howard Temperley, *British Antislavery 1833–1870* (London: Longman, 1972), p. 237; George Armstrong to the editor, Clifton, 25 August, 1853, *Inquirer,* 28 August 1852, p. 554; Philip P. Carpenter to William Lloyd Garrison, Warrington, 4 June 1858, Garrison Papers, MB; "Obituary. Miss Estlin," *Inquirer,* 22 November 1902, p. 743; A. Cobden Smith, *Rev. S. Alfred Steinthal, 1826–1910. A Memorial Address Delivered to the Congregation of the Lower Mosley Street Sunday School, Manchester, on Sunday Evening, 8th May, 1910* (Manchester: Co-operative Printing Society, Ltd., 1910), p. 6; "The (American) Unitarian Churches," *ASA* (September 1853), pp. 89–90, (October 1853), pp. 97–98.

18. "The Rev. S. A. Steinthal," *Inquirer,* 14 May 1910, pp. 314–16; "The Rev. S. A. Steinthal," *Manchester Guardian,* 7 May 1910, n.p. no.; Mary Estlin to Maria Weston Chapman, Bristol, 19 December 1853, Weston Papers, MB; S. Alfred Steinthal, *Address on the Assassination of Abraham Lincoln, Delivered at Platt Chapel on the Morning, and in the Ashton Town Hall on the Afternoon of Sunday, the 7th May, 1865* (London: Whitfield, Green, and Son, 1865), p. 4.

19. Eliza Lee Follen to Mary Estlin, Headingley, 14 July, n.y.; "From Rev. S. Alfred Steinthal acknowleding the memoir of W. L. Garrison," 23 April 1880, MS fragment; Estlin Papers, Dr. Williams's Library, London, cited hereafter as LDW.

20. S. Alfred Steinthal to Mary Estlin, Bridgwater, 9 November 1853, Steinthal to Maria Weston Chapman, Bridgwater, 28 December 1853, Weston Papers, MB; Steinthal to Samuel May, Jr., Bridgwater, 4 May 1854, May papers, MB.

21. S. Alfred Steinthal to the editor, Bridgwater, 8 April 1854, *ASA* (May 1854), p. 155; Steinthal, "American Slavery," p. 8; Steinthal to Samuel May, Jr., Bridgwater, 7 November 1853, May Papers, MB; Steinthal to the editor, Bridgwater, 24 October 1855, *Inquirer,* 27 October 1855, p. 681; Steinthal to the editor, Bridgwater, 18 October [1856], *Inquirer,* 8 November 1856, p. 724.

22. Steinthal, *American Slavery,* pp. 25–26.

23. Maria Weston Chapman to Mary Estlin, Clarens, Switzerland, 1 August 1855, Estlin Papers, LDW; [Maria Weston Chapman], *Report of the Twenty-third National Anti-Slavery Bazaar, 1856–1857* (Boston: J. B. Yerrington, 1857), pp. 21–22; Fladeland, *Men and Brothers,* p. 364; Temperley, *British Antislavery,* p. 245.

24. "Importance of British Sympathy," *ASA* (February 1853), p. 33; Chapman, *Report of 23rd Bazaar,* pp. 10, 24; Mary Grew to Mary Estlin, Philadelphia, 10 January 1853, Abby Kimber to Mary Estlin, Philadelphia, 28 March 1853, Estlin Papers, LDW; *Proceedings of the Massachusetts Anti-Slavery Society at the Annual Meetings Held in 1854, 1855, 1856.* . . . (n.p.: n.d.), pp. 64, 65.

25. Mary Carpenter to Eliza Lee Follen, Bristol, 8 December 1846, Carpenter to Abiel Abbott Livermore, Bristol, 11 February 1848, J. Estlin Carpenter, *The Life and Work of Mary Carpenter,* 2nd ed. (London: Macmillan and Co., 1881), pp. 95, 98; Edwin Chapman to Samuel May, Jr., Bristol, 25 October 1848, May Papers, MB; James Haughton, "American Slavery," *ASA* (October 1853), p. 101; S. Alfred Steinthal to Samuel May, Jr., Bridgwater, 29 September 1854, May Papers, MB.

26. "American Slavery An English Question," *ASA* (November 1852), p. 9; George Armstrong to the editor, Clifton, 25 August 1852, *Inquirer,* 28 August 1852, p. 555; S. Alfred Steinthal to the editor, Bridgwater, 8 April 1854, *ASA* (May 1854), p. 156; Edmund Kell to the editor, Newport, Isle of Wight, 17 August [1852], *Inquirer,* 21 August 1852, pp. 538–39; Steinthal, *American Slavery,* pp. 16–18. See also C. Duncan Rice, "The Scots Abolitionists, 1833–1861" (unpublished manuscript, 1975), pp. 15–16.

27. "Introductory Notice," *ASA* (October 1852), p. 1; "Appeal to the Friends of the *Anti-Slavery Advocate,*" *ASA* (1 September 1855), p. 294; S. Alfred Steinthal to the editor, London, 19 May 1853, *ASA* (June 1853), p. 70; "[Letter by H. Martineau read at] Anti-Slavery Meeting at Manchester," *ASA* (September 1854), pp. 190, 200; [Harriet Martineau], "Freedom, or Slavery?" *Household Words* 9 (1854): 537–42; Edmund Kell to the editor, Newport, Isle of Wight, 17 August [1852], *Inquirer,* 21 August 1852, p. 538; Estlin, *Brief Notice,* pp. 465–47, 50–52.

28. "Anti-Slavery Conference at Manchester," *ASA* (September 1854), 199; "Our American Visitors," *ASA* (January 1853), p. 29; S. Alfred Steinthal to Samuel May, Jr., Bridgwater, 4 December 1855, May Papers, WM; Steinthal, "Anti-Slavery Speech . . . at the Recent Meeting of the Western Unitarian Christian Union," *ASA* (June 1855), pp. 275–76; Henry Solly to the editor, n.p., 26 August 1852, *Inquirer,* 28 August 1852, p. 555; George Armstrong to the editor, Clifton, 2 September 1852, *Inquirer,* 4 September 1852, p. 573.

29. "Anti-Slavery Conference at Manchester," *ASA* (September 1854), p. 200; S. Alfred Steinthal to Samuel May, Jr., Bridgwater, 17 August 1854, May Papers, MB.

30. Montgomery, "Working Classes' Association Lecture," p. 92; Henry Solly to the editor, n.p., n.d., *Inquirer,* 14 August 1852, p. 525; Solly to the editor, n.p., 26 August 1852, *Inquirer,* 28 August 1852, p. 555; S. Alfred Steinthal to Samuel May, Jr., Bridgwater, 8 March 1854, May Papers, MB; George Armstrong to the editor, Clifton, 2 September 1852, *Inquirer,* 4 September 1852, p. 573. See also C. Duncan Rice, "'Humanity Sold for Sugar!' The British Abolitionist Response to Free Trade in Slave-Grown Sugar," *Historical Journal* 13 (1970): 402–18.

31. [Anne Warren Weston], *Report of the Twenty-first National Anti-Slavery Bazaar* (Bos-

ton: J. B. Yerrington & Son, 1855), pp. 7–8, 10, 23–24; Estlin, *Brief Notice*, pp. 29, 49–50.

32. Fladeland, *Men and Brothers*, p. 364; Temperley, *British Antislavery*, p. 241; William Lloyd Garrison to the editor of the *London Morning Advertiser*, [Boston], 19 September 1851, *Letters of Garrison*, 4: 71–82; Margaret Smith, Jane Barclay, et al., "Anti-Slavery Cause," Glasgow, May, 1850, Richard D. Webb to Mrs. W. C. Barclay, Dublin, 3 June 1850, Henry Wigham to [Garrison], Edinburgh, 16 July 1850, Samuel May, Jr., to Mary Carpenter, Leicester, 2 August 1850, Taylor, *British and American Abolitionists*, pp. 342–44, 344, 345, 347; "[Francis Bishop at] Edinburgh, Anti-Slavery Conference," *ASA* (November 1853), p. 107; "The Infidelity of the Abolitionists," *ASA* (1 March 1856), p. 346; John Bishop Estlin, *Reply to a Circular Issued by the Glasgow Association for the Abolition of Slavery Recommending a Discontinuance of British Support to the Boston Anti-Slavery Bazaar* (Paris: E. Briere, 1850), p. 4; see also Bristol and Clifton Ladies' Anti-Slavery Society, *Statements Respecting the American Abolitionists; by Their Opponents and Their Friends: Indicating the Present Struggle Between Slavery and Freedom in the United States of America* (Dublin: Webb and Chapman, 1852), pp. 3, 5, 6, 13.

33. Francis Bishop to Mary Estlin, Liverpool, 4 October 1850, Estlin Papers, LDW. See also Bishop to Estlin, 27 August 1854, Estlin Papers, LDW, and S. Alfred Steinthal to Samuel May, Jr., Bridgwater, 7 November 1853, May Papers, MB; Henry Solly, *"These Eighty Years" or, The Story of an Unfinished Life* (London: Simpkin, Marshall, and Co., 1893), 1: 337.

34. Anne Tribe to [Anne Warren] Weston, Bristol, 29 October 1852, Weston Papers, MB; S. Aflred Steinthal to Mary Estlin, Bridgwater, 9 November 1853, Weston papers, MB.

35. Lydia Maria Child to Sarah Blake (Sturgis) Shaw, Wayland, 7 July 1857, Lydia Maria Child Papers, Houghton Library, Harvard University, William Lloyd Garrison to Harriet Martineau, Boston, 4 December 1855, *Letters of Garrison*, 4: 372. When Steinthal expressed a need in England for a full time antislavery agent, he wrote to Samuel May, Jr., that the person had to be orthodox in religion for the English were "very suspicious of heretics as every Unitarian [found] out to his cost." S. Alfred Steinthal to May, Bridgwater, 28 March 1855, May Papers, MB.

36. Fladeland, *Men and Brothers*, pp. 360–61, 364–65; John Bishop Estlin to Louis A. Chamerovzow, Bristol, 13 February 1855, Weston Papers, MB; S. Alfred Steinthal to Samuel May, Jr., Bridgwater, 8 March 1854, Steinthal to May, Bridgwater, 17 August 1854, May Papers, MB; Estlin to Louis A. Chamerovzow, Bristol, 20 April 1853, BFASS Papers, Rhodes House, Oxford University, cited hereafter as ORH; Steinthal to Chamerovzow, Bridgwater, 3 May 1853, BFASS Papers, ORH; Henderson, *Memoir of Armstrong*, p. 276; Richard D. Webb to Samuel May, Jr., Dublin, 16 August 1854, Webb to May, Dublin, 25 October 1854, Webb to May, 7 November 1854, Taylor, *British and American Abolitionists*, pp. 408, 412–13, 413–14; William Lloyd Garrison to Mary Estlin, Leicester, 27 August 1854, *Letters of Garrison*, 4: 308.

37. Fladeland, *Men and Brothers*, pp. 360–63; Temperley, *British Antislavery*, pp. 242–43; S. Alfred Steinthal to Samuel May, Jr., Bridgwater, 28 March 1855, May Papers, MB; "Schism in the Anti-Slavery Union, and Temporary Suspension of *The Anti-Slavery Watchman*," *ASA* (February 1854), p. 132. See also Frederick William Chesson, "The Manchester Union and Rev. F. Hemming," *Anti-Slavery Watchman* (January 1854), pp. 64–65, 69.

38. John R. Beard, et. al., to the editor, Manchester, 20 July 1854, *Inquirer*, 22 July 1854, pp. 450–51.

39. Francis Bishop to Mary Estlin, Town Hall, Manchester, 1 August 1854 [copy], Weston Papers, MB.

40. "Anti-Slavery Conference and Meeting," *Inquirer*, 12 August 1854, pp. 506–8.

41. S. Alfred Steinthal to Samuel May, Jr., Bridgwater, 17 August 1854, May Papers, MB; "The Anti-Slavery Conference," *Inquirer*, 5 August 1854, p. 482; Steinthal to the editor, n.p., n.d., *Inquirer*, 12 August 1854, p. 505; Armstrong to the editor, Bristol, 10 August 1854, *Inquirer*, 12 August 1854, p. 505; "The Relation of England to the Anti-Slavery Agitation," *Inquirer*, 19 August 1854, pp. 513–14.

42. "Anti-Slavery Conference at Manchester," *ASA* (September 1854), p. 200; "Proceedings of the London Anti-Slavery Conference," *ASA* (January 1855), pp. 226–27, 229, 232; Francis Bishop to the editor, London, 30 November 1854, ibid., p. 232; Fladeland, *Men and Brothers*, pp. 363–64.

43. John Bishop Estlin to Louis A. Chamerovzow, Bristol, 21 May 1855, BFASS Papers, ORH; S. Alfred Steinthal to Chamerovzow, Bridgwater, 4 April 1855, BFASS Papers, ORH; Rice, "Scots Abolitionists," p. 233.

44. "Mr. Parker Pillsbury and His Anti-Slavery Labors in England," *ASA* (March 1855), pp. 245–46; *"Guilty or Not Guilty?" A Few Facts and Feelings Regarding the Religious Bodies of America in the Matter of Slavery; Being a Report of an Anti-Slavery Meeting Held in Belgrave Chapel, Leeds, December 10th, 1855. Containing Addresses of Parker Pillsbury, Esq., and the Rev. G. W. Conder: Revised from the Columns of the Leeds Mercury,* 2nd ed., with additions (Leeds: Edward Barnes & Sons, 1855), p. 3.

45. Entry for 8 June 155, "Bristol and Clifton Ladies' Anti-Slavery Society Minutes," MS, Estlin Papers, LDW; S. Alfred Steinthal to Samuel May, Jr., Bridgwater, 4 December 1855, May Papers, MB; Samuel May, Jr., to Richard D. Webb, Leicester, 24 July 1855, Taylor, *British and American Abolitionists*, pp. 415–16; Samuel J. May to Mary Estlin, Liverpool, 18 October 1859, Estlin Papers, LDW.

46. Samples of the eulogies and praise for Estlin are George Armstrong, *A Sermon on the Death of John Bishop Estlin, Esq., F.L.S., F.R.C.S. . . . Delivered at Lewin's Mead Chapel, Bristol, June 17th, 1855* (Bristol: Evans and Arrowsmith, [1855]); "The Late John Bishop Estlin," *Anti-Slavery Reporter* 3 (2 July 1855): 156–57; "The Late J. B. Estlin, Esq.," *ASA* (1 August 1855), p. 290; Wilson Armistead, *Resolutions Passed at a Committee of the Leeds Anti-slavery Association, September 25th, 1855* (n.p.: n.d.). The BFASS experienced a decline in antislavery interest and activity corresponding to that of the Garrisonians. See Temperley, *British Antislavery*, pp. 229–32, 246.

47. William James, *The Grateful Remembrance of Departed Ministers. A Sermon Delivered on Sunday Morning, August 16th, 1857, in Lewin's Mead Chapel, Bristol, On the Occasion of the Death of the Rev. George Armstrong, B.A.* (London: Edward Whitfield, 1857); "Bristol and Clifton Ladies' Anti-Slavery Society Minutes," MS, Estlin Papers, LDW; Temperley, *British Antislavery*, p. 244; Samuel May, Jr., to Richard D. Webb, Boston, 30 March 1858, [Extract of letter], Estlin Papers, LDW.

48. Maria Weston Chapman to Mrs. Wigham, n.p., 11 February 1859, Estlin Papers, LDW; Philip P. Carpenter to William Lloyd Garrison, Warrington, 4 June 1858, Garrison Papers, MB; "Extracts from Letters from Mrs. Chapman," *ASA* (April 1858), pp. 124–25; May to Webb, Boston, 30 March 1858; Webb to May, Dublin, 16 April 1858; Taylor, *British and American Abolitionists*, pp. 429–30, 430–32, 432–33.

49. "Inaugural Address of the President of the United States," *Inquirer*, 19 March 1853, pp. 177–78; "The Annexation of Nebraska," *Inquirer*, 1 April 1853, p. 193; George Armstrong to the editor, Bristol, 14 October 1856, *ASA* (1 November 1856), p. 407; "The Fruits of Slavery [Brooks-Sumner affair]," *Inquirer*, 14 June 1856, pp. 377–78.

50. "The Home Politics of the United States," *Inquirer*, 30 August 1856, p. 555.

51. "The Struggle in the United States," *Inquirer*, 1 November 1856, p. 698; George Armstrong to Samuel May, Jr., Bristol, 12 August 1856, May Papers, MB; James

Martineau to Joseph Henry Allen, Liverpool, 30 December 1856, Allen Papers, MH-AH.

52. "Slavery in the United States [Dred Scott Decision]," *Inquirer*, 4 April 1857, p. 210; Fladeland, *Men and Brothers*, pp. 340–41; "The Echo," *Inquirer*, 2 October 1858, p. 633.

53. [James Martineau], "The Slave Empire of the West," *National Review* 4 (January 1857): 212–13, 220, 228, 231, 233–35.

54. Maria Weston Chapman to Miss Whitelegge, Weymouth, 18 December 1859, Estlin Papers, LDW; "The Rev. George Armstrong of Bristol," *ASA* (January 1857), p. 5. *Cf.* Henderson, "Memoir of Armstrong," p. 557.

55. George Armstrong, "Flummery! American Generosity—British Gratitude," *ASA* (March 1857), p. 17; Armstrong to Lord Broughman, Bristol, 15 May 1857, Henderson, "Memoir of Armstrong," p. 562.

56. Richard D. Webb to Samuel May, Jr., Dublin, 25 June 1858, Taylor, [*British and American Abotitionists*, p. 435; S. Alfred Steinthal to Samuel May, Jr., Bridgwater, 28 June 1854, May Papers, MB.

57. S. Alfred Steinthal to Samuel May, Jr., Bridgwater, 23 January 1855, May Papers, MB.

58. S. Alfred Steinthal to Samuel May, Jr., Bridgwater, 23 January 1855, May Papers, MB; Steinthal to May, Bridgwater, 28 March 1855, May Papers, MB; Maria Weston Chapman to Mary Estlin, The Knoll, 29 October [1855], Estlin Papers, LDW; "Rev. S. May on the Dissolution of the American Union," *ASA* (1 November 1856), p. 406; Harriet Martineau, "'Manifest Destiny' of the American Union," *Westminister Review* 68 (July 1857): 140.

59. Russell Lant Carpenter to the editor, Halifax, 20 July 1858, *Inquirer*, 24 July 1858, p. 484; "The First of August," *Inquirer*, 24 July 1858, pp. 473–74; "The First of August," *Inquirer*, 7 August 1858.

60. James Haughton, *Statistics of Free and Slave Labour in the United States of America. A Paper Read at the Dublin Statistical Society, on the 8th January, 1859* (n.p.: n.d.); Haughton, *Progress of the British West Indian Colonies Under Freedom: and the Inexpediency of Legislative Interference with Immigration Into them [and] Immigration Into the British West Indian Colonies. Two Papers, Read Before the Dublin Statistical Society, March 25th, 1859, and February 26th, 1860* (Dublin: Hodges, Smith, & Co., 1860); Richard D. Webb to Samuel May, Jr., Dublin, 10 March 1859, Taylor, *British and American Abolitionists*, pp. 438–40.

61. Maria Weston Chapman to Philip P. Carpenter, Weymouth, 7 January 1858 [sic, should be 1859], Carpenter Autograph Collection, Dorset Record Office; Russell Lant Carpenter, ed., *Memoirs of the Life and Work of Philip Pearsall Carpenter, B.A., London, Ph.D., New York, Chiefly Derived from His Letters*, 2nd ed. (London: C. Kegan Paul & Co., 1880), pp. 198–99, 205–6, 208, 212, 214–17, 232.

62. Philip P. Carpenter to William Lloyd Garrison, Ogdensburg, N.Y., 23 October 1859, Garrison Papers, MB; W. Freeman Galpin, "Samuel Joseph May 'God's Chore Boy,'" *New York History* 21 (April 1940): 139–41; Samuel J. May to Mary Estlin, Liverpool, 18 October 1850, Estlin Papers, LDW; Samuel J. May, *The Duty of the United Kingdom towards the Slaves of the United States. A Letter.* . . . (Bristol: I. Arrowsmith, [1860], p. 7.

63. "The Rev. S. J. May at Tenterden," *Inquirer*, 20 August 1859, p. 749; Edward Talbot to the editor, Tenterden, 28 February 1860, *Inquirer*, 3 March 1860, p. 192; "Anti-Slavery Meeting in Leeds," *Inquirer*, 10 September 1859, p. 818; "Our Metropolitan Correspondence" and "Rev. S. J. May in London," *ASA* (1 November 1859), pp. 277, 277–280.

64. "Rev. S. J. May in London," pp. 278–79; May, *Duty of the UK*, pp. 4, 7–8; "An

English Lawyer" to the Rev. R. Brook Aspland, London, 21 October 1859, *Christian Reformer* 15 (December 1859): 721–29.

65. Galpin, "Samuel Joseph May," p. 140; Maria Weston Chapman to Miss Whitelegge, n.p., 18 December 1859, [copy], Chapman to Mrs. Michell, n.p., 6 December 1859 [copy], Estlin Papers, LDW; "American Slavery," *Inquirer*, 31 December, 1859, pp. 1182–83.

66. "The Abolitionist Martyr," *Inquirer*, 24 December 1859, pp. 1162–63; R. L. Carpenter, *Memoirs of P. P. Carpenter*, p. 230; J. E. Carpenter, *Mary Carpenter*, pp. 208–9.

67. John Bowring, Edwin Chapman, and William James, "Address to the Ministers and Churches in the United States of America," *Christian Register*, 3 November 1860, p. 173; Samuel J. May and James Freeman Clarke, "Reply to the English Unitarian Address on Slavery," *Christian Register*, 20 [sic, should be 27] October 1860, pp. 169–70.

7

Unitarians in Religion, Unitarians in Race: Teaching America Equality—1844–60

"One Blood of All Nations":
A Theological Doctrine Opposed to Racism

"I wish I were black!" exclaimed a boy at Mary Carpenter's Ragged School at Bristol. The words would have been unthinkable in America. But in Bristol, where there was a remnant population of blacks as a result of the slave trade, the community had grown used to them, and Mary Carpenter, testing to see if her children had any prejudice against color, found that the contrary was the case—so much so that she had to tell her pupils to "be content with the colour God made [them]."[1] Indeed, Mary Carpenter found that what was characteristic of her schoolboys was also characteristic of Bristol in general and, indeed, of the whole country. She seldom saw a black man walking alone; he was "generally in animated conversation with a white companion."[2] Earlier she had testified to Maria Weston Chapman that she never saw a "coloured person" in England "without desiring to congratulate him, that he [was] in a country where he [was] looked upon as a man and a brother, and regarded with peculiar interest and sympathy."[3]

Most of Carpenter's Unitarian coreligionists were remarkably free of color phobia and they fought against racial misconceptions and prejudice. They were undoubtedly pleased that American fugitive slaves such as William Wells Brown and Frederick Douglass found Great Britain wonderously free of racial conflict. Brown for his part testified that there was no "negro pew" in the London churches.[4] And in writing of Douglass's visit to England during 1845–1846, Frances Armstrong suggested that the former slave's return to America might be painful because of the "perfect absence of prejudice against colour [in England], indeed the interest his colour [had] excited, would make [his] return even to New England, painful to him."[5] Here then was one reason that the British Unitarians had a liberal attitude to the problem of racism. They lived in a country where there was little racial prejudice.

But Unitarians had another, deeper and more powerful reason for hating racial prejudice. They themselves had suffered as a persecuted minority, they knew what it was to be "theological negroes." They understood the meaning of oppression and developed an empathy for the victims of oppression.[6]

Still another reason for the British Unitarians' progressive attitude on race was their theological doctrine. Universal brotherhood was a cardinal tenet of their faith. And unlike many of their American brethren, they practiced it as they preached it.

No Unitarian escaped this message of interracial unity, the idea that as children of the "Universal Father" all men and women, regardless of race, were brothers and sisters. Sermons, essays, books, and periodicals preached it. "One of the essential features of Christianity," Steinthal taught, was "its doctrine of universal brotherhood. Before it . . . all distinctions of ranks or race [had to] disappear." John Relly Beard, in his *People's Dictionary of the Bible,* attacked the "anti-social, anti-human, antichristian, and hateful distinction" of race. All people were one in Christ Jesus. Russell Carpenter proclaimed in the *Christian Reformer* that "the divine nature . . . in every soul, awaken[ed] a solemn conviction of brotherhood. No complexion conceal[ed] it." He believed that generally blacks had no reason to complain about the treatment they received in England.[7]

Pride—the belief that England was superior to America in the treatment of black people—also encouraged British Unitarians in their progressive views of race. They clearly understood the magnitude and significance of America's racial prejudice. Dr. Joseph Hutton thought the persuasivness of the "almost miraculous prevalence of anti-African feeling" in America had led some Englishmen to oppose black emancipation. It had certainly prevented the Northern states, explained Russell Carpenter, from properly dealing with slavery. The

free states held the blacks in contempt. Had they respected
them as they did "persons of their own colour, they would
never submit to their enslavement." James Haughton was appalled that Boston Unitarians found physical contact with
"their coloured brethren" distasteful. He maintained that this
"shameful prejudice" disgraced all the churches in the North.
When Philip Carpenter traveled in the states he was horrified
to see on a bus something "*ESSENTIALLY* American,"—
" 'Coloured Persons *allowed* here'!!!!" On board a river steamer
he lectured against slavery and was asked how he would "like to
sleep with a nigger?" He answered: "much better" than with
some whites.[8] The vivid contrast, therefore, between American
slavery and racial prejudice, and English freedom and brotherhood fed the vanity of the British Unitarians. During Douglass's visit to England, for example, they pointed out with
alacrity that in "democratical, republican America" the great
man was a slave and despised, but in "aristocratical, monarchi-
cal England" he was a free man and respected. Philip Carpenter found that American racial prejudice was enough "to make
any Englishman, however democratic, turn Tory."[9]

However, prejudice certainly did exist in England and, as
Steinthal explained, few churches were "quite free" from its
taint, including his own. Philip Carpenter informed Samuel
May that the parents of a mutual friend of theirs opposed her
"union with a coloured man." When fugitive slaves fled to England in the 1850s, they were usually offered menial labor or
passage to the West Indies. The celebrated Crafts spurned the
former in favor of the self-sufficiency of managing a boarding-
house.[10]

The taint of racial prejudice of some Unitarians was most
evident in their conviction that Europeans were superior in
intelligence. Edwin Chapman, in 1834, could not deny absolutely that the black might be "inferior in his mental and moral
organization." He declared that the black ought to be allowed
"to rise as high as the nature which God [had] given him
permitt[ed]." Sir John Bowring had observed on his world
travels that blacks were more teachable and ready to learn than
Europeans at an early age, but upon reaching a certain point
they fell behind. They had difficulty understanding "complicated mathematical problems" and lacked the ability to study
"the abstract sciences." Chapman later changed his views as his
knowledge of black intelligence increased, but Bowring held his
observations in 1861 with the benefit of almost a generation of

discussion on race. Robert Hibbert was convinced of the natural inferiority of Negroes and denied a black civilization ever existed. Any Negro achievement was simply the result of the influence of other races. Charles Beard argued that blacks would improve with the development of the "Anglo-Saxon element" within mulattoes—and he cited Frederick Douglass as a prime example.[11]

These statements exhibit ignorance and naïveté, but no evidence of color phobia or racial hatred. With the exception of Hibbert's views, which could be discounted as a slaveholder's rationalization, all the statements were made in the context of calls for sympathy or aid for blacks. Russell Carpenter's confession regarding the Negro accommodated them all: "How little the colour of his skin repel[led them], how deeply his wrongs move[d them]."[12]

"Impassable Barriers": The Failure of Unitarian Brotherhood across the Sea

Russell Carpenter had suggested that Northern lethargy in antislavery reform was related to racial prejudice, and proposed that British abolitionists ought to aid the elevation of the blacks as "one of the most feasible methods of promoting emancipation." British Unitarians who wanted to aid emancipation had to combat the racial prejudice of those whom they could influence most, their American brethren.

There was much to be done. Unhappily, the saintly leader of the American Unitarians, William Ellery Channing, offered them little help. His prejudicial views were revealed in an interview with Edward Strutt Abdy, an Anglican abolitionist who visited America in 1833–34. Channing had told Abdy that the cause of much racial prejudice was due to the Negro's rank in society. He hinted that there were different races of men "with various degrees of intellect" and declared that prejudice only infected the "uneducated classes." He denied that customs of prejudice inflicted "any pain or humiliation" upon blacks. He argued that only time erased prejudice; remonstrances made no impression. He thought that, if "some great genius" would arise among the blacks, "their lot [might] be ameliorated through the admiration and sympathy [the great one] would excite." He was convinced "that the best and only way" to educate blacks was in separate schools and boasted that Boston's "African schools" had "originated with him." Abdy maintained that, throughout their interview, Channing held that blacks were naturally inferior, were doomed to labor for their superiors, and were beset by a prejudice so "invincible" that "no effort [ought to] be made to subdue it." Even if half of Abdy's recorded observations were true—and the propensity for abolitionist exaggeration cannot be discounted—they were a strong indictment against Channing.[13]

Whether or not the indictment of Channing for racism was widely read, for Abdy published their interview in 1835, he managed to maintain his international reputation. But Orville Dewey did not, and he bore the burden of British wrath against prejudice. During his pilgrimage to England in the early 1830s, he had obtained the high esteem of many British Unitarians.[14] But his proclamations on slavery and race that came later grieved his former admirers. James Martineau called his policy on slavery the "silent system"—see no slavery, hear no slavery, speak against no slavery. His conduct on slavery was "utterly disgraceful," declared Martineau, a "downright betrayal of 'the Son of Man with a Kiss.'"[15]

In 1844, Dewey wrote an article, "On American Morals and Manners," that was partially directed to British readers. He published it in the *Christian Examiner* and as a pamphlet. In it Dewey censured the abolitionists, and told the antislavery stalwarts in Britain to tend their own hearths: "We say simply that we do not like the tone of *English* criticism upon us." These statements alone piqued the abolitionists, but other statements were even more provocative. On American blacks, Dewey declared that the colored race had "to ever be a small and depressed minority." They were separated from whites by "impassable physical, if not mental barriers," and probably could only achieve happiness through their "entire removal from the country."[16]

British criticism was immediate and enduring. Dewey's phrase "impassable barriers" echoed in England for years. George Harris ridiculed the comment in the *Christian Pioneer;* Estlin held that the blacks shared Dewey's right to inhabit America, "the soil of their birth"; and Joseph Hutton said that, instead of talk about barriers and exile for blacks, Dewey ought to be proclaiming the Negroes as "children of [their] common Father" and "joint heirs" with them of the Christian promise.

Charles Wicksteed declared that Dewey, as well as Daniel Webster, wished the "whole black race were at the bottom of the sea—or far into the Sahara." They think them, he continued,

> a bad breed. They look at them as something worse than the scum of Ireland and Europe. . . . They do not hate slavery so much as the slaves themselves. They wish they had never had them; they do not want to see them multiplied: . . . they would send them back to Africa: they would give two hundred million dollars to be rid of them: but they will not *free* them.[17]

When Frederick Douglass lectured in the British Isles he condemned Dewey for using the doctrine of "impassable barriers" to justify slavery.[18]

The most important response to Dewey's remarks was a letter to the editors of the *Christian Examiner* from William Carpenter. He felt well qualified to speak on the practical and scientific aspects of the controversy because of his experience in the West Indies and his training as a physiologist. He focused his attack upon Dewey's unfortunate phrase "impassable barriers." He explained tersely that there were "no definite races, . . . which [could] justify the belief that they [were] to be regarded as distinct species." They were all from a "common stock" and "various external circumstances [caused] the diversities." Placed in "favorable external circumstances," blacks could in several generations be on par with whites in every respect. A "favorable" environment meant equal educational and social opportunities and the absence of prejudice. The differences between black children and white children *of educated parents* were the same as between the children of uneducated European parents and the children of educated and cultured families. The racial "barriers" were thus artificial and removable.[19]

Carpenter attempted to refute two "impassable barriers" that were popularly held by white Americans to exist. The first was that blacks exuded an obnoxious odor, and, therefore, ought to be denied social intercourse. He explained that any noticeable odor was produced by a lack of cleanliness, not by the perspiration itself. Recalling his visit to the West Indies, he could safely say that he would "as soon sit in a room-full of negroes, as in the midst of an equal number of the 'great unwashed' of [his] own country." The second barrier was the white American's "instinctive repugnance" to miscegenation. He was puzzled to account for this feeling, except to attribute it to the particular social conditions in which the colored races were placed in the United States. Interracial marriages in England were not "uncommon": West Indian black stewards and servants frequently married white women ("often very handsome ones") in English seaport towns. No "impassable barrier" existed as to miscegenation. It was a matter of caste or rank, not of race. Remove the difference in social position and the barrier crumbled. He believed that in a generation or two, "the daughter of an American merchant might find the descendant of the despised Negro not unworthy of her attachment."[20]

Carpenter's formula to improve the condition of blacks and to achieve harmonious racial relations was to offer the colored races "elevation in the social scale." Offer "the reward and it will be speedily attained." He recited as success stories the black integration of the church, military, government, economy, and social life of the West Indies, and the achievements of blacks at the University of Edinburgh and the Inns of Court, London, and he ended with a gibe at Dewey: leaders of public opinion on race ought not to put forth "such strong and sweeping assertions without examining . . . the evidence on which they [were] based, through some other medium than the mists of hereditary and national repugnance."[21]

A Unitarian physician, S. Henry Dickson, in Charleston, South Carolina, rebutted Carpenter in a letter to the *Examiner*. At his friends' request, he also published his remarks as a pamphlet and included those the *Examiner* found too rude or crude to print. He was recommended by the magazine as a doctor of "high standing," "entitled to respect," who would answer Carpenter "scientifically."[22]

His treatment follows—with those remarks expurgated by the *Examiner* given in brackets: Dickson wished to reply to Carpenter. He could not remain silent on a subject [so "revolting"]. There *were* "impassable barriers" between black and white and the blacks were [and "ought to be"] refused social intercourse with whites. No attempt ought to be made ["or even thought of"] to raise them by intermarriage. As evidence for the diversity of the human races, he quoted Dr. Samuel George Morton, a Philadelphia physician and professor of anatomy, who had "proved" the diversity through skull measurements. He also selected statements from Carpenter's own writings to support the marked differences "between the races."[23] The black could not improve his standing among the races. ["The tendency of the race (had) always been to retrograde. . . . The fact of his downward progress (was) undeniable and undenied."] To avert this retrogression, he had to "cease to be a Negro." Carpenter held out to him intermarriage with a white. ["Has Dr. C. a sister or daughter" to offer as "a prize"?] Like Carpenter, Dickson had known black men to marry white women.

> [That a poor and destitute Caucasian should thus ally herself to a black man, however revolting, is not strange nor unaccountable. The average condition of the negro in reference to physical comfort, is infinitely above that of the wretched white slave of the British manufactory, or worse still, of the coal mine, trained from infancy to push with her forehead a loaded wagon. . . . With these . . . let the negro "amalgamate" or intermarry, and we will thank Providence if it give them even this foul alternative.]

To elevate blacks by intermarriage, Dickson concluded, was completely unacceptable. ["Indeed that as a race and a people (he and his fellow Southerners would) rather die a thousand deaths than consent to (it)."][24]

The British and Irish Unitarian awareness of, and sensitivity to the American racism typified by Dewey and Dickson eventually led the Irish to protest against it in their reply to the Boston Invitation of 1847. In boldly raising the issue of ecclesiastical racism, their protest was perhaps unique among the many British antislavery remonstrances.[25] In it, the Irish spoke of the Americans

> denying to the free coloured inhabitants . . . the participation of equal Rights and Privileges with their Fellow-citizens, as Members of the Church of Christ. [In] many churches, coloured persons are not allowed to have vote or voice in the election of officers, or the management of church affairs; that during public worship they are restricted to particular seats, and a particular part of the building; . . . and that they have even been refused permission to place themselves at the Lord's Table beside their Fellow-Christians of a different complexion, but are compelled either to abstain from the Lord's Supper, or to assemble themselves together, in order to partake of it, at a different hour from other members. [Such measures are] utterly opposed . . . to the precepts of Christ, and to the spirit of the Gospel; and we trust that Unitarian Christians will show the efficacy of their pure,

mild, and comprehensive faith, by discarding, in all their churches, a system of procedure, founded only upon local and temporary prejudice; by which . . . the church is rendered an instrument for degrading, not elevating, those for whom Christ died.

It will be remembered that the most distinguished members of the denomination all signed it, and that the *Christian Register* published it without comment.[26] On the question of racism, the Unitarian denomination in America, as a body, remained silent.

Monogenesis vs. Polygenesis: Testimonials to the Unity of Humankind

Unsuccessful in their attempt to affect their coreligionists' racial prejudice in America, the British Unitarians turned to sustain the racial tolerance, and to counter the appearance of American racial thinking, in their own country. They undertook no concerted campaign, but effectively conducted two types of propaganda. The first was the scientific treatise for scholars, sometimes popularized for the laity. The second was the historical novel or literary biography. William Carpenter excelled in the use of the first, and John Relly Beard, the second.

In Carpenter's education at his father's school, religion and science received equal time, and to his very last days, he was equally devoted to his Greek New Testament and his scientific manuals. His lifelong "cautious and moderate" stance on slavery was the result of observing the humane treatment of slaves by a kind planter in the British West Indies.[27] In 1834, he began his medical studies at the University College, London, and later completed them at the University of Edinburgh.[28] In 1844, he was appointed Fullerian Professor of Physiology in the Royal Institution and was elected to the Royal Society. From 1851 he served as the principal of University Hall, and from 1856 to 1879, as registrar of the University of London. In 1871 Edinburgh conferred upon him the degree of LL.D., and two years later he was chosen over Charles Darwin as a corresponding member of the Institute of France.[29]

He worshiped for nearly forty years at the Rosslyn Hill Chapel, Hampstead, where he played the organ, conducted psalmody, and compiled a *Handbook of Psalmody.* He pursued the harmony of science and religion throughout his life, and in 1845 wrote eighteen essays on that theme for the *Inquirer.* He was a vice-president of the British and Foreign Unitarian Association and an enthusiastic benefactor of the London Domestic Mission. Despite his "Catholic spirit," his close clerical friends in prominent orthodox churches, and his claim that he never suffered discrimination as a Unitarian, his "infidel" faith in fact denied him a faculty appointment at the University of Edinburgh. The few days before his tragic death from burns incurred in an accident in 1885 were spent preparing for a lecture on miracles at a denomination conference.[30]

Carpenter wrote nearly 300 books, essays, and encyclopedia articles. Several of his major works to be published in numerous editions were his *Principles of General and Comparative Physiology, Popular Cyclopedia of Science, Principles of Human Physiology,* and *A Manual of Physiology.* With the exception of the *Cyclopedia,* all of his books were basic medical texts that were read by thousands of English and American students. He reached wider audiences as an editor and a writer for the *British and Foreign Medico-Chirurgical Review,* and as a popular essayist for the *Edinburgh Review, National Review,* and *Westminster Review.*[31] When he died, the *Popular Science Monthly* wrote that his science, catholicity, reform interests, personality, and tragic death all invested "the history of his career with an unusual degree of interest."[32]

Whether it was Dewey's remark on impassable racial barriers that inspired Carpenter to lend his scientific testimony to the cause of racial equality is not known. However, in his major writings on the subject, he never failed to quote Dewey's phrase almost as if to regard his writings as refutations of Dewey's racism. Moreover, he included in the edition of his *Principles of Human Physiology* that followed his article against Dewey in the *Christian Examiner* a chapter on the "Varieties of the Human Race." In the chapter, he taught that the black people were "not separated, by any impassable barrier, from the most civilized and cultivated nations of the globe."[33] He acknowledged his heavy dependence upon the research of Dr. James Cowles Prichard, a learned British anthropologist, who was his brother-in-law and mentor. With Prichard, he held to the unity of the human race. He wrote that the question of race was of great social as well as scientific interest. Those peoples who differed in appearance from Europeans were thought by some to be a distinct species. It had been "a favourite idea," he explained,

> among those who wished to excuse the horrors of slavery, or the extirpation of savage tribes, that the races thus treated might be considered as inferior species, incapable of being raised by any treatment to our own elevation; and as thus falling legitimately under the domination of the superior races. . . . This doctrine, which has had its origin in the desire to justify as expedient what could not be defended as morally right, finds no support from scientific inquiries conducted in an enlarged spirit.

He devoted the next twenty-five pages to prove the "just conclusion" that there was no impassable barrier between black and white.[34]

Carpenter's next writing on race was a review article of Dr. Prichard's *Researches into the Physical History of Mankind*. Carpenter declared that the varieties of people in the world prompted questions of their relationship to each other. Some persons believed in the "common origin of all races of mankind" on scriptural authority. However, there were many Bible-loving people in the American South who completely disregarded the biblical and "historical testimony" in support of the "Unity of Origin of the Human Races." Instead, they proclaimed that the Negroes were not of the "*Adamic* race," and not "*men* in the full sense of the term." They propounded, Carpenter continued, that blacks were "organically different," separated by "impassable barriers," incapable of any improvement, and fit only for slavery. Acceptance of this racism, he declared, meant that a hungry European in Africa could conscientiously kill and eat "the first native he might happen to meet."[35]

For his part, Carpenter declared that, as a result of reading Prichard's work, he had become convinced of the probable existence of "a single original pair" of human parents. He sought not to confirm a literal interpretation of the Genesis account of Adam and Eve, for he appreciated "modern" biblical criticism; he only wished to put forward Prichard's thesis that humanity had emerged from a single center, that climate, diet, and cultural influences—particularly hunger and ignorance—caused the differences among the people of the earth. He concluded again that the "barriers" were passable, that careful and extensive ethnological research tended "to break down the barriers which ignorance and prejudice [had] erected." A unity rather than a plurality of races existed as it had at the genesis of humanity.[36]

A year later, this time for a general audience, Carpenter reviewed once more the work of Prichard. Entitled "Ethnology, or the Science of Races," his article praised this new science which furnished a strong argument for the "*common,* or at least the *similar* origin of all races." Opponents of this unity of origins cited the "Negro type" as a race that possessed unique characteristics. They argued that, if external stimuli such as hunger and climate affected the physical and mental form of blacks, why did they not improve when placed in a European or white environment? Carpenter claimed that changes had in fact taken place among Africans who had been transported to temperate climates and to more civilized nations. He did not disclaim the cultural or civilized background of many blacks; rather, he paid due respects to the African achievement in Egyptian society. However, the general elevation of blacks would in time come with their removal from the African continent. Moreover, it would come "*without any actual intermixture of races.*" Carpenter, unlike Charles Beard and others, did not feel that the African race needed an infusion of Anglo-Saxon blood to achieve intelligence, ambition, and cultural growth.[37]

Carpenter taught that the British ought to dispense with the idea of "racial" differences when judging Negroes as a people. The true relation of the Negro to the cultivated European had to be based upon the same claims as those of the "outcast and degraded" among the British people. The capabilities of blacks ought not to be judged by their manner of life, albeit sometimes wretched, because that was "often forced upon them by external circumstances." Moreover, they ought not be judged as being "incapable of entertaining any particular class of ideas" simply because Europeans could not discern those ideas in the blacks' "existing forms of expression." Again, Carpenter dismissed Dewey's racial pronouncement:

It will only be when the influence of perfect equality in civilization and in social position has been ineffectually brought to bear on [the blacks] for several consecutive generations, that we shall be entitled to say, of the Negro . . . race, that it is separated by an "impassable barrier" from those which arrogate to themselves an inalienable superiority in intellectual and social endowments. All our present knowledge on this subject tends rather to show that no such barrier exists.[38]

Negroes were regarded by some in England, he continued, and many more in the United States, as a people unable to reach the heights of white civilization. But his comparison of the capacities of Negro and white children in Bristol revealed that they were "in every respect equal." There was a "super docility" on the part of some of the Negroes and their progress in learning seemed to be checked at an early age. These observations he attributed to the many discouragements placed in their paths and to their knowledge that they could never be "admitted within the pale of white civilization." Carpenter suggested that Britons might recall their own uncivilized state when Caesar and his soldiers arrived on their shores. His article was not only a book review, but a Unitarian's homily on the unity and equality of humankind.[39]

Carpenter would again write on race. He continued to acknowledge Prichard as his master, to repeat the same arguments, and to give a refutation of Dewey's "impassable barrier" doctrine an appropriate place.[40] Although not free himself from some erroneous views in ethnology or anthropology, Carpenter showed a healthful and refreshing liberality on the controversy of race. His many writings in a broad variety of publications reached many people and surely made some impact. Most historians, however, have ignored this Unitarian layman and recent volumes devoted to nineteenth-century British attitudes on race fail to mention him.[41]

Few readers would have faulted the scientific credentials and reputation of Carpenter and fewer still would dismiss the work of the Reverend John Relly Beard as the sentimental and exaggerated outpourings of an abolitionist propagandist. Although conservative in his theology, Beard was somewhat radical in his social outlook. He was a friend to "unlimited education" for "all ages and all ranks," and wrote educational manuals for the working and impoverished classes. One impressive project was his *People's Biographical Dictionary,* which included Lancashire working men and other "obscure worthies." Another was his *People's Dictionary of the Bible.* He described himself as "an anti-war, anti-slavery, and anti-capital punishment man to the backbone," and he dedicated his forty-year ministry in Manchester to the spread of freedom and liberty at home and abroad.[42]

Beard was as much a scholar as a social reformer. He established and edited *The Christian Teacher and Chronicle,* edited for a time the *Foreign Quarterly Review,* contributed frequently to denominational and national periodicals, wrote and translated thirty-eight volumes on religion and theology, edited Cassell's *Latin Dictionary,* and founded, and served as its first principal, the Unitarian College of Manchester. In 1853, he published *The Life of Toussaint L'Ouverture, The Negro Patriot of Hayti.*[43] Carpenter, one of the Unitarian denomination's most distinguished scientists, had presented a scientific antidote to American racism, and now Beard, one of its most distinguished educators, provided a scholarly and literary answer to the same.

Channing had called for a Negro avatar to prove the ability of the blacks. In Beard's mind the black champion had already emerged. Toussaint was not a new subject to Unitarian authors. In 1841, Harriet Martineau had written *The Hour and the Man,* a laudatory account of the black leader. But while her hero's race was probably not her primary reason for writing about him, to Beard it was.[44]

In his preface, Beard admitted that Toussaint's life was of permanent interest and value in itself, but it had an added dimension: it could aid "the sacred cause of freedom" and "the removal of the prejudices on which servitude mainly depend[ed]." Providence, he explained in his opening chapter, periodically brought forth "extraordinary men" to accomplish great and important objects. He would "supply the clearest evidence [to Orville Dewey?] that there [was] no insuperable barrier between the light and dark-coloured tribes of our common species."[45]

In narrating his story, Beard attacked slavery and slaveholders. He told of the prejudice directed toward freed slaves and how they were denied political and social rights. The situation called for a liberator, "the appearance of a hero of negro blood [to afford] the best proof of negro capability." The person, of course, was Toussaint L'Ouverture, who in a short time transformed the state of Haiti into a country comparable to "the higher forms of white and European civilization," and best of all, into a country in which "the prejudices of colour" seemed to lose "their former power."[46] But his rule was overthrown and he died in a French prison. It was European prejudice against the color of the liberator's skin that caused his unhappy end. "How long, O reason," Beard asked,

> shall so potent and flimsy a pretext prevail? A brown complexion, commonly called white, ensures and justifies personal immunity and personal freedom; a rather deeper brown, [or black] complexion . . . ensures and justifies the loss

of personal liberty. . . . The relation of master and slave when reduced to its last link, is the relation of . . . the hues of the skin, . . . which extend from the fair Circassian to the raven-black negro. Where in this minutely graduated scale, is the point at which liberty ends, and slavery begins?

His biography of Toussaint was not only a testimony to a great black leader and an attack on racial prejudice, it was a tract against slavery, the "essence and concentration of injustice."[47]
In his book, Beard was not free of popular notions regarding blacks: they were excellent dancers, emotional people, paragons of familial affection. But to his credit he viewed Toussaint as a world hero, not a black hero. He saw in the story of Haiti many great black men, not a freak or solitary example of black achievement. He seemed to welcome interracial marriage and found it *mutually* benefiting the races. Finally, in a very modern way, he accepted a Haitian life-style that differed from the English view of labor and ambition, and he saw "no ground whatever" on which Europeans could "justifiably interfere" with it. He was no nineteenth-century imperialist. His book was for the period impressive propaganda against racial prejudice and slavery. There was irony in its publication and Beard's standing as an abolitionist. To escape the poverty of their family's surroundings, two of his brothers had sought their fortune in America while he had chosen the ministry. One brother found his in New Orleans—as a prosperous auctioneer selling slaves.[48]

Noble Specimens of a Common Race: British Unitarians and Their Equals in Black

Given the noble theological pronouncements on universal brotherhood, the remonstrances against American racism, the scientific treatises on the unity of the human race, and the praise of a black hero, the proof of the Unitarians' commitment to racial equality had to be their personal conduct toward blacks. Because so few blacks resided in Great Britain and Ireland, contact with them was rare and limited to specific groups: West Indian and British black artisans (especially in Bristol), American fugitive slaves, and Northern middle-class blacks. The encounters ranged from the superficial meetings with West Indian blacks at the World's Anti-Slavery Convention—

who showed Haughton that "the image of the beneficent Creator [had] been imparted to all alike"—to the prolonged visits by fugitive blacks at the Estlins'.[49] The most memorable encounter, of course, was with Frederick Douglass during 1845–47.

Several Unitarian abolitionists met blacks when they traveled in the United States. Philip Carpenter stayed at the home of the noted black author, William Still, in Philadelphia, and tried to be so civil to the blacks as to wonder if his conduct "were not almost an insult." He was appalled by the harsh treatment of free blacks in the North and South, but was most grieved in seeing a beautiful young slave "without scarcely a tinge of colour." That so many slaves were nearly white surprised him.[50]

When Russell Carpenter visited the slave states, he was at first, like his brother Philip, sensitive to showing blacks social courtesies lest he "transgress the usages of the place." But his conscience so troubled him that he threw caution aside. Some of the blacks he met were of the "lowest grade of humanity," not because of their color, "for some of the finest men that [he had] seen had the same," but because of their slavery. He was pleased to find that everyone assumed that as an Englishman he opposed slavery. However, they had no assumptions as to his racial views, and were "half amused, half surprised" on hearing of his "friendly equality" with blacks in England. Inevitably, he was asked how he would like to have his sister marry a Negro. He replied that there were a great many men, including white Europeans, for whom he "desired equal rights," but did not "desire as brothers-in-law." Yet, he believed that he was ready to welcome anyone whom his sisters decided to marry. In the North, he visited the Douglass family. He saw blacks on first-class railway cars and omnibuses, at civic processions and public meetings. He felt a great deal of prejudice was abating due to the abolitionists, in particular, to Douglass himself.[51]

In 1853, Carpenter used his experiences in America to rebut a racist tract called *Free Blacks and Slaves. Would Immediate Abolition Be a Blessing?* Written under the pseudonym "A Cambridge Man," it warned that blacks did not fare well in freedom. It spoke of the high incidence of mental disorders of the free blacks, the short life of mulattoes, the general dangers of amalgamation, the blessings of colonization, and the replacement of America's slaves by "an influx of Chinese, via California"! Carpenter replied that any "faults" relative to the free blacks were "more fairly" charged to their former slavery than to their liberty. There was no scientific evidence that mulattoes were short-lived. He believed that "some of the finest specimens of humanity" were of the "mixed race," because in their persons the "peculiar excellences" of both races were combined. For scientific evidence, he quoted extensively from his brother William's writings. As for colonization, Americans had no more right to take blacks back against their will than they had in carrying them away.[52]

Francis Bishop was another Unitarian minister who was much impressed with the blacks he met in America. Even some of the slaves surprised him by their "good sense and quiet capacity, . . . acuteness and discernment." In Philadelphia, he visited blacks in their homes and churches, and was very favorably impressed with their "intelligence, propriety, happiness, and virtue."[53]

These favorable impressions were published in Unitarian periodicals and read by people already convinced of their veracity. For although many Unitarians had never observed or visited blacks in the United States, most had met or heard fugitive slaves or free blacks speak in their own country. Many had the unforgettable experience of meeting Frederick Douglass. The general history of his activities in Great Britain from 1845 to 1847 is well known. In Scotland, he was an effective spokesman for the "Send Back the Money" campaign against the Free Church of Scotland, which had accepted funds from Southern slaveowners.[54] He also generally excited antislavery feeling in Britain. Moreover, as an American fugitive slave under the protection of the English flag, he symbolized "the moral superiority of the British society."[55] A great variety of articles in Unitarian publications during and after his visit invariably mentioned that in America this "man of great native gifts" was a slave, in England a free man, "an equal, and [a] brother."[56]

The *Inquirer* gave him considerable publicity. It reported his letters, speeches, commemorations, and, at the close of his tour, commended him in a full front-page editorial. It defended him when he was rudely treated aboard a British steamship. Numerous English citizens, it stated, considered Douglass their "equal" and were appalled that an English firm had "truckled to American prejudice." A few years later, it praised his newspaper, the *North Star,* as "a standing refutation of that monstrous theory which denie[d] to the negro race the highest moral and intellectual qualities."[57]

Among the British Unitarians, the closest friends of Douglass were probably Russell Carpenter and his wife, Mary. Russell was pleased with Douglass's independent course and he believed him to be right "on his main principles." He believed that "every triumph" that Douglass achieved with his "remarkable powers" benefited all blacks.[58] He and his wife solicitied funds from their rich friends to help him aid fugitives, and to keep his newspaper solvent.[59] In England, Russell defended Douglass from those who made unfair demands upon him or would condemn his conduct—particularly his alleged role in John Brown's raid. Douglass gratefully acknowledged the Carpenters' assistance in his autobiography.[60]

For a time, Douglass was also the darling of the British Garrisonians. George Armstrong called him that "noble specimen of [their] common race," and to Mary Carpenter, he was "one of nature's true nobility." Armstrong's ardor for Douglass cooled when the latter in an antislavery harangue "was unguarded in one of his expressions," as Garrison put it, "in regard to the Unitarian communion tables." But Douglass's apology soothed Armstrong's hurt, and just before he departed for the States, Armstrong and his Bristol friends gave him a silver inkstand as a farewell gift. Unfortunately, when he split with the American Garrisonians, Douglass destroyed his relationship with their British allies as well.[61]

The English Unitarian who knew Douglass and other prominent fugitive slaves the best was Estlin. He welcomed to his home the Crafts and William Wells Brown, and they boarded with him for long periods of time. Douglass was also his guest. Such tolerance Sam May found "worth *everything*—[for] its [powerful] influence," and he mentioned it at numerous antislavery meetings. Brown found that among the hundreds of British abolitionists he had met Estlin was the most fervent leader of the cause; a "model Christian," who always opened "his home, his heart, and his purse" to those in need "without respect to sect, color or country."[62]

Estlin and his daughter commented on the blacks who visited and boarded at their home. Mary Estlin had but one opinion of Douglass—wonderful. Wherever he went he aroused "sympathy for [their] cause and love for himself." His "outward graces, intellectual power and culture, and eloquence" impressed her. He was certainly a "very remarkable man," declared her father, but the good doctor feared that his frequent association with "white women of education & refined taste & manners" would create a "craving void" when he returned home. Dr Estlin was perhaps more impressed with Ellen Craft. He had not realized, he confided to May, the real "inequity of slavery" until he heard "Ellen's quiet, tea-table, incidental details of her experience." He liked her work habits, but found her husband a "little indolent." He praised William Wells Brown for the same reason—energy and ambition. He lamented the methods employed to publicize the lectures of his house guests. Some announcements, he complained, had declared, " 'Arrival of 3 Fugitive Slaves from America!!!' as if 3 monkeys had been imported."[63] Indeed, were they not three human beings, whom he looked upon as not only his equals, but as his sister and brothers?

Estlin's views on race were shaped by his friends William Carpenter and James Prichard. He maintained that people, whether black or white, were largely shaped by external influences. In his important tract, *A Brief Notice on American Slavery*, he included sections on the free blacks and the "origin and intellect of the Negro." He declared that American racism had no analogies in the English class system where no "impassable barriers" existed. He belittled the views of Orville Dewey, and declared that "no sincere advocate of emancipation" ever treated "the coloured people otherwise than as 'men and brothers.' "[64]

As the five years following Estlin's death in 1855 coincided with a general decline in antislavery enthusiasm in England, there was proportionally less occasion to comment or to act upon American racism. However, when the need did arise, Unitarians sought to meet it. In 1859, Sarah Remond, a black abolitionist, visited England. She spoke on American slavery and racial prejudice before numerous groups, and stayed in several Unitarian homes. When she attempted to proceed to France, George M. Dallas, the American minister to England, refused to visa her passport.[65] The *Inquirer* took up her cause and John Relly Beard chaired an antislavery meeting at his chapel in Manchester that protested her mistreatment. But worse was yet to befall her. When she sailed on the Cunard liner to Boston, she was prohibited from eating with the rest of the passengers. Edwin Chapman and a local Bristol official complained to Sir Samuel Cunard that since "Great Britain recognize[d] no distinction of rights because of colour," the captains of his ships ought not be permitted to make his vessels "the scenes of social oppression." The *Inquirer* was fearful that British commerce might degenerate to the standard of the American slave-holding community. . . . According to the healthy English sentiment, the prejudice of colour [was] a monstrous absurdity. . . . It was a duty to [their] own high standard of civilization and social equality, and not to lower it to the American platform.[66]

The testimony of British Unitarians against racism prior to the American Civil War was against a cancerous racism that, as physicians of the body, mind, and soul, they diagnosed as contagious. It could possibly infect them and they believed in stopping it from spreading, in fact, in stifling the disease at its source. They chose to quarantine this particular disease of American life.

Notes

1. Mary Carpenter to Maria Weston Chapman, Bristol, 31 October 1847, Weston Papers, Boston Public Library, cited hereafter as MB.

2. Ibid.

3. Mary Carpenter to Maria Weston Chapman, Bristol, 14 October 1844, Weston Papers, MB.

4. William Wells Brown, *Sketches of Places and People Abroad* (Boston: John P. Jewett and Co., 1855), p. 306; Howard Temperley, *British Antislavery 1833–1870* (London: Longman Group Ltd., 1972), p. 223.

5. Frances Armstrong to Samuel May, Jr., Clifton Vale, 16 February 1846, May Papers.

6. "[The Twenty-Second Annual Meeting of the] British and Foreign Unitarian Association," *Inquirer*, 29 May 1847, p. 348; Raymond V. Holt, *The Unitarian Contribution to Social Progress in England*, 2nd rev. ed. (London: Lindsey Press, 1952), passim.

7. S. Alfred Steinthal, *American Slavery. A Sermon, Preached at Christ Church Chapel, Bridgwater, on Sunday, May the First, 1853* (Bridgwater: J. Whitby, 1853), p. 3; John Relly Beard, *The People's Dictionary of the Bible*, 3rd ed. (London: Simpkin, Marshall & Co., 1859), 1:185; Russell Lant Carpenter, "American Slavery. No. III," *Christian Reformer* 7 (October 1852): 597; R. L. Carpenter, "Our Conflict with American Slavery," *Christian Reformer* 9 (October 1853): 651.

8. "Sunday-School Association," *Unitarian Magazine and Chronicle* 2 (August 1835): 251; Russell Lant Carpenter to the editor, n.p., n.d., *Inquirer*, 11 December 1858, p. 801; James Haughton to the editor, Dublin, 21 December 1845, *Inquirer*, 10 January 1846, p. 19; Haughton to the editor, Dublin, 3 October 1844 [sic], *Inquirer*, 18 October 1845, p. 659; Philip P. Carpenter to William Lloyd Garrison, Albany, N.Y., 30 December 1858, Garrison Papers, MB.

9. "Anti-Slavery meetings in Bristol," *Inquirer*, 12 September 1846, p. 588; Philip P. Carpenter to William Lloyd Garrison, Carpenterville, 19 August 1859, Garrison Papers, MB.

10. Steinthal, *American Slavery*, p. 13; Philip P. Carpenter to Samuel May, Jr., Warrington, 21 September 1860, May Papers, MB; Francis Bishop, "An Appeal in Behalf of Two Distressed Fugitive Slave Families," *Inquirer*, 12 July 1851, p. 439; Bishop, "The

Distressed Fugitives from America," *Inquirer,* 2 August 1851, 486; J. B. Estlin to _____, Bristol, December, 1853 [printed letter on the progress of the Crafts], Weston Papers, MB.

11. Edwin Chapman, "Abolition of West Indian Slavery," *Unitarian Magazine and Chronicle* 1 (1834): 261; John Bowring, *Autobiographical Recollections of Sir John Bowring. With a Brief Memoir by Lewin B. Bowring* (London: Henry S. King & Co., 1877), p. 393; Robert Hibbert, *Hints to the Young Jamaica Sugar Planter* (London: T. and G. Underwood, 1825), p. 7, see also pp. 5–6, 15–16; [Charles Beard], "Uncle Tom's Cabin," *Prospective Review* 8 (1852): 508.

12. Russell Lant Carpenter to the editor, n.p., 26 May [1851], *Inquirer,* 7 June 1851, p. 360.

13. Edward Strutt Abdy, *Journal of Residence and Tour in the United States of North America, from April, 1833, to October, 1834* (London: John Murray 1835), 3:218–22, 224–25, 227–34.

14. Samuel A. Eliot, ed., *Heralds of a Liberal Faith,* (Boston: American Unitarian Association, 1910), 3:84–89.

15. George Armstrong to Samuel May, Jr., Clifton, Bristol, 3 May 1847, May Papers, MB; James Martineau to J. B. Estlin, Liverpool, 24 November 1845, Estlin Papers, Dr. Williams's Library. Cited hereafter as LDW.

16. Orville Dewey, "On American Morals and Manners," *Christian Examiner* 26 (March 1844): 265–68. Cf. also the pamphlet under the same title (Boston: William Crosby, 1844).

17. [George Harris], "Review of *American Morals and Manners* by Rev. Dr. Dewey," *Christian Pioneer,* 18 (October 1844): 477–78; J. B. Estlin to the editor, Bristol, 7 June 1847, *Inquirer,* 12 June 1847, p. 373; Joseph Hutton to the editor, [London], 29 September 1847, *Inquirer,* 2 October 1847, p. 632; [Charles Wicksteed], "The American Fugitive Slave Act," *Prospective Review* 7 (1851): 456–57.

18. "The Anti-Slavery League," *Inquirer,* 22 August 1846, p. 530.

19. William B. Carpenter, "Letter from W. B. Carpenter, M.C.," *Christian Examiner* 27 (July 1844): 139, 140–41.

20. Ibid., pp. 142–43.

21. Ibid., pp. 143–44.

22. S. Henry Dickson, "Letter from S. H. Dickson, M.D.," *Christian Examiner* 36 (November 1844): 427. The pamphlet was published as S. H. Dickson, *Remarks on Certain Topics Connected with the General Subject of Slavery* (Charleston: Observer Office Press, 1845). For more on Dickson, see Douglas C. Stange, "Abolitionism as Maleficence: Southern Unitarians Versus 'Puritan Fanaticism'—1831–1860," *Harvard Library Bulletin* 26 (April 1978): 155–56.

23. Dickson, "Letter from S. H. Dickson," pp. 427–28. For the material in brackets, see Dickson, *Remarks,* pp. 24, 25. For a study of the ideas of Morton, see William Stanton, *The Leopard's Spots: Scientific Attitudes Toward Race in America 1815–1859* (Chicago: University of Chicago Press, 1966).

24. Dickson, "Letter from S. H. Dickson," pp. 428–32; Dickson, *Remarks,* pp. 27, 28–29, 35.

25. See above, chapter 4, section "Notes of No Thank You: The Irish and British Unitarians Reply"; "Address of the Irish Christian Unitarian Society to Their Brethren in America," *Inquirer,* 23 September 1843.

26. John Scott Porter to James Haughton, n.p., 4 April 1848, May Papers, MB; Ezra S. Gannett to the editor, Boston, 1 May 1848, *Christian Register,* 6 May 1848, pp. 74–75.

27. "Dr. W. B. Carpenter, C.B., F.R.S.," *Inquirer,* 14 November 1885, pp. 728–29;

William B. Carpenter, *Nature and Man: Essays Scientific and Philosophical.* With an Introductory Memoir by J. Estlin Carpenter (New York: D. Appleton and Co., 1889), pp. 8–10; Leslie Stephen and Sidney Lee, eds., *The Dictionary of National Biography* (Oxford: Oxford University Press, 1921–22), 3:1075.

28. Carpenter, *Nature and Man*, pp. 13–15.

29. "Dr. W. B. Carpenter," p. 728.

30. Ibid. Carpenter, *Nature and Man*, pp. 31, 44; William Benjamin Carpenter to the Rev. Dr. Booth, [London], 15 April 1856, David E. Smith Collection, Columbia University Library.

31. For a bibliography of his writings, see Carpenter, *Nature and Man*, pp. 467–83.

32. "Sketch of Dr. W. B. Carpenter," *Popular Science Monthly* 28 (1885): 538; "Dr. W. B. Carpenter," *Eclectic Magazine* 85 (September 1875): 374–75.

33. William Benjamin Carpenter, *Principles of Human Physiology, with Their Chief Applications to Pathology, Hygiene, and Forensic Medicine*, 3rd ed. (Philadelphia: Lea and Blanchard, 1847), p. 99. His explanation for the addition of another chapter was dated October 1846.

34. Carpenter, *Principles of Human Physiology*, pp. 76–77. The chapter's pages are 76–99. Prichard has been called by a recent historian "by far the most influential ethnologist in England in the first half of the nineteenth century." See Reginald Horsman, "Origins of Racial Anglo-Saxonism in Great Britain Before 1850," *Journal of the History of Ideas* 37 (July–September 1976): 396.

35. William Benjamin Carpenter, "Dr. Prichard on the History of Mankind, etc.," *British and Foreign Medico-Chirurgical Review* 47 (July 1847): 49–50.

36. Ibid. (October 1847), pp. 441–42, 450, 447–78, 480–81.

37. William B. Carpenter, "Ethnology, or the Science of Races," *Edinburgh Review* 89 (October 1848): 429, 432, 440.

38. Carpenter, "Ethnology, or the Science of Races," p. 461.

39. Ibid., pp. 465, 468–70.

40. See, for example, William Benjamin Carpenter, "Varieties of Mankind," *The Cyclopaedia of Anatomy and Physiology*, Robert B. Todd, ed. vol. 4, part 2 (London: Longman, Brown, Green, Longmans, & Roberts, 1849–1852), pp. 1316–17, 1319, 1324–25, 1337–39.

41. Christine Bolt, *Victorian Attitudes to Race* (London: Routledge & Kegan Paul, 1971); Douglas A. Lorimer, *Colour, Class and the Victorians: English attitudes to the Negro in the mid-nineteenth Century* ([Leicester]: Leicester University Press, 1978).

42. Herbert McLachlan, *Records of a Family 1800–1933: Pioneers in Education, Social Service and Liberal Religion* (Manchester: Manchester University Press, 1935), pp. 9, 11, 14–18, 27.

43. Ibid., pp. 11, 26–29; John Relly Beard, *The Life of Toussaint L'Ouverture, The Negro Patriot of Hayti* (London: Ingram, Cooke, and Co., 1853).

44. Harriet Martineau, *The Hour and the Man. An Historical Romance*, 2 vols. (New York: Harper & Bros., 1841); Beard, *Toussaint*, p. 23.

45. Beard, *Toussaint*, pp. v, 1.

46. Ibid., pp. 18, 20, 23, 137–38.

47. Ibid., pp. 233–34.

48. Ibid., 256–57, 280, 302, 316–18; McLachlan, *Records of a Family*, p. 1.

49. Samuel Haughton, *Memoir of James Haughton, With Extracts from His Private and Published Letters* (Dublin: E. Ponsonby, 1877), p. 49; John Bishop Estlin to Samuel May, Jr., Bristol, 2 May 1851, Clare Taylor, *British and American Abolitionists. An Episode in Transatlantic Understanding* (Edinburgh: Edinburgh University Press, 1974), p. 377.

50. Russell Lant Carpenter, ed., *Memoirs of the Life and Work of Philip Pearsall Carpen-

ter, *B.A., London, Ph.D., New York, Chiefly Derived from His Letters,* 2nd ed. (London: C. Kegan Paul & Co., 1880), pp. 202, 207, 221, 233.

51. Russell Lant Carpenter, "American Slavery. No. II," *Christian Reformer* 7 (September 1851): 544, 547; Carpenter, "American Slavery. No. V," *Christian Reformer* 7 (December 1851): 721, 724.

52. "A Cambridge Man," *Free Blacks and Slaves. Would Immediate Abolition Be a Blessing? A Letter to the Editor of the Anti-Slavery advocate* (London: Arthur Hall Virtue & Co., 1853), pp. 12, 15–16, 20, 22, 27; Russell Lant Carpenter, "Free Blacks and Slaves," *Christian Reformer,* 9 (August 1853): 473, 483, 484–85.

53. [Francis Bishop], "Key to Uncle Tom's Cabin," *Prospective Review* 9 (1853): 268–69.

54. Benjamin Quarles, "Ministers without Portfolio," *Journal of Negro History,* 39 (January 1954): 27–42; George Shepperson, "Frederick Douglass and Scotland," *Journal of Negro History* 38 (1953): 307–21; Shepperson, "The Free Church and American Slavery," *Scottish Historical Review* 30 (October 1951): 126–43.

55. Gerald Fulkerson, "Exile as Emergence: Frederick Douglass in Great Britain, 1845–1847," *Quarterly Journal of Speech* 60 (February 1974): 71.

56. Ralph Varian to the editor, Cork, Ireland, 4 November 1845, *Inquirer,* 15 November 1845, p. 724; "Farewell Soiree to F. Douglass," *Inquirer,* 3 March 1847, p. 219.

57. "Frederick Douglas and the Anti-Slavery Movement," *Inquirer,* 3 April 1847, pp. 209–10; "Prejudice of Colour," *Inquirer,* 10 April 1847, p. 226; "Frederick Douglass," ibid., pp. 228–29; "Pirates and Mobs in America," *Inquirer,* 15 June 1850, p. 370.

58. R. L. Carpenter, "Douglass's Bondage," p. 295.

59. Mary Carpenter to Frederick Douglass, Bridport, 22 April n.y.; Mary Carpenter to Frederick Douglass, Bridport, 8 June n.y.; Russell Lant Carpenter to Frederick Douglass, n.p.d., n.d.; Frederick Douglass Papers, Library of Congress.

60. Russell Lant Carpenter to the editor, Bridgwater, 3 August [1847], *Inquirer,* 14 August 1847, p. 522; Carpenter to the editor, Halifax, 12 December 1859, *Inquirer,* 17 December 1859, p. 1146; Frederick Douglass, *Life and Times of Frederick Douglass Written by Himself* (Hartford, Conn.: Park Publishing Co., 1882), pp. 324, 330–31.

61. George Armstrong, "American Slavery—The Late Discussion on the Boston Invitation," *Christian Reformer* 3 (July 1847): 427; Mary Carpenter to Maria Weston Chapman, Bristol, 1 April n.y Weston Papers, MB; "American Slavery, Correspondence between the Reverend George Armstrong and Mr. Frederick Douglass," *Inquirer,* 26 September 1846, p. 620; William Lloyd Garrison to John B. Estlin, London, 8 September 1846, Walter M. Merrill, ed., *Letters of William Lloyd Garrison* (Cambridge, Mass.: The Belknap Press of Harvard University Press, 1973), 3:400; George Armstrong to Frederick Douglass, Clifton-vale, Bristol, 17 January 1847, *Inquirer,* 6 February 1847, p. 92; Douglass's break with the Garrisonians has been well documented. See, for example, William H. Pease and Jane H. Pease, "Boston Garrisonians and the Problem of Frederick Douglass," *Canadian Journal of History* 2 (September 1967): 29–48. See also Maria Weston Chapman to [Harriet Beecher Stowe], Weymouth, 5 February [1858], Beecher-Stowe Papers, Schlesinger Library, Radcliffe College.

62. John Bishop Estlin to Samuel May, Jr., Bristol, 2 May 1851, Taylor, *British and American Abolitionists,* p. 377; May to Estlin, Leicester, 26 February 1846, Taylor, *British and American Abolitionists,* p. 255; Brown, *Sketches of Places and People Abroad,* pp. 304–5.

63. Mary Estlin to Maria Weston Chapman, Bristol, September, 1846; J. B. Estlin to Samuel May, Bristol, 12 January 1847; J. B. Estlin to May, Bristol, 2 May 1851; Taylor, *British and American Abolitionists,* pp. 282, 305, 377–78.

64. John Bishop Estlin to Maria Weston Chapman, Bristol, 9 December 1853, Wes-

190 British Unitarians against American Slavery, 1833–65

ton Papers, MB: [John Bishop Estlin], *A Brief Notice of American Slavery and the Abolition Movement* (Bristol: H. C. Evans, 1846), pp. 11–13.

65. Howard Temperley, *British Antislavery 1833–1870* (London: Longman Group Ltd., 1972), p. 231; "Minutes of the Bristol and Clifton Ladies Anti-Slavery Society," entry for 15 August 1859, Estlin Papers, LDW; Sarah P. Remond to the editor, 4 December 1859, *Inquirer*, 10 December 1859, p. 1125. See also above, chapter 6, n. 64.

66. "Anti-Slavery Meeting at Manchester," *Inquirer*, 21 January 1860, p. 57; "Coloured Passengers and the Cunard Ships," *Inquirer*, 7 July 1860, p. 574; "The Prejudice of Colour," *Inquirer*, 14 July 1860, pp. 586–87.

8

Fratricidal War: Censuring America's Second Revolution—1861–65.

The Wars between North and South and Old and New England Begin—1861

Given their aversion to American racial prejudice and their anxiety over the corrupting influence of the "United States of Slavery," the attitude of British Unitarians toward the two sides in America's Civil War was predictable—they cursed both houses.[1] Of course, there were some who publicly favored the North and a few the South, but the general feeling in the denomination was a neutrality of contempt for both sides. Whether North or South gained victory mattered little; most believed that America's curse would continue to thrive. The task of those who favored the North, mostly the Garrisonians, was to show that the policies of the federal government tended toward emancipation. The task of Southern sympathizers was to show that Southern independence meant the isolation and withering away of slavery. Neither side was very successful and Unitarians changed from an attitude of neutrality and disinterest to partisanship only after the Union's victory, Lincoln's assassination, and Congress's constitutional amendment to abolish slavery in 1865.

Victors are normally guaranteed an accession of belated allies and the North found a profusion of supporters at the end of the war. Contemporaries of the conflict and historians who followed it fabricated a mythology that extolled the wonderful support given the Union cause by the British people, particularly the working classes. Anyone who had opposed the North's "war of emancipation" was certainly a member of the aristocracy.[2] Even the Unitarians were praised by denominational and secular historians alike for their sympathy for the Northern side.[3] Recently, demythologizing has proceeded at a rapid pace. Current investigations have shown that personal opinion among English conservatives and aristocrats was sharply divided on the issue of the American war and that their public policy was largely uniform—a strict neutrality that could not help but aid the North.[4] England's largest market outside of Europe being the United States, the managers and merchants of the middle classes saw commercial preservation dependent upon neutrality.[5] Among the working classes, universal and unshakable support either for the North or the South did not exist. In the case of the Lancashire cotton operatives, economic hardship correlated with their desire for an early cessation of the war, and only in some local instances with their desire for Confederate victories that would restore Britain's cotton supply.[6] Several researchers have proclaimed the "new" discovery that actually opinions and allegiances varied among all classes and political and philosophical persuasions in Britain.[7] But James Martineau made this observation at the time of the conflict: proponents of both sides were found in every class. Still, dedicated partisans were few, he declared; the English people held to a "general neutrality" and viewed the war with "impartial sorrow."[8]

It was symbolic that at almost the same time that South Carolina passed its ordinance of secession in December 1860, a Canadian court handed down a judgment against William Anderson, a fugitive slave. In his flight to Canada, Anderson had slain a white man in the slave state of Missouri. Under treaty with the United States, Canada was required to extradite him to his master and to certain death. His case incensed the English abolitionists. "For the first time," Russell Carpenter wrote, "English law [had] been made to serve the purposes of American lawlessness." Anderson was "a hero," he declared, and "under no circumstances" ought England to surrender him or any slave who sought her protection. The Anderson case confirmed the warnings of the 1850s by Carpenter and the Garrisonians. America's curse had corrupted England and a slave such as Anderson, breathing free English air, remained enslaved.[9] Symbolically, the secession of South Carolina separated slavery from the North at the very time that the slave power had contaminated English soil. Lasting protection of the Northern states and Great Britain from slavery could be achieved by letting the South go—just as the Garrisonians had suggested for so many years. Mary Carpenter congratulated James Freeman Clarke that the disintegration of the Union had begun. Before, the North had "disgracefully" been a "*partaker*" of slavery and racism. Now it could be free. "How marvelously [did] the Father order the course of the universe."[10]

South Carolina was followed by ten other states to form ultimately the Confederate States of America. Lincoln, in his inaugural address on the fourth of March 1861, assured the slave states that he contemplated no interference with their slavery, but that he could not countenance secession. He would employ no violence, unless it was "forced upon the national authority." That violence erupted when the Confederate shore batteries began firing upon Fort Sumter, the federal fort situated in the harbor of Charleston. On 13 April 1861 the installation was surrendered. Two days later Lincoln called for 75,000 volunteers to put down the rebellion, and on 19 April decreed a naval blockade of all Southern ports. This halted foreign trade with the South and strangled the supply of cotton to Britain. On 21 May, Queen Victoria issued a Proclamation of Neutrality, which forbade any participation in the American conflict by British subjects. Her proclamation was severely criticized in the American newspapers, but Samuel May, Jr., liked it. He felt a "great confidence in the sympathy of the *British people*" in support of the North's war against the "Seceding Slaveholders & slavetraders."[11]

It was a confidence misplaced, however, for it became very quickly apparent that British support was shallow indeed. The *Inquirer* was at first sympathetic and declared in January 1861 that the North had every right to oppose the "armed violence of the South" rather than to face "political suicide." But in a few months, the conduct of the Northern states had cooled its sympathy: the North had told the South that slavery need not fear Northern interference. At the BFUA annual meeting in May, James Stansfeld, M.P., told his fellow Unitarians that their duty as a people had to be "an absolute neutrality." He contemplated the forthcoming "cost in sufferings and loss of life . . . [with] horror and dismay."[12] By the summer, the *Inquirer* and the *Unitarian Herald,* a new denominational newspaper, began to be censorious of the North. The former carried weekly news of the American conflict and both maintained columns by American correspondents. Unitarians, therefore, had full coverage of the political, social, and military cost of the war and many deplored what they read. That the American Garrisonians jettisoned their peace principles and embraced the war saddened them.[13] That American Unitarian leaders labeled the conflict a "holy war" and an event "in essence religious" shocked them.[14] That Lincoln and the North pursued the war to preserve the Union rather than to destroy slavery angered them. "The strength of the Union," declared the *Unitarian Herald,* had "for years been devoted to girding the fetters of the slave more tightly." The paper could not now lend "enthusiastic sympathy" to a war for union; it had sympathy only for a "struggle for liberty."[15]

Great Britain's general lack of sympathy for the North and her policy of neutrality were unacceptable to American Unitarians. Their denomination was absolutely committed to the war effort. The American Unitarian Association distributed to Union servicemen over 800,000 religious tracts, song books, and handbooks. Proportionately, the denomination had more chaplains in the field than any other religious body. Over fifty minister served the North as chaplains, several fought as officers, and some led Negro troops. One prominent Unitarian minister remarked that his denomination supported Lincoln and the war in a way unequaled by any other Christian body.[16]

Any group that exerted this much effort in behalf of the Union cause could only object strenuously to any criticism of their president and their nation. In sermons and articles they accused England of giving the South her "only ray of hope." England's confounded neutrality, exclaimed William Henry Furness (1802–96) of the Unitarian Church in Philadelphia, was a "neutrality between Freedom and Bondage!" In order to get cotton, he continued, she claimed "to be neither for God nor for the Devil."[17] The Reverend William Henry Channing (1810–84), an American who served an English Unitarian congregation, became a self-appointed propagandist for the North's fight against a "barbarous anarchy." He outlined the Northern cause in a hundred-page tract subtitled "The Slaveholders' Conspiracy." Anxious to participate directly in his country's "holy war," he left England and took charge of the Unitarian church in Washington. The chasm between British and American Unitarian thinking on the war had become so wide that James Martineau cancelled a proposed trip to the United States. Any comment, he declared, that he could offer Americans on their great struggle would be a "profane Impertinence."[18]

Although the supporters of the British and Foreign Anti-Slavery Society early lent their aid to Lincoln and the North, the British antislavery forces generally were ill-prepared to rise to the opportunities arising out of the American war. In 1861, the Garrisonians were at their weakest. The London Emancipation Committee, founded by George Thompson, was but a phantom. The Hibernian Anti-Slavery Society consisted mainly of James Haughton and Richard D. Webb, and the former's anti-Northern views interrupted for the duration his lifelong friendships with the American Garrisonians. The Bristol and Clifton Ladies' Anti-Slavery Society met for the last time in 1861. The Liverpool Anti-Slavery League, Steinthal's local organizational effort, was too weak to sponsor an antislavery lecture. The tottering *Anti-Slavery Advocate* could not decide to back the North until September 1862, and died eight months later.[19] Typically, the Garrisonian position on the war had to be presented by individuals, and as individuals each viewed it differently. Philip Carpenter was disturbed by Lincoln's truckling to the border slave states to keep them in the Union. His sister Mary disliked the Northern "Union worshippers" and confessed she could never trust the Americans again until they freed the slaves. Haughton held anti-North views because the region "detested the coloured people," and he saw "the dissolution of the misnamed Union" as a blessing. This kind of talk angered and frustrated Samuel May, Jr., and he wrote his cousin, Samuel J. May, in December 1861, that England's anti-slavery feeling had apparently "oozed out in [the] Remonstrances and Rebukes" sent to America.[20] May's chastisement was directed generally at the English people, not particularly at his old Garrisonian friends, but he was aware that their "backsliding" contributed to the general public opinion. Happily, he could find solace in the support offered by other Garrisonians: Solly, William Shaen, Mary Estlin, Bishop, Steinthal, and Harriet Martineau. Martineau was said to have done much more than anyone else "to uphold the northern cause in England," more than George Thompson and the pro-North politicians, John Bright and Richard Cobden, "rolled into one." Actually, Garrisonians such as she provided the only consistent support for the Union among the Unitarians. "But with few exceptions," Steinthal remarked, the old British Garrisonians were loyal to the North.[21]

It was a loyalty, however, that was severely tested when a crisis exploded between Great Britain and the United States in November and December 1861. A Union warship, the U.S.S.

San Jacinto, commanded by Captain Charles Wilkes, halted the British steamer *Trent* and forcibly removed James M. Mason and John Slidell, Confederate commissioners en route to Europe. Wilkes was hailed as a hero in the North, but his action created an alarming war fever in England. Harriet Martineau, as British correspondent of the *National Anti-Slavery Standard,* strongly condemned the *Trent* affair and drew the wrath of the paper's readers. A bellicose Samuel May told an Irish friend that, if the English wanted war, they could have it. But cooler tempers prevailed. Maria Weston Chapman agreed that Wilkes's conduct was impetuous, illegal, and a mistake. Abolitionists such as Haughton and conservatives such as Martineau both tried to dampen the war hysteria. Eventually, Lincoln's common sense, the gracious diplomacy of the Prince Consort, and the friendly intervention of John Bright and Richard Cobden brought about the release of Mason and Slidell, thus avoiding an Anglo-American war.[22]

Britain's Workers and America's Slaves: The Cotton Crisis and Emancipation—1862–63

If an Anglo-American war had been averted, the Civil War in America and the contest for British sympathy and support continued unabated. The war went badly for the North in both the areas of public opinion and military operations. Lincoln and his government were plagued with the question of emancipation and to complicate the issue, two Union generals, John C. Frémont and David Hunter, ordered all slaves within their military jurisdictions emancipated. Lincoln countermanded their orders, preferring that his generals win battles rather than emancipate slaves, but victories by the Union forces were few. They were routed in the first major battle of the war at Manassas Junction, Virginia, July 1861. In Tennessee, in 1862, after victories at Fort Donelson and Fort Henry in February, they suffered heavy losses at the Battle of Shiloh in April. From March through June, they were unable to overcome the brilliant generalship of "Stonewall" Jackson, in his masterful campaign in Virginia's Shenandoah Valley. Under pressure from Jackson and General Robert E. Lee, they were hard pressed to defend the federal capital. At the end of June, they suffered heavy casualties in a week-long clash with Confederate forces on the Virginia Peninsula. Although the Union forces claimed a victory, they did not press their advantage and Lee's army escaped to fight again. In a second battle at Manassas, in August, the federal troops were again defeated and fled in full retreat to Washington. The survival of the Union was precarious.

Early in 1862, the *Inquirer* complained about how badly the war was going for the North and how shrill the American response to English criticism was becoming. Its remarks were indiscreet: it termed the Confederacy a "great nation . . . struggling for independent power in opposition to the aggression of the North." These audacious remarks thoroughly piqued conservative Unitarian minister George E. Ellis of Charlestown, Massachusetts, and he accused the newspaper of being "as ignorant as a child" regarding the facts of the war.[23] America was faced with dismemberment and fought to survive as a nation. Britain would have acted no differently if faced with internal revolt. The *Christian Register* commented cynically: the American war was "of course wholly wrong in the eyes of the British press, because it impoverish[ed] their cotton spinners," and prevented "the disruption of [the] powerful Union, a confessedly formidable rival. No war could be right which did that."[24]

Public comment on the American war was frequently connected with expressions of concern for the poverty and distress that emerged out of the "Cotton Crisis." Economic distress was most acute in 1862 and depression in Lancashire and Cheshire lingered until the late summer and fall of 1863. Many Unitarians were involved in a Manchester relief organization that served 5,000 cases a week in 1862. During one week in November of that year, 431,395 persons applied for relief in the whole of the distressed manufacturing districts.[25] In Manchester, John Relly Beard and his wife, Mary, organized sewing classes for a hundred girls, fed them, and taught them to read and to write. Moreover, they sponsored a soup kitchen that fed more than a hundred families a week. In Gee Cross, their son, Charles, worked with an interdenominational relief committee that included Church of England and Roman Catholic representatives. He had also under his personal care some twenty-five families.[26] John Relly Beard was one of the principals of a Unitarian relief committee that tried to meet the physical needs of "the poor Lancashire lads and lasses."[27] At the annual spring meeting of the BFUA in May 1863, a fund was established to meet their spiritual needs.[28] Both the *Inquirer* and the *Unitarian Herald* publicized the wants of the distressed and the projects created to help them.[29]

Naturally, such hardship and taxing of denominational resources could be expected to elicit a call from Unitarians for Great Britain either to end her neutrality or to intervene directly in the American conflict. However, this did not occur. Dr. Beard in his initial report on the Lancashire populace, in November 1861, admitted that their plight was the result of America's "unnecessary," "blameable," and "insane" war. But he conceded that the guilt of the war fell on their shoulders as well:

> In social life we are all members one of another. Even in the misdeeds of others we have a share—it may be with, or it may be against our will. Certainly it is the spindles of Manchester that have filled the slave market of New Orleans. The same influence has deadened our moral sentiments to the atrocity of holding property in human beings, and in so doing have silenced our tongues when they ought to have been loud and constant in protesting against a wrong, baneful, not less to the slaves than to the masters. No wonder, then, that we are in peril. We have shared the crime, and must not expect to escape without sharing the punishment.

A year later, he extolled the opportunities created by the crisis. In a nationally circulated sermon, *The Cotton Crisis,* he urged the church to come forward as "a fellow-worker with the State," and become a vehicle for social justice. There was nowhere a call by Beard to depart from his country's position of neutrality.[30]

Neither did such a call come from John Hamilton Thom (1808–94). In a sermon entitled *Distress in the Manufacturing Districts,* the Liverpool minister declared that their "National Righteousness" and "duty to the American People" compelled them "to maintain the conditions" that prolonged their sufferings. He praised the patience and reasonableness of the distressed factory operatives,

> and though Southern sympathizers have been busy among them, expecting cold and hunger to make ready tools, they have been found deliberately opposed to Intervention. . . . These men are among us the Vindicators of the National sentiment, the true martyrs of human Freedom.

In the Lancashire area, the Beards and the Reverend James C. Street in Manchester; Steinthal, Thom, and the Unitarian laymen, the Rathbones, in Liverpool; Howorth in Bury; and

Philip Carpenter in Warrington opposed any departure from Great Britain's policy of neutrality.[31]

The solitary public voice among Unitarians for recognition of the Confederacy was a minister who lived for a short time in the distressed areas—John Page Hopps (1834–1911). Until 1864, he served Upper Chapel, Sheffield, Yorkshire, and during the last year of the war, at the Old Chapel, in Dukinfield, Cheshire. He was only twenty-seven years old at the start of the Civil War and he defended the cause of Southern independence with youthful, hardheaded impetuosity. He claimed to be an abolitionist who deplored Northern procrastination on emancipation, and a servant of peace who despised war for any reason. In 1863, at the great pro-Confederate rally in Sheffield, he revealed his intense commitment to the South by moving to obtain England's acknowledgment of the Confederacy's independence. He shared the podium at the rally with John Arthur Roebuck, the Southerners' champion in the House of Commons. Tenaciously, Hopps clung to the recognition of the Confederacy as the means to end America's "unjust," "useless," and "shameful" war. He continued to preach this idea as late as September 1864.[32] His fellow Unitarians and the English press in general strongly disagreed with his stand.[33] Neither could many British citizens agree to the sale of warships to the Confederacy. With the exception of James Martineau, who believed it to be just for England to sell to both sides in the American conflict, Unitarians opposed the outfitting of vessels for the Confederate navy.[34]

During the midsummer of 1862 Lincoln had become convinced that a presidential proclamation of emancipation was essential for the survival of the Union. He took the favorable occasion of Lee's reversal at the battle of Antietam to issue on 22 September his preliminary proclamation. On 1 January 1863, slaves in the rebellious states and parts of the states still in Confederate hands would be "then, thenceforward, and forever free." Hopps ridiculed the president's document as "an instrument of terror . . . in the hands of desperate men." The BFASS seized the opportunity to distribute thousands of copies of an address encouraging Lincoln on emancipation. The *Inquirer* was unimpressed with this initial stage of the proclamation and it continued to maintain its anti-Union position. In two editorials in October and November 1862, it held that the continuance of the Union was *"impossible and undesirable."* Both Bishop and Steinthal in letters to the *Inquirer* praised the preliminary proclamation. It pained Steinthal deeply that his denomination had not "unanimously expressed sympathy with the righteous cause which [lay] at the root of the great [American] struggle."[35]

When the Emancipation Proclamation took effect on 1 January 1863, its reception by Unitarians varied widely. Maria Weston Chapmen exclaimed to Mary Estlin: "Hosanna! Hallelujah! Te deum! Jubilate!" The *Inquirer* suggested that Unitarians ought to rejoice over the North's "repentance." Edmund Kell felt that they now could shout, "All hail to President Lincoln!" Others were not so ecstatic. Russell Carpenter told Frederick Douglass that the horrors of the war dampened the rapture he felt for emancipation.[36] Jerom Murch and James Martineau doubted that the proclamation was either wise or just. The latter felt his opinion was possibly shared by all of England's "most experienced and high-minded men of affairs, including the anti-slavery leaders themselves." He wrote to an American correspondent:

> The removal of slavery is, . . . no proper *object* of a war. . . . It is pre-eminently a work of peace; needing deliberation, time, and organized vigilance and control: and to inaugurate it in the heat and haste of conflict, to impose it as a military penalty, . . . is to do all that is possible to make it hateful and hopeless. . . . The proclamation of Lincoln . . . if I mistake not, has had upon our responsible men of action a deeper and more unfavorable effect than any incident since the beginning of the struggle.[37]

Martineau had been mistaken. Overall, the proclamation had a good effect upon the North's standing in Great Britain.[38]

Comic Relief: The Conway-Mason Imbroglio—1863.

In the spring of 1863, an American abolitionist of Southern birth arrived in England "to lecture and persuade the English that the North [was] right." He carried letters from Garrison that recommended him as an "uncompromising and earnest abolitionist." Such a witness "against slavery and the rebellion" had not yet stood before British audiences, and Garrison thought he could help the antislavery cause. The abolitionist was the Reverend Moncure Daniel Conway (1832–1907), formerly minister of the Unitarian churches in Washington and

Cincinnati. He had made an impressive pilgrimage from being a Methodist lay preacher and heir to an estate of slaves in Virginia to being a Unitarian abolitionist ambassador to England. His terrestrial pilgrimage stopped for a generation in England, but his spiritual quest continued until even Unitarianism proved too confining for his fiercely independent nature. Neither did Garrisonianism satisfy him as the ultimate in righteous abolitionism and he soon isolated himself from "militant America" and her sword-bearing abolitionists.[39]

Conway, an inveterate name-dropper, suffered from recurring attacks of megalomania. He possessed a facile pen and an unrelenting intellectual curiosity. European sophisticates admired his "Virginia valour" as the French had Benjamin Franklin's coonskin cap. He took advantage of the invitations to the drawing rooms of the elite, which a letter of introduction in those times secured.[40] His story here is simply a comical interlude. Modern historians have ignored, or have refused to accept, his own measure of his contribution to discrediting the Confederate cause in England and France. The most comprehensive study of "Anglo-American Antislavery Cooperation" fails to mention his name.[41]

Conway was essentially an intellectual journalist and was in fact employed by the Boston *Commonwealth* at the time of his antislavery mission to England. In the beginning all went well for him, as he brandished his letters of introduction and kept in tow a life-sized bust of John Brown, a gift for Victor Hugo. He charmed the women of the London Ladies' Emancipation Society, and was promptly, to use his words, "raised to the dignity of an 'emissary.'" He sympathized with the English disdain for the Union cause. "Why . . . [ought] Englishmen," he asked, to "feel any interest in a murderous struggle to preserve a Union which American antislavery men had for years tried to dissolve?" Yet he claimed two-thirds of the English literati espoused the Northern cause. He soon found that he was preaching to the already converted. Antislavery activity was the province of Dissenting preachers, he recorded, and their meetings were held in Dissenting chapels. Their movement was conventicular. In Conway's opinion it somehow had to broaden its influence.[42]

The Confederate commissioner, James M. Mason, a fellow Virginian, was also in England trying to secure the diplomatic recognition of the South. Conway hit upon the foolish, albeit daring idea of challenging the Confederate emissary on the point of emancipation. With reckless abandon, he wrote to Mason on June 10 that he had the "authority . . . on behalf of the leading antislavery men of America" to trade abolitionist opposition to the further prosecution of the war for emancipation of the slaves in the Confederate States. Since the abolitionists held "the balance of power" in the United States government, their action would "certainly cause the war to cease." Mason replied the following day and asked Conway for "evidence" of his right to make such an offer. Not dismayed, Conway answered that he would "write out to America and obtain the [needed] evidence." Mason, in a stinging reply, told him not to bother. He had fully realized all along that Conway's proposal was preposterous and, he declared, the North would never be in a position to bargain with the South over the question of emancipation. He then turned the correspondence over to the London *Times*. It produced a sensational outcry, and Conway admitted that it embarrassed his English abolitionist friends a good deal. His American friends were not only embarrassed, they were enraged. "To think of the abominable *conceit,* in the first place," Sam May exploded, "of his assumption of the office of an Envoy! and then of the *audacity* of recognizing [the Rebel] Mason . . . !" He thought it was "insufferable that . . . the Anti-Slavery Cause [had] to bear the burden of such transparent stupidity and conceit." Most abolitionists believed Conway had made a fool of himself. He went "for wool," snapped May, "and came away shorn."[43]

Conway tried to salvage his reputation by means of a public confession in the *Times*. He had acted alone, he explained, without the blessings of the abolitionists and was inexperienced in "diplomatic and political affairs." But in his own "blundering way," he boasted, he had forced Mason to admit that every "gateway" to emancipation "except that of war [was] closed." Conway also confessed to the American ambassador, Charles Francis Adams, and for penance he sent an apology to Lincoln and Seward, which was accepted.[44]

For all practical purposes, his antislavery mission in England was at an end. Eventually, he accepted the pulpit of the South Place Society, London, and wrote for a number of American and British newspapers and magazines. He had no faith in the Union and could not promote the continuance of the war even to secure emancipation. He sharply attacked Lincoln and berated Charles Sumner for the senator's attacks on England. It was likely that his loyalties had really always remained with the

Southern people. He advocated disunion with emancipation until March 1865, a month before the war's end. His imbroglio with Mason probably made him feel somewhat reluctant to return home. His antislavery mission to England was intended to last a few months. He stayed thirty years.[45]

The War Drags On—1863–64

In 1863, the Confederacy experienced a number of devastating reverses. In May, Lee and Jackson trounced the Union forces at Chancellorsville, but the battle proved to be the South's costliest victory, for Jackson was accidentally killed by his own men. In July, two great battles occurred, one in the West at Vicksburg, Mississippi, and another in the East, at Gettysburg, Pennsylvania. Both were Confederate defeats. The casualties at Gettysburg were frightful; together, the two sides lost 7,000 men killed and over 40,000 wounded. Confederate defeats at Vicksburg and Gettysburg crushed any hope that the South continued to hold for European recognition and intervention. At the end of 1863 the Mississippi valley was securely in Union hands and the year 1864 was spent in wearing down Lee's army in the East. While Ulysses S. Grant hammered away at Lee's tired troops, Philip H. Sheridan turned the rich Shenandoah Valley in Virginia into a wasteland that could not provision a crow, and William T. Sherman burned and desolated a swath through Georgia on his "march to the sea." Sherman took Savannah at the end of December 1864, as a "Christmas-gift" for Lincoln. The president had only recently been reelected in a tough campaign in which defeatism and the war-weariness of the Northern people were major issues. Although the total surrender of the Confederacy was a few months away, the war seemed endless.

During 1863 and 1864 as the frightful news of the war's slaughter and destruction filtered across the Atlantic, British Unitarians, like so many of their fellow citizens, debated incessantly the war's cause, continuation, and possible outcome. As to its cause, most Unitarians believed it to be slavery. It was, taught Kell, "clear as noon-day that the Southern States . . . rushed into the horrors of war for the sole object of living on other men's unrequited labour."[46] The Reverend Robert Spears (1825–99) of Stamford Street Chapel, London, declared that the only reason the "rebel chiefs" resorted to arms was because "slavery was in danger." Spears had four nephews fighting for the Union side and he saw them destroying a rebellion whose cornerstone was slavery.[47] Not so, countered opponents of the North. The South was fighting, cried a Unitarian minister in Preston, Lancashire, "not for SLAVERY but for INDEPENDENCE." Others, including James Haughton, concurred. They declared that the right of self-determination gave the South as much justification to rebel as the American colonies had to rebel against England.[48] The bulk of the Garrisonians and other Northern supporters condemned this idea as sheer nonsense. The South always had self-government, taught Spears. There were many pro-Unionists in the South, explained Bishop; the South in fact had not been united on secession. Besides, he declared, "the right of secession would, indeed, render stable government impossible." It was "irrational" to believe, remarked a partially converted *Inquirer*, that the federal government could have tolerated "the loss of half its power." And the newspaper now declared with certainty "that Slavery was the cause of the war and that Slavery depend[ed] upon its issue."[49]

In the argument over the war's genesis, most accepted the view that slavery had indeed been its cause. But given the justice of the North in resisting its own dismemberment by trying to annul a secession movement spawned by slavery, could the continuation of the war with its enormous cost in human suffering be justified? James Martineau said no. The North's right "to vindicate its authority and property [was] unimpeachable," but to prolong a war so unlikely to obtain success was to go against "nature and Providence." Sir John Bowring, a consistent critic of the North, believed that the South could never be subjugated by Northern arms. Hatred between the two regions, he maintained, could never be reconciled, so why prolong the slaughter? Kell, Spears, and Bishop marveled at Great Britain censuring another nation's war. England was always ready, Kell reminded the North's opponents, to "unsheathe the sword" on the most "doubtful occasions." Great Britain's "abusive language" against the North, preached Spears, ill became a nation that fought "so many battles against the natives of foreign lands." Bishop liked to recall Great Britain's treatment of Ireland and India whenever he heard criticism of the North's suppression of an "independence movement."[50] Their continual advocacy of the North's belligerence gained these men the designation "priests of Mars."[51] Their arguments with their opponents in letters to the *Inquirer* became so numerous and so heated that the newspaper refused to continue to publish them.[52]

In the minds of Garrisonians Steinthal and Bishop the fact that day by day the war hastened freedom for America's blacks justified its continuance. Steinthal lamented the bloodshed caused by the war, but he could not comprehend the heaping of criticism upon the North. How could anyone, Bishop asked, call the South's position a "gallant struggle for freedom" in any sense except freedom to enslave and to oppress?[53] Why could the North's critics not realize, Bishop demanded, that it was a "holy war" to stop the South's "bold and blasphemous attempt to fight against the laws of God [and] to turn back the tide of civilization and Christianity?" Americans such as Samuel J. May and William Henry Furness continued to believe that the answer lay in the "aristocratic biases" of the English ruling class. It had an "enmity to democratic institutions" and was jealous of America's growth and prosperity.[54] Howorth believed this. He saw a "miserable jealousy" of the United States that led many Englishmen to desire its dismemberment.[55] Although the *Inquirer* consistently attributed its censure of the North to its abhorrence of war, it did not conceal its apprehension over the growing power of the United States nor its near delight that America had "become a spectacle of pity to the effete monarchies it was to regenerate."[56]

A fairly common expression of opposition to the North that both embellished Britain's own superiority and at the same time damaged the credibility of the federal cause was to attack Northern racism. How could they support the North when its law permitted blacks to suffer "the greatest indignity" on public conveyances and at public places, and to be even cast out from churches?[57] They had to give the North time, answered Kell; prejudice was rooted in slavery and when slavery was uprooted, prejudice would wither. Union supporters such as Kell did not understate the intensity of Northern racism. They always spoke in terms of its future resolution and how much better freedom with prejudice was in the North compared to slavery in the South. Bishop reminded critics of the North that black fugitives fled only in one direction.[58] Unitarians warmly discussed this subject to the end of the war.[59]

As the Union began to achieve military victories, supporters of the Union in Great Britain began to achieve propaganda victories. In the early summer of 1863, 750 French Protestant pastors exhorted their fellow ministers in Great Britain "to speak strongly against American slavery, and especially against the attempt now being made by the Southern States to make slavery the basis of their Government." Over 4,000 ministers in Great Britain complied by issuing an appropriate antislavery protest. Among the many Unitarian signers were James, Bishop, Crosskey, Kell, Spears, Russell Carpenter, John Scott Porter, J. J. Tayler, and John Hamilton Thom.[60]

Also helpful to Union partisans in Great Britain was William Henry Channing's two-month speaking tour of England and Scotland in the fall of 1863. Channing, who had turned his Washington church into a hospital for wounded soldiers, had been appointed chaplain to the House of Representatives. Because of his standing in the federal government and because he was the nephew of his denomination's most adored and honored leader, Channing was the best pro-Union spokesman American Unitarians could have sent. At a large gathering in the Concert Hall in Liverpool, he talked about the American war being governed by "Divine Providence." He told of his support for the enlistment of Negro troops and reported that four of his cousins were Union officers of Negro regiments. He testified that emancipation was progressing smoothly.[61] He repeated his patriotic message to large rallies in Leeds, Manchester, and Edinburgh.[62] His speaking tour pleased immensely Edmund Kell and other pro-Northern advocates.[63] But his tour, and his later statements from America praising his country's "holy war," stimulated numerous, and usually anonymous, letters of protest against "Channing the preacher of war."[64] The *Inquirer* also had difficulty with Channing's divine self-assurance. It was amazed that by some wondrous means Channing had learned "the purpose of the Almighty."[65]

In 1863, British antislavery support of the North was at its height. George Thompson claimed that by the end of that year most towns and cities in Great Britain had a branch on the order of the London Emancipation Society, a revitalized metamorphosis of his London Emancipation Committee.[66] No longer a distinctly Garrisonian organization, the society now included in its membership "some of the best men of the country, without distinction of sect or party."[67] Its elite committee of John Bright, Richard Cobden, John Stuart Mill, Herbert Spencer, and others made it a formidable agency for pro-Northern propaganda. In the society and others like it, members of the BFASS and Garrisonians were able to overcome past differences to work together.[68] The Manchester Union and Emancipation Society, whose founder and president was Unitarian merchant Thomas Bayley Potter (1817–98), also intensified its activities during 1863. Potter had established the organization in Manchester in 1861 and contributed over £5,000 to its continued operation. Unitarians were prominent among its leadership: Bishop, Crosskey, William Shaen, and Professor Francis W. Newman (1805–97) were only a few of the Unitarians who served the organization as vice-presidents. Newman also was active on the committee of the London Emancipation Society.[69] In opposition to the pro-North organizations stood the Southern Independence Association, which, the *Inquirer* recorded, a few Unitarian laymen and ministers were gullible enough to join. The association could not possibly duplicate the massive and elaborate rallies held by the pro-Northern groups.[70] Essentially those groups sought expressions of support for non-intervention and emancipation, whereas supporters of the South sought intervention and ignored emancipation. The vigorous activity of the friends of the North and the warm cooperation demonstrated among the abolitionists improved the image of the Garrisonians. Harriet Martineau wrote in the fall of 1864 that the British people were beginning to revere the Garrisonians for helping to bring about America's "national repentance" and emancipation.[71]

A Martyred President, A Freed People, A Redeemed Nation—1865

As the Confederacy collapsed in the early months of 1865, a realignment of loyalties on the war took place in Britain. This was to be expected. Consistent critics of the North became its "summer friends." There was no joy in backing a loser. Unitarians who had been caustic opponents of the North became repentant, especially after the tragic event of Lincoln's assassination. John Page Hopps lingered as a proponent of Southern independence. "Love [was] sometimes blind," quipped the *Inquirer*. But even Hopps confessed his sins upon Lincoln's death. A certain ambivalence plagued the *Inquirer* as it reported the Confederacy's fall. It greeted emancipation in the slave state of Missouri as an event that was witness "to the truth that God reign[ed] on the earth," but in an editorial on the fall of Richmond, it waxed eloquent on the South's courage in defending her "native land from invaders."[72] It pleaded for mercy for the captured Confederate president, and could not denounce him for trying to found an independent nation.[73] The *Inquirer* believed (having mastered Channing's magic of knowing "the purpose of the Almighty") "that Providence, more than the Northern armies or Northern patriotism," had defeated the South.[74]

These remarks Northern Americans could only find offensive, and they diminished any positive effect produced by the *Inquirer's* expression of sympathy on the death of Lincoln. The president had been shot by a Confederate on 14 April 1865 and had died the following day. The newspaper eulogized him as "one of the greatest and best of [the] earth's rulers." It saw in his martyrdom perhaps a "providential method" of initiating a "new reign of brotherhood in America." That "reign of brotherhood" took a long time to arrive in America, but the event of Lincoln's assassination did help to begin to restore the friendly or familial feeling between American and British Unitarians. Generally, British Unitarian statements on the president's death appeared to express genuine grief, compassion, and repentance. Unitarian ministers delivered memorial sermons in Liverpool, London, Manchester, Birmingham, Bradford, Leeds, Chesterfield, Bridport, Banbury, Southampton, and many other places.[75] Several of the sermons were later printed.[76] John Page Hopps was but one longtime opponent of the North who expressed his sorrow over Lincoln's death. At a large meeting in Stalybridge, he went so far as to move a resolution of sympathy with the North. Other Unitarian critics of the North experienced a corresponding change of heart. Conway regretted his harsh words against Lincoln. Haughton helped to secure an address of condolence to the American people from the citizens of Dublin.[77] Five to six thousand people packed St. George's Hall in Liverpool, "the head-quarters of the Southern Confederacy in England," and unanimously passed a motion of sympathy proposed by William Rathbone and two fellow Unitarians. Unitarian participation at the Liverpool meeting pleased the *Inquirer*. There all the "grandeur of English integrity" beamed, but most important was the ecumenical nature of the meeting, where "Romanists, Trinitarians, and Unitarians ceased to be representatives of sects, and rose into the higher realm of practical Christianity."[78] The change of heart exhibited by the Unitarians was generally displayed by the British nation as a whole. All the "old hostile, and pro-confederate journals," Mary Estlin told an American Garrisonian, "have attempted to bury their harsh words." The British people were proceeding to be, the *Inquirer* asserted, almost one in their "universal devotion to Union and Emancipation." This "deathbed" repentance sickened Steinthal. In a strongly worded sermon he held pro-Confederate sympathizers in Great Britain partially accountable for Lincoln's death.[79]

Of all the memorial sermons reviewed by the *Inquirer*, one by an American, Charles Lowe (1828–74), troubled it very much. Lowe was in the South attempting to revive the denomination's war-ravaged congregations. His sermon, delivered at the Unitarian Church in Charleston, South Carolina, disturbed the *Inquirer* because it contained no direct reference to slavery; there were "no pleas for *freedom,* no word of sympathy for the coloured people."[80] This boded ill for the future. It was a particularly sensitive matter because the newspaper felt the British had a special responsibility to America's new freedmen. They had planted the blacks in America and they had shared in the profits from the slaves' unrequited toil. If it was charitable to help them, it was also prudent. The blacks would again raise the staple that fed England's textile mills. The *Inquirer* recalled that America had been generous in her relief during the Irish famine and the cotton crisis; Britain ought to display a similar generosity.[81]

British relief efforts for the freedmen had actually begun with the foundation of the London Freedmen's Aid Society in April 1863. By 1865 some forty to fifty such organizations were in operation. All denominations, especially the Quakers and the Congregationalists, took part. In proportion to their numbers, Unitarians were no less important. The *Inquirer* was pleased that other Christian creeds welcomed the Unitarians in this "philanthropic labour."[82] Two notable supporters of the cause were William Rathbone and William Trimble. The latter was a central figure in supervising the transmission of money and goods from England to America.[83] British Unitarians were stimulated in their efforts to assist when the American Unitarian Association appealed to them to help finance a special mission to the freedmen and poor whites in the South.[84] By the end of 1865, they had pledged nearly £ 300 to this "Freedmen's Mission."[85] Unitarians were one in their desire to help. The Western Unitarian Christian Union, the Southern Unitarian Society, and the British and Foreign Unitarian Association each pledged its support.[86] Veteran Garrisonians such as

Mary Estlin, Edwin Chapman, Haughton, Bishop, Kell, and others joined with independent antislavery folk such as Russell Carpenter, and conservatives such as Bache, Madge, and J. J. Tayler, to help their "brothers in black." Beyond the Unitarians' own special project, the freedmen's aid movement in Great Britain produced nearly £ 120,000 in money and goods by 1868. "This extraordinary burst of generosity," Howard Temperley has written, "represented the culmination of Britain's efforts on behalf of the American Negro. After the frustrations of the forties and fifties, here was an opportunity of giving positive assistance."[87]

The outburst of help for the freedmen also revealed that the British had correctly seen that the emancipation of the American blacks had to be an ongoing movement. The fight had to continue, but who would carry it on? The London Emancipation Society disbanded in September 1865, because "the dream of a slave empire" was dead. The American Anti-Slavery Society had also voted on whether to disband. It had decided to continue, but why, asked the *Inquirer,* did it ever entertain the question in the first place? The abolitionists were still needed to counteract America's "negro-phobia." They were popular now. Garrison was honored in Boston, applauded in Baltimore, and, in Charleston, South Carolina, could watch his British co-worker, George Thompson, help to hoist the Stars and Stripes over Fort Sumter. The abolitionists were popular now, admonished the *Inquirer,* and they were never more needed "to awaken, direct, and strengthen the conscience of [America]."[88] The slave empire was dead, long live the free republic!

Lincoln's death and the conclusion of the war brought a spate of resolutions from Unitarian annual meetings in the spring of 1865. The Western Unitarian Christian Union, the Southern Unitarian Society, the Provincial Assembly, and the North-Midland Presbyterian and Unitarian Association all passed resolutions of sympathy and fraternity with their American brethren. But the most important action came at the meeting of the BFUA, when James Martineau moved and eloquently defended resolutions on behalf of America.[89] Although all the resolutions supported British-American reconciliation, central to most of them was an expression of concern for the freedmen. Martineau saw the mission to the freedmen as "a holy work." The resolution of the North-Midland Association called for raising "the coloured man . . . to an equality with the white in regard to all legal rights and the privileges of citizenship."

The Provincial Assembly's resolution went further; it demanded "perfect equality" with the white.[90]

The American response to the resolutions repeated the pattern of disappointment of previous decades. James Freeman Clarke had been the mediator for the resolution of the Southern Unitarian Society to the AUA. His letter was bitter. In his opinion goodwill toward England had "ceased to exist in the United States."[91] Charles Lowe, responding as the secretary of the AUA, made a conciliatory reply. In each of his answers to the resolutions he accentuated "the cordial fellowship" and "common religious faith" of the Unitarians on both sides of the Atlantic.[92] But nowhere did he mention the freedmen, nothing was said of the "holy work," no response was forthcoming on "perfect equality." The omission was conspicuous and ominous. Was the mission of the American church on race to be silence? The slave empire was dead, but the free republic, the truly free republic, was yet to be born. America's redemption had been partial, her second revolution, like her first, incomplete.

Notes

1. Douglas A. Lorimer argues as well about English observers of the American conflict in general. He based his thesis on the "almost universal commitment against slavery and a widespread acceptance of abolitionist views" by the English people. That observation would bring smiles to the celestial countenances of Armstrong and Estlin. See Lorimer, "The Role of Anti-Slavery Sentiment in English Reactions to the American Civil War," *Historical Journal,* 19 (1976): 406, 420.

2. Joseph M. Hernon, Jr., "British Sympathies in the American Civil War: A Reconsideration," *Journal of Southern History* 33 (August 1967): 367; Joseph H. Park, "The English Workingmen and the American Civil War," *Political Science Quarterly* 39 (1924): 432.

3. Raymond V. Holt, *The Unitarian Contribution to Social Progress in England,* 2nd rev. ed. (London: the Lindsey Press, 1952), p. 138; Donaldson Jordan and Edwin J. Pratt, *Europe and the American Civil War* (Boston: Houghton Mifflin Co., 1931), p. 94.

4. See, for example, Wilbur Devereux Jones, "The British Conservatives and the American Civil War," *American Historical Review* 58 (April 1953): 542.

5. Martin P. Claussen, "Peace Factors in Anglo-American Relations, 1861–1865," *Mississippi Valley Historical Review* 26 (March 1939–1940): 516, 517.

6. Royden Harrison, "British Labor and the Confederacy," *International Review of Social History,* 2 (1957): 79; Harrison, "British Labor and American Slavery," *Science and Society,* 25 (1961): 292, 304, 315, 317; Mary Ellison, *Support for Secession: Lancashire and the American Civil War* (Chicago: University of Chicago Press, 1972), p. 5.

7. Arnold Whitridge, "British Liberals and the American Civil War," *History Today* 12 (1962): 689; D. G. Wright, "Bradford and the American Civil War," *Journal of British Studies* 8 (1969): 83; D. P. Crook, "Portents of War: English Opinion on Secession," *Journal of American Studies* 4 (1970): 175.

8. James Martineau to Joseph Henry Allen, London, 14 April 1863, Allen Papers, Andover-Harvard Theological Library, cited hereafter as MH-AH. *Cf.* same letter in "Letters of James Martineau to Joseph Henry Allen," *Publications of the Colonial Society of Massachusetts* 6 (March 1900): 428–30, cited hereafter as PCSM.

9. Russell Lant Carpenter, "Can England Protect Fugitive Slaves?," *Christian Reformer* 17 (February 1861): 101, 108, 110, 112. Edwin Chapman, Mary Estlin, James Haughton, and the *Inquirer* all expressed an interest in Anderson's case. See entry for 11 January 1861, "Bristol and Clifton auxilary Ladies' Anti-Slavery Society. Minutes," MS, Estlin Papers, Dr. William's Library, London, cited hereafter as LDW; Samuel Haughton, *Memoir of James Haughton. With Extracts from His Private and Published Letters* (Dublin: E. Ponsonby, 1877, p. 159; "Have We a Fugitive Slave Law?," *Inquirer*, 12 January 1861, pp. 17–18. Eventually, Anderson was released on a technicality. See Howard Temperley, *British Antislavery 1833–1870* (London: Longman Group Ltd., 1972), p. 205.

10. Mary Carpenter to James Freeman Clarke, Bristol, 7 January 1861; Carpenter to Clarke, Bristol, 12 April 1861; James Freeman Clarke Papers, Houghton Library, Harvard University.

11. Abraham Lincoln, *Collected Works of Abraham Lincoln*, Roy B. Basler, ed. (New Brunswick: Rutgers University Press, 1953), 4:266; Samuel May to Richard D. Webb, Leicester, 3 June 1861, Clare Taylor, *British and American Abolitionists. An Episode in Transatlantic Understanding* (Edinburgh: Edinburgh University Press), p. 454.

12. "Civil War in America," *Inquirer*, 26 January 1861, p. 50; "'Slaveownia,'" *Inquirer*, 13 April 1861, p. 241; James Stansfeld, Jr., to the editor, London, 18 June 1861, *Inquirer*, 22 June 1861, p. 449.

13. "American Notes. A Sermon by the Rev. S. J. May," *Unitarian Herald*, 13 July 1861, p. 122, cited hereafter as *UH;* "A Letter from America," *UH*, 27 July 1861, p. 146; "Slavery," *Inquirer*, 3 August 1861, pp. 553–54; "Abolitionists and the War," *Inquirer*, 28 September 1861, pp. 697–698.

14. "Thirty-sixth Anniversary of the American Unitarian Association," *Quarterly Journal of the American Unitarian Association* 2 (1961): 304, cited hereafter as *QJAUA;* "America," *UH*, 1 June 1861, pp. 54–55; "American Unitarian Association," *UH*, 15 June 1861, p. 79; "American Notes," *UH*, 22 June 1861, p. 91; "American Notes," *UH*, pp. 232–233.

15. "American Demands for Sympathy," *UH*, 14 September 1861, p. 226. See also "Octogenerian" to the editor, London, 5 June 186l, *Inquirer*, 8 June 1861, p. 409; "The American War and American Slavery," *Inquirer*, 13 July 1861, p. 497; John Page Hopps to the editor, Sheffield, n.d., *Inquirer*, 13 July 1861, p. 506.

16. Charles Richard Denton, "An American War That Unitarians Approved: The Civil War," *Proceedings of the Unitarian Historical Society* 17, part 1 (1970–72): 47–48. See also Douglas C. Stange, "United for Sovereignty and Freedom: Unitarians and the Civil War," *Proceedings of the Unitarian Universalist Historical Society* 19, part 1 (1980–81): 16–38.

17. Edward Everett Hall, "England and America," *Christian Examiner* 121 (September 1861): 189; George E. Ellis, "Why has the North felt aggrieved with England?" *Atlantic Monthly* 7 (November 1861): 616, 620; William Henry Furness, *England and America. A Discourse Delivered by W. H. Furness, Minister of the First Congregational Unitarian Church, Sunday, December 22, 1861* (Philadelphia: C. Sherman & Son, printers, n.d.), pp. 4, 7.

18. Octavius Brooks Frothingham, *Memoir of William Henry Channing* (Boston: Houghton, Mifflin & Co., 1886), pp. 279, 285, 298, 307–8; William Henry Channing to the editor, Liverpool, 1 May 1861, *Inquirer*, 4 May 1861, p. 295; "The Rev. W. H.

Channing on the American War," *Inquirer,* 31 August 1861, p. 626; Ellison, *Support for Secession,* p. 105; "Farewell from the Rev. W. H. Channing," *UH,* 2 November 1861, pp. 315–16; William Henry Channing, *The Civil War in America: Or, the Slaveholders' Conspiracy. An Address . . .* (Liverpool: W. Vaughan, [1861]); James Martineau to W. R. Alger, London, 27 June 1861, James Drummond, *The Life and Letters of James Martineau, LL.D., S.T.D., Etc.* (New York: Dodd, Mead & Co., 1902), 1:391.

19. Betty Fladeland, *Men and Brothers: Anglo-American Antislavery Cooperation* (Urbana, Ill.: University of Illinois Press, 1972), pp. 382–83; Temperley, *British Antislavery,* pp. 252–53; Haughton, *Memoir,* p. 161; Sarah Steinthal to George B. Cheever, Liverpool, 22 March 1861, Cheever Family Papers, American Antiquarian Society.

20. Russell Lant Carpenter, ed. *Memoirs of the Life and Work of Philip Pearsall Carpenter, B.A., London, Ph.D., New York, Chiefly Derived from His Letters,* 2nd ed. (London: C. Kegan Paul & Co., 1880) p. 258; J. Estlin Carpenter, *The Life and Work of Mary Carpenter,* 2nd ed. (London: Macmillan & Co., 1881), pp. 229, 231; Haughton, *Memoir,* pp. 156, 159, 163; Samuel May to Samuel J. May, Leicester, 22 December 1861, Taylor, *British and American Abolitionists,* p. 470.

21. Henry Solly, *"These Eighty Years" or, The Story of an Unfinished Life.* (London: Simpkin, Marshall, & Co., 1898), 2:247–48; Margaret J. Shaen, *William Shaen. A Brief Sketch* (London: Longmans, Green, & Co., 1912), p. 21; Richard D. Webb to the Westons, Dublin, n.d., Taylor, *British and American Abolitionists,* pp. 458–59; Samuel J. May to Mary Estlin, Syracuse, 13 December 1863, Taylor, *British and American Abolitionists,* p. 515; S. Alfred Steinthal to the editor, Manchester, 6 December 1864, *Inquirer,* 10 December 1864, p. 809.

22. Samuel May, Jr., to Richard D. Webb, Leicester, 20 December 1861, Taylor, *British and American Abolitionists,* p. 467; Maria Weston Chapman to Mary Estlin, Weymouth, 3 February 1862, Estlin Papers, LDW; Haughton, *Memoir,* pp. 160–61; James Martineau to Joseph Henry Allen, London, 29 November 1861, Allen Papers, MH-AH; see same letter, PCSM, pp. 424–25.

23. "England and America," *Inquirer,* 8 February 1862, p. 105; George E. Ellis to the editor of "The London Inquirer," Charlestown, 25 February [1862], *Christian Register,* 5 April 1862, pp. 53–54.

24. "Dr. Ellis's Second Letter," *Christian Register,* 17 May 1862, p. 77; "London Inquirer on the War," *Christian Register,* 14 June 1862, p. 94.

25. Fladeland, *Men and Brothers,* p. 408; Holt, *Unitarian Contribution,* p. 138; John Hamilton Thom, *Distress in the Manufacturing Districts. A Sermon Preached on Sunday, 7th December, 1862, in Renshaw Street Chapel, Liverpool* (London: E. T. Whitfield, [1862]), p. 6.

26. Herbert McLachlan, *Records of a Family 1800–1933. Pioneers in Education, Social Service and Liberal Religion* (Manchester: Manchester University Press, 1935), pp. 14, 52.

27. "Relief Fund," *UH,* 15 November 1862, p. 388; "Distress in the Cotton District," ibid., p. 382; "Relief for Lancashire and Cheshire," *UH,* 13 September 1862, p. 310.

28. "[The Thirty-eighth Annual Meeting of the] British and Foreign Unitarian Association," *Inquirer,* 30 May 1863, p. 343; "Our Poorer Congregations in the North," *UH,* 12 June 1863; "Appeal on behalf of the Unitarian Congregations suffering through the Cotton Famine," *Inquirer,* 3 October 1863, p. 644; "Help for the Brethren," *Inquirer,* 24 October 1863, pp. 678–79.

29. See, for example, "The Cotton Famine," *UH,* 2 August 1862, p. 262; "The Cotton Famine," *Inquirer,* 4 October 1862, p. 698; "The Cotton Distress: Is Lancashire Doing Its Duty?" *UH,* 29 November 1862, p. 398; "Mission Congregations in the Distressed Districts," *UH,* 9 January 1863, p. 10; "A Thank Offering," *UH,* 23 January

1863; et al. The *Unitarian Herald* was besieged with so many relief appeals that it began to charge them an advertising fee! See "Relief Appeals," *UH*, 29 November 1862, p. 397.

30. John R. Beard, "The Cotton Crisis," *UH*, 16 November 1861, pp. 335, 336; John R. Beard, *The Cotton Crisis. A Discourse. . . . Disciples Ministering to Their Needy Brethren* (London: E. T. Whitfield, [1862], pp. 5, 11–12.

31. Thom, *Distress in the Manufacturing Districts*, pp. 8, 14; James C. Street to the editor, Manchester, n.d., *Inquirer*, 18 April 1863, 248; Ellison *Support for Secession* p. 105; Thomas H. Gill *The Triumph of Christ. Memorials of Franklin Howorth* (London: Hodder and Stoughton, 1883), pp. 120–21.

32. "A Unitarian Minister for the Recognition of the South," *Inquirer*, 30 May 1863, p. 353; John Page Hopps, *Southern Independence: A Lecture* (London: Whitfield, Green, and Son, 1865), pp. 2, 3, 11, 14–16.

33. [William Binns?], "English Sympathy with Confederates;" *Inquirer*, 30 May 1863, p. 340; "A Unitarian Minister for the Recognition of the South," p. 353.

34. James Martineau to Joseph Henry Allen, London, 14 April 1863, Allen Papers, MH-AH. See same letter, PCSM, 429; Francis Bishop, Edmund Kell, Philip Carpenter, and William Rathbone are but a few of the Unitarians who opposed the sale of ships to the South. See Francis Bishop to the editor, Chesterfield, 25 March 1863, *Inquirer*, 4 April 1863, p. 217; Edmund Kell to the editor, Southampton, 23 September 1863, *Inquirer*, 26 September 1863, p. 620; Philip P. Carpenter to William Lloyd Garrison, Manchester, 5 April 1863, Garrison Papers, Boston Public Library, cited hereafter as MB; Eleanor F. Rathbone, *William Rathbone: A Memoir* (London: Macmillan & Co., 1905), p. 197.

35. Lincoln, *Works*, 6:29; John Page Hopps to the editor, n.p., n.d., *Inquirer*, 8 November 1862, p. 790; British and Foreign Anti-Slavery Society, *The Crisis in the United States*, No. II, Tracts on Slavery in America (London: BFASS, 1862), p. 4; Fladeland, *Men and Brothers*, p. 399; "Shall the American Union Be Preserved?," *Inquirer*, 4 October 1862, p. 698; "The American War," *Inquirer*, 22 November 1862, pp. 813–14; Francis Bishop to the editor, Chesterfield, 4 November 1862, *Inquirer*, , 11 November 1862, pp. 807–8; S. Alfred Steinthal to the editor, Liverpool, 10 November 1862, *Inquirer*, 11 November 1862, p. 808.

36. Maria Weston Chapman to Mary Estlin, New York, 7 February 1863, Estlin Papers, LDW; "Sympathy with the North," *Inquirer*, 28 February 1863, p. 130; Edmund Kell to the editor, Southampton, 16 June 1863, *Inquirer*, 20 June 1863, p. 397; Russell Lant Carpenter to Frederick Douglass, Bridport, 28 March n.y., Frederick Douglass Papers, Library of Congress.

37. "Anti-Slavery Meeting at Bath—Speech of Mr. Jerom Murch," *Inquirer*, 7 February 1863, p. 92; James Martineau to Joseph Henry Allen, Ty Mawr, Penmaenmawr, Conway, 8 July 1863, Allen Papers, MH-AH. See same letter, PCSM, 434–35.

38. D. G. Wright, "Leeds Politics and the American Civil War," *Northern History*, 9 (1974): 98, 118.

39. Moncure Daniel Conway, *Autobiography Memories and Experiences* (Boston: Houghton Mifflin & Co., 1904), 1:388, 417, 426, 428; see also 2:45; William Lloyd Garrison to Mary Estlin, Boston, 10 April 1863, Estlin Papers, LDW.

40. Moncure Daniel Conway, *Addresses and Reprints, 1850–1907* (Boston: Houghton, Mifflin & Co., 1909), pp. vii–ix, xi–xii.

41. Fladeland, *Men and Brothers*.

42. Conway, *Autobiography*, 1:388–92, 406–7, 409.

43. *Ibid*, pp. 410, 412–18, 424. For the correspondence between Conway and Mason, see pp. 413–15, or "Abolitionism and Southern Independence." *William and Mary Quar-*

terly 21 (April 1913): 221–23; Samuel May, Jr., to Richard Webb, Leicester, 1 July 1863, May Papers, MB.

44. Conway, *Autobiography*, 1:422–24; 426, 434.

45. Ibid., pp. 434–35; 2:2, 45, 86–94. Some of Conway's writings during this time were Moncure Daniel Conway, "North & South, and Slavery," *Pitman's Popular Lecturer and Reader* (August 1863), pp. 225–36 [corrected copy reads 127–38]; Conway, "The American War as an English Question," *Christian Examiner* 76 (May 1964): 392–409; Conway *Testimonies Concerning Slavery* (London: Chapman and Hall, 1864); [Conway], "President Lincoln," *Fraser's Magazine* 71 (January 1865): 1–21; [Conway], "The Assassination of President Lincoln," *Fraser's Magazine* 71 (June 1865): 791–806. For a bibliography of Conway's writings, see his *Addresses and Reprints*, pp. 437–44.

46. Edmund Kell to the editor, Southampton, 30 November 1864, *Inquirer*, 17 December 1864, 822; Gill, p. 121.

47. Robert Spears to the editor, London, n.d., *Inquirer*, 5 September 1863, p. 573; *Memorials of Robert Spears 1825–1899* (Belfast Ulster Unitarian Christian Association, 1903), p. 27; Spears to the editor, London, n.d., *Inquirer*, 19 November 1864, p. 760.

48. William Croke Squier, Unitarian minister of Percy Street Church, Preston, quoted by Ellison, *Support for Secession*, p. 38; Haughton, *Memoir*, p. 157; John Dendy to the editor, Patricroft, 5 April 1863, *Inquirer*, 11 April 1863, p. 230; "Pax" to the editor, n.p., 12 October 1863, *Inquirer*, 31 October 1863, p. 702.

49. Robert Spears to the editor, London, n.d., *Inquirer*, 19 November 1864, p. 760; Francis Bishop to the editor, Chesterfield, 30 April 1863, *Inquirer*, 2 May 1863, p. 280; Bishop to the editor, Chesterfield, 9 November 1864, *Inquirer*, 16 May 1863, p. 305.

50. James Martineau to Joseph Henry Allen, Ty Manor, Penmaenmawr, Conway, 8 July 1863, Allen Papers, MH-AH; see same, PCSM, p. 434; "Sir John Bowring on the American War," *Inquirer*, 14 February 1863, p. 105; John Bowring, "The American Conflict," *Inquirer*, 15 August 1863, p. 526; Edmund Kell to the editor, Southampton, 4 November 1863, *Inquirer*, 21 November 1863, p. 747; Robert Spears to the editor, n.p., n.d., *Inquirer*, 3 December 1864, p. 792; Francis Bishop to the editor, Chesterfield, 26 October 1864, *Inquirer*, 29 October 1864, p. 711.

51. Francis Bishop to the editor, Chesterfield, 6 December 1864, *Inquirer*, 10 December 1864, p. 809.

52. See the *Inquirer's* statement following the miscellaneous letters under the combined heading "The American War," *Inquirer*, 17 December 1864, p. 823.

53. S. Alfred Steinthal to the editor, Manchester, 6 December 1864, *Inquirer*, 10 December 1864, p. 809; Francis Bishop to the editor, Chesterfield, 15 April 1863, *Inquirer*, 18 April 1863, p. 248.

54. Francis Bishop to the editor, Chesterfield, 26 October 1864, *Inquirer*, 29 October 1864, p. 711; Samuel J. May to Edmund Kell, Syracuse, 27 July 1863, *Inquirer*, 22 August 1863, p. 538; William Henry Furness, *Our American Institutions. A Thanksgiving Discourse Delivered in the First Congregational Unitarian Church in Philadelphia, August 6th, 1863* (Philadelphia: T. B. Pugh, 1863), pp. 16–17, 19.

55. Gill, *Triumph of Christ*, pp. 120–21.

56. "The *Christian Examiner* on the War," *Inquirer*, 24 October 1863, p. 678; "Union or Disunion?," *Inquirer*, 31 October 1863, p. 694.

57. James Taplin to the editor, Crediton, 23 June 1863, *Inquirer*, 23 June 1863, p. 429.

58. Edmund Kell to the editor, Southampton, 8 July 1863, *Inquirer*, 11 July 1863, p. 446; Francis Bishop to the editor, Chesterfield, 15 April 1863, *Inquirer*, 18 April 1863, p. 248.

59. See for example, Moncure D. Conway to the editor, London, 22 March [1865],

Inquirer, 25 March 1865, p. 184; Russell Lant Carpenter to the editor, Bridport, 28 March 1865, *Inquirer*, 1 April 1865, p. 199.

60. "Ministers of Religion on American Slavery," *Inquirer*, 6 June 1863, p. 367.

61. Frothingham, *Memoir of Channing*, pp. 312–13, 316, 318–19; William Henry Channing, "The American War," *Inquirer*, 19 September 1863, pp. 605–6.

62. "Emancipation Meetings," *Inquirer*, 26 September 1863, pp. 622–23; "Speech of the Rev. W. H. Channing at Edinburgh," *Inquirer*, 17 October 1863, pp. 672–73.

63. Edmund Kell to the editor, Southampton, 23 September 1863, *Inquirer*, 26 September 1863, p. 620.

64. "Emancipation, Not Extermination" to the editor, 29 September 1863, and "Pax" to the editor, 1 October 1863, *Inquirer*, 10 October 1863, p. 652. See also the exchange of letters that took place in 1864: "Letter on the War from the Rev. W. H. Channing," *Inquirer*, 15 October 1864, p. 678, "B." to the editor, n.p., n.d., "W." to the editor, n.p., 2 November 1864, "W.H." to the editor, n.p., n.d., *Inquirer*, 5 November 1864, p. 729.

65. "Statesmanship *Versus* Philanthropy," *Inquirer*, 3 October 1863.

66. Temperley, *British Antislavery*, p. 254.

67. Frederick W. Chesson to William Lloyd Garrison, London, 9 January 1863, Taylor, *British and American Abolitionists*, p. 494.

68. Lorimer, "English Reactions to the American Civil War," p. 419; Fladeland, *Men and Brothers*, p. 390.

69. Ellison, *Support for Secession*, pp. 79–81; Fladeland, *Men and Brothers*, p. 394; Temperley, *British Antislavery*, p. 255; Union and Emancipation Society," *Inquirer*, 6 February 1864, p. 100.

70. "Southern Independence Association," *Inquirer*, 28 November 1863, p. 758; Harrison, "British Labor and American Slavery," p. 316; D. G. Wright, "Leeds Politics," p. 98.

71. Harriet Martineau to [William Lloyd Garrison?], Ambleside, 10 August 1864, Taylor, *British and American Abolitionists*, p. 525.

72. "Review of *Southern Independence* by John Page Hopps, London: Whitfield, Green & Son, 1865," *Inquirer*, 11 March 1865, p. 148; "Missouri a Free State," *Inquirer*, 4 February 1865, p. 67; "Richmond," *Inquirer*, 22 April 1865, p. 242.

73. "Jefferson Davis," *Inquirer*, 24 June 1865, pp. 394–395.

74. "The End of the Civil War in America," *Inquirer*, 29 April 1865, p. 258.

75. "The Assassination of President Lincoln," *Inquirer*, 29 April 1865, p. 258; "Liverpool and President Lincoln," and "Sermons on the Assassination of President Lincoln," *Inquirer*, 6 May 1865, p. 275.

76. See, for example, William Binns, *A Sermon on the Death of President Lincoln Preached by the Rev. W. Binns, in the Unitarian Chapel, Birkenhead, On Sunday Evening, April 30th, 1865* (Birkenhead: J. Oliver, 1865); Robert Blackley Drummond, *President Lincoln and the American War. A Funeral Address Delivered on Sunday, April 30, 1865* (Edinburgh: W. P. Nimmo, 1865); S. Alfred Steinthal, *Address on the Assassination of Abraham Lincoln, Delivered at Platt Chapel on the Morning, and in the Ashton Town Hall on the Afternoon of Sunday, the 7th May, 1865. . . .*(London: Whitfield, Green, and Son, 1865).

77. "Liverpool and President Lincoln," p. 275; Ellison, *Support for Secession*, p. 175, 181; "The Rev. J. Page Hopps on the Assassination of President Lincoln," *Inquirer*, 29 April 1865, p. 269; [Conway], "Assassination of Lincoln," p. 793; Haughton, *Memoir*, p. 165.

78. "Liverpool and President Lincoln," pp. 274–75; Ellison, *Support for Secession*, p. 185.

79. Mary Estlin to Miss Weston, Bristol, 17, 19 May 1865, Weston Papers, MB;

"Liverpool and President Lincoln," p. 275; Steinthal, *Address on the Assassination of Lincoln*, p. 6.

80. "Review of *Death of President Lincoln* by Charles Lowe, Boston: American Unitarian Association, 1865," *Inquirer*, 17 June 1865, p. 380.

81. "Help the Freedmen," *Inquirer*, 25 March 1865, pp. 178–79.

82. Temperley, *British Antislavery*, pp. 259–60; "Unitarians and Freedmen," *Inquirer*, 2 December 1865, p. 762.

83. "Help the Freedmen," p. 179.

84. "An Appeal from the American Unitarian Association," *UH*, 24 November 1865, p. 374; "Help the Freedmen," *Inquirer*, 25 November 1865, p. 757; "Unitarians and Freedmen," pp. 761–62.

85. "Mission to the Freedmen of the Southern States," *UH*, 29 December 1865, p. 413.

86. "Western Unitarian Society," *Inquirer*, 19 August 1865, pp. 531–32; "Southern Unitarian Societies," *Inquirer*, 7 October 1865, p. 641; "Help the Freedmen," p. 757.

87. Contributors to the "Mission of the Freedmen" and the amount of their contributions were listed in both the *Inquirer* and the *Unitarian Herald* on an almost weekly basis. Temperley, *British Antislavery*, pp. 259–60. For a history of British assistance to the American freedmen, see Christine Bolt's *The Anti-Slavery Movement and Reconstruction: A Study of Anglo-American Cooperation 1833–1877* (London: Oxford University Press, 1969).

88. "The American Anti-Slavery Society," *Inquirer*, 1 July 1865, pp. 410–11; "Dissolution of the Emancipation Society," *Inquirer*, 2 September 1865, p. 565; "Work for the Abolitionists," *Inquirer*, 8 July 1865, pp. 426–27.

89. "The Western Unitarian Christian Union," *Inquirer*, 6 May 1865, pp. 280–81; "[Southern Unitarian Society at] Southampton," *UH*, 23 June 1865, p. 204; "The Provincial Assembly," *Inquirer*, 24 June 1865, p. 402; "North Midland Presbyterian and Unitarian Association," *Inquirer*, 8 July 1865, p. 432; "[Fortieth Annual Meeting of the] British and Foreign Unitarian Association," *Inquirer*, 10 June 1865, p. 363.

90. "Fortieth Annual Meeting of the BFUA," p. 363; "North Midland Presbyterian and Unitarian Association," p. 432; "Provincial Assembly," p. 402.

91. "The Rev. J. Freeman Clarke's Reply to the Address of Sympathy from English Unitarians," *Inquirer*, 5 August 1865, p. 499.

92. "Sympathy with America," [Lowe's reply to the Southern Unitarian Society], *Inquirer*, 29 July 1865, p. 483; "Reply of the American Unitarian Association to the Address of the Provincial Assembly," *UH*, 15 September 1865, p. 295; "North Midland Association and the American Association," *UH*, 22 September 1865, p. 307; "The American Unitarian Association and the British and Foreign Unitarian Association," *Inquirer*, 14 October 1865, p. 658. *Cf.* the British letters and replies in "Meetings of the Executive Committee [of the AUA]," *QJAUA* 6 (1865): 419–22, 465–70. See also the editorial "American Responses" in the *Inquirer*, 5 August 1865, pp. 490–91.

Epilogue

In 1853, when Harriet Beecher Stowe had visited England, and Estlin had published a revision of his *Brief Notice of American Slavery*, and the BFUA had entertained its first resolution on slavery asking American Unitarians to testify against slavery in some way corresponding to their "social position and elevated religious principles," a slim volume was published in London called *The Unitarian Almanac*. It listed Unitarian ministers, chapels, periodicals, tracts, and societies in the British Isles. It recorded members of the royal family, "European Sovereign Princes," London bankers, "Stamps and Taxes," and transfer and dividend days. It announced the university terms at Oxford and Cambridge, even though Unitarians could not attend them. Tables to "Cast Up Expenses" and Calculate Wages" were provided, the latter given presumably to pay them, not earn them. Advertisements for insurance companies were scattered throughout the *Almanac* and its only article, nine pages long, instructed Unitarians on "Productive Investments." Later *Almanacs* commemorated the abolition of British West Indian slavery on 1 August 1834, but they also advertised "Double Guns, Breech Loaders [and] Double Rifles"[1]—which prompts one to ask: did a Unitarian layman ever meditate on slavery while hunting big game in darkest Africa? That question may never be answered, but another question ought to be: why for Servetus's[2] sake did any Unitarian demonstrate the slightest interest in a domestic institution of a foreign nation thousands of miles away?

For many generations the interpreters of the abolition of British slavery have spoken of a triumph of "humanitarian" over "interest" politics. For example, Frank J. Klingberg, a member of this humanitarian tradition, entitled his work *The*

Anti-Slavery Movement in England: A Study in English Humanitarianism. But Eric Williams toppled the lofty humanitarian tradition with his *Capitalism and Slavery,* published in 1944. He agreed that the "humanitarians were the spearhead of the onslaught which destroyed the West Indian system and freed the Negro. But their importance [had] been seriously misunderstood and grossly exaggerated by men who sacrificed scholarship to sentimentality and, like the scholastics of old, placed faith before reason and evidence." Williams had in mind the imperial historian Reginald Coupland, but Klingberg was of the same ilk. Williams argued that, while the work of individual humanitarians was important, the antislavery movement was a response of a rising industrial middle class in Great Britain to a protectionist West Indian plantation economy. The antislavery attack could be best explained as a part of the overall strategy of the British middle-class campaign for free trade. It succeeded because of the relative decline of the economic importance of West Indian plantation slavery. "One of the charms of [Williams's] hypothesis," Seymour Drescher has written, "was its aesthetic simplicity: a see-saw of rising industrial metropolis and falling agricultural colony."[3]

Williams's thesis that economic, not humanitarian forces were behind the overthrow of West Indian slavery, came under fire a generation later. In 1968 Roger Anstey suggested that the relationship between humanitarian and economic motives was far more complex than Williams allowed. Two years later, Duncan Rice showed that few abolitionists gave up their antislavery interests following the abolition of West Indian slavery. Many even advocated the continued protection of British West Indian sugar in opposition to the easy admission into Great Britain of slave-grown produce. They in effect repudiated their free-trade principles, which Williams had said were uppermost in their minds. Howard Temperley, in an appendix to his *British Antislavery 1833–1870* published in 1972, suggested that nineteenth-century industrialism was not necessarily at odds with plantation slavery and that the motivation and success of the campaign against British slavery had to be found elsewhere. "On present evidence," he declared, "it would appear that [the motivations] were primarily religious and idealistic in origin." Success was achieved because economic changes combined with humanitarian zeal to make abolition inevitable. David Brion Davis also felt that the motivations for the antislavery campaign rested elsewhere than where Williams had placed them. He believed that the British interest in plantation slavery abroad might be attributable to a guilty conscience about the lack of concern about wage slavery at home. Common to all of these scholars from Anstey to Williams was the opinion that British West Indian slavery was in decline.[4]

Seymour Drescher contested that view in his meticulously researched *Econocide: British Slavery in the Era of Abolition.* He demonstrated that slavery was "not a wasted machine which the British government could phase out like a bankrupt venture. . . , but a dynamic system." Although not central to British economic survival or growth, slavery was economically important to Great Britain at the very time the crusade against it was securing political success. It would be wrong for scholars, taught Drescher, "to view abolition as an economic appendectomy."[5] Drescher also questioned the opinion that the rising industrial class in Britain was aligned against the slave trade and slavery. He could find no evidence for such an assertion, and he further pointed out that, as far as the slave trade was concerned, opposition against it was mobilized before the industrial class in Britain was numerous enough and strong enough to attribute to it the strength of the antislavery movement. "Abolition," he explained,

> was neither a calculated winding down of a falling overseas enterprise, nor demonstrably a means by which emergent industrialists, or their unwitting spokesmen, made Britain safer for the factory. . . . It was more a vehicle adopted by underrepresented and dynamic social, regional, and religious groups. . . . It was a dramatic assertion of political power in the name of humanity. The petitioners were offered not merely exemption from national guilt, but a personal opportunity to use abolition as a lever to move the entire world forward.[6]

Drescher's exciting study converted both Anstey and Temperley to an acceptance of the "decline of the decline theory" of West Indian slavery.[7] Moreover, their recent contributions toward locating the wellsprings of the drive against British West Indian slavery are particularly helpful to the present study. Anstey emphasizes in his *The Atlantic Slave Trade and British Abolition 1760–1810* the important role of the Evangelicals and Quakers as "active agents of reform, as the actual instigators of abolition." Propelling many of these abolitionists forward, he believes, was the fuel of a providential and dynamic theology. That theology, which he maintains was primarily at work among Evangelicals and Quakers, called its professors to overcome the evil in their own hearts, but also the evils of the world. The theology held that "reform was a part of the divine plan" and to ignore slavery, that greatest of iniquities, could lead to divine retribution.[8]

Temperley, in an article on "Capitalism, Slavery and Ideology," helps to explain how the capitalist ideology of the period could sympathize with an attack upon the slave trade and West Indian slavery even though that ideology extolled "the pursuit of individual self-interest" and its advocates could expect no economic gain from the demise of either slavery or the slave trade. Whether or not Great Britain's rising industrial class saw slavery as immoral or moral was not perhaps so important as whether they viewed capitalism as an "emancipation from traditional restraints, a liberation of energies, a letting go." If the latter was the case, it was likely they would lend their aid to close slavery down. Their suspicions anyway were that it was bankrupt; no matter that their suspicions were unfounded.[9] One could combine the findings of Anstey and Temperley to conclude that the wealth of a liberating Gospel deftly joined the liberating Gospel of Wealth to drive slavery into a receivership that sold it for £20 million.

Although the observations of these two scholars are directed at British slavery, they are useful in comprehending why many British Unitarians turned their attention to American slavery. Anstey states that the providential theology of the Evangelicals and Quakers was a product of their age from which both groups drew; "a corpus of commonly held ideas to which they could appeal." In his documentation of the theology of "Divine Providence" and Progress, he quotes Joseph Priestley, but typically, as Unitarian historians are wont to remind everyone, he does not identify him as a Unitarian.[10] This failure is unfortunate, for the Unitarians, as much as the Evangelicals and Quakers, could identify "the corpus" as their own. Unitarians such as Priestley in the eighteenth century, who believed in "God's Indubitable Progress," or Henry Solly in the nineteenth century, who intended "to right all the wrongs of the universe," were the kinds of recruits an antislavery crusade was likely to enlist.

In addition to providential theology, Anstey explains that the Evangelicals and some of the Quakers placed considerable emphasis upon personal sin and redemption, that they believed that salvation from sin meant liberation from bondage, and that they easily made the projection of this concern to the liberation of slaves from physical bondage.[11] At first blush this particular emphasis would seem to exclude the Unitarians. But the blush is the embarrassment by Unitarians not for being excluded, but in remembering their own "evangelicals." Admittedly, the Unitarians did not share with the Evangelicals an intense anxiety over personal redemption. It will be remembered that that has never been a major concern of their denomination nor among them as individuals. The evangelical Unitarians, however, did share three identifying characteristics of the Evangelicals: an adoration of Jesus Christ as the bread of life, rather than Priestley's loaf of bread; an intense warmth of feeling; and a deep and abiding concern for all sorts and conditions of humankind. Mary Carpenter provided the following summation of the evangelical Unitarian creed:

> I believe "Evangelical Unitarian," as my revered and beloved father [Lant Carpenter] expressed it, to be the "doctrine of the gospel," *i.e.*, simple Christianity, and as such I desire its extension. I value the holy truth, and without it I could not do the work which my Heavenly Father has given me to do. . . . I value it . . . as a *living reality*, which is to be carried with vivifying warmth to bear on every great social evil.

Carpenter, one of her biographers has written, placed "a far greater emphasis on the figure of Christ than [was] common to the mainstream of Unitarian belief." So did her brother, Philip, who wrote how he felt "a great delight in pleading for Christ." He later became an Anglican. Their father's persistent references to Jesus Christ had prompted damning rumors among the Unitarians that he was converting to the orthodox.[12] Joseph Hutton, Franklin Howorth, and Henry Solly were all Arians. The first had been ejected from his chapel because of his Christology and joined the Church of England, the second resigned his ministerial charge for the same reason, and the third was voted down when he moved that his denomination place itself on the "teachings and example of Jesus Christ." Solly became agitated and warned his fellow Unitarians:

> The "religious improvement of human life" cannot be effected except by an organization which has a Leader, a Captain, a Deliverer, an invisible King, like the Christ, the Son of God, *as its Head.* He must be the head and front, "the

spearhead" of the army which is to conquer evil in all its forms, and establish the kingdom of righteousness, peace, and joy.[13]

Similar references could be made to John Bishop Estlin, Henry Montgomery, John Scott Porter, George Armstrong, John Relly Beard, and Francis Bishop.[14] They held a common adoration of Jesus Christ. Most of them possessed a warm, compassionate, and sentimental nature whether it was Beard, who stood with tears in his eyes at the Provincial Assembly of Lancashire and Cheshire, or Solly, whose "steam was up," or Bishop, who ran from the Richmond slave mart crying hysterically.[15] They were all dedicated to reform. They were all evangelical Unitarians. And incidentally, they were all Garrisonians.

Therefore, Anstey's correlation between evangelical theology and antislavery reform does enhance the suggestion of a similar analogue among the Unitarians. Temperley's observations are also useful. The capitalist ideology he describes was prevalent among the Unitarians, particularly the manufacturers, merchants, and managers among them. His observations tend to suggest that the lay readers of the *Unitarian Almanac* who clipped dividend coupons, computed wages, and poured over actuarial tables really did not mind whether their ministers preached against slavery, joined antislavery societies, entertained American abolitionists, or passed the hat for the latest fugitive slave. And it did matter very much if they did mind. They paid their ministers' salaries. And while Joseph Hutton lost his job for preaching too much about Jesus and Solly his for preaching abstinence when his chapel's central benefactor, a brewer, sat before him, no record remains of any Unitarian minister being fired for preaching abolition. The successful capitalists who controlled most British Unitarian chapels might even on occasion join in the antislavery fun, whether it was Josiah Wedgwood against British slavery or Thomas Bayley Potter against American slavery.

Sometimes the different wellsprings of Unitarian antislavery reform flowed into a common stream. Robert Kiefer Webb has written that the Garrisonian radicalism of Harriet Martineau could be attributed to her acceptance of Priestley's necessarian philosophy of progress and to her being the daughter of a Unitarian manufacturer. Martineau read both Priestley and Priestley's mentor, David Hartley, and she embraced their doctrines "completely." Their doctrines directed her toward activism and reform: "Since necessarianism, as she understood it," Webb explains, "put a premium on enlightened self-discipline and enforced the moral of laboring to bring about the millennium, the life which she foresaw was necessarily an active one."[16] The second influence arose "from her position in the liberal, educated, and ambitious manufacturing middle class." She was the sixth child of a Norwich manufacturer and her capitalist ideology was founded upon household discussion, her father's management of workers in his factory, and the labor unrest in the city of Norwich. Her education in capitalism was duplicated in the lives of Unitarians throughout England. As a result of this education her radicalism became "a manufacturer's radicalism," writes Webb, "the rationalization of a growing power and the justification of its continuance. . . . The manufacturers and their daughters were going to inherit the earth— a prospect that hardly makes for meekness."[17] And the mention of meekness is a reminder to suggest a possible third influence operating upon (as well as within) Harriet Martineau— evangelical Unitarianism. Webb does not consider the influence of evangelical Unitarianism, but if that influence is added to those already cited as having an impact upon Martineau, a composite emerges of the British Unitarian abolitionist opposed to American slavery. Martineau was a student of Lant Carpenter, whom she called "a very earnest pietist." She "worshipped" him; his influence upon her was "overpowering." He made her "desperately superstitious, living wholly in and for religion, and fiercely fanatical about it."[18]

When Harriet Martineau traveled to America in 1834, she carried this baggage of influence with her. As one of the "theological lepers" of Great Britain and as a manufacturer's daughter, she cautiously sought out the hospitality of the American Unitarian elite. As a Unitarian and a devotee of Joseph Priestley, she was predisposed to a favorable impression of revolutionary America; excepting, of course, its slavery, "the greatest crime against American principles." As a radical, she soon found herself in the midst of the Garrisonians. She attended a meeting of the Boston Female Antislavery Society led by the Unitarian bluestocking, Maria Weston Chapman. While a boorish mob ranted outside their meeting place, Martineau affirmed her agreement with Garrisonian principles. Webb declares that in the battle by the various American antislavery parties for the allegiance of Martineau, the Garrisonians won her "mind."[19] But it was more likely that they won her "heart," for during her American tour she was yet an evangelical Unitarian. It was true that she later publicly abandoned her faith, but behind her "conversion" to Garrisonianism in Boston was probably Lant Carpenter's pietistic influence, an influence that could have lingered throughout her life to charge continually her emotive drive against American slavery. Neither Carpenter nor Priestley would have been displeased with the title she selected for her history of her beloved Garrisonians: *The Martyr Age of the United States.*[20]

To the question as to why Unitarians demonstrated an interest in a domestic institution of a foreign nation thousands of miles away, the witness of Harriet Martineau as a composite British Unitarian abolitionist provides the answer. Whether the Unitarians sought social acceptance by joining antislavery and other reforms, or whether Priestley's necessarian philosophy enlisted them as God's instruments to eradicate slavery, or whether their capitalist ideology sought to discard slavery as an economic anachronism, or whether an evangelical warmth and Christian concern for the world's multitudes drove them on, or whether it was a composite of all of the above, they moved to act. They saw with George Armstrong that slavery was "the one great master question of [their] age."[21] It affronted their Unitarian beliefs and threatened their own nation's liberty. They had the theology, ideology, experience, wealth, empathy, interest, and world view to work against American slavery. After all, to them there was a double meaning to the question of the slave on Wedgwood's cameo, "Am I Not a Man and a Brother?" As "theological negroes," they could answer it in two ways: "Yes, you are—and—yes, I am."

Notes

1. John Webb, ed., *The Unitarian Almanac, for 1854* (London: Edward T. Whitfield, [1853]), pp. 16–38, 42–45, 61–63, 66–74; *The Unitarian Almanac for 1859, Being the third after Bisextile, or Leap Year* (London: Edward T. Whitfield, [1858]), p. 10; *The Unitarian Almanac, for 1860 . . .* (London: Edward T. Whitfield, [1860]), n.p. no.

2. Michael Servetus (1511–53), Unitarian martyr. Burned at the stake in Geneva by John Calvin for publishing his heretical *De Trinitatis Erroribus.*

3. Frank J. Klingberg, *The Anti-Slavery Movement in England: A Study in English Humanitarianism* (n.p.: Archon Books, 1968 [1st edition, 1926]); Eric Williams, *Capitalism and Slavery* (New York: Perigee Books, 1980 [1st edition, 1944]), pp. 178, 209–12; Reginald Coupland, *The British Anti-Slavery Movement* (London: Frank Cass & Co., 1964 [1st edition, 1933]); Seymour Drescher, *Econocide: British Slavery in the Era of Abolition* (Pittsburgh: University of Pittsburgh Press, 1977), p. 5.

4. Roger Anstey, "Capitalism and Slavery: a Critique," *Economic History Review,* 2nd Series, 21 (1968): 307–20; C. Duncan Rice, "'Humanity Sold for Sugar!' The British Abolitionist Response to Free Trade in Slave-Grown Sugar," *Historical Journal* 13 (1970): 404, 405, 408, 417–418; Howard Temperley, *British Antislavery 1833–1870* (London: Longman Group, Ltd., 1972), pp. 273–76; David Brion Davis, *The Problem of Slavery in the Age of Revolution 1770–1823* (Ithaca, N.Y.: Cornell University Press, 1975), pp. 254, 348–50, 366.

5. Drescher, *Econocide,* pp. 165, 184, 185.

6. Seymour Drescher, "Capitalism and the Decline of Slavery: The British Case in Comparative Perspective," *Annals of the New York Academy of Sciences* 292 (1977): 134, 139, 140.

7. Roger Anstey, *The Atlantic Slave Trade and British Abolition 1760–1810* (London: Macmillan Press, 1975), pp. 52, 407; Howard Temperley, "Capitalism, Slavery and Ideology," *Past and Present* 75 (May 1977): 102.

8. Anstey, *Atlantic Slave Trade,* pp. 127, 140–41, 160, 164, 194, 198, 230.

9. Temperley, "Capitalism, Slavery and Ideology," pp. 106, 117–18.

10. Anstey, *Atlantic Slave Trade,* pp. 127, 133.

11. Anstey, *Atlantic Slave Trade,* pp. 190–93, 234, 235.

12. Mary Carpenter to the Reverend Theodore Parker, Bristol, 12 June 1859, J. Estlin Carpenter, *The Life and Work of Mary Carpenter,* 2nd ed. (London: Macmillan & Co., 1881), p. 207; Harriet Warm Schupf, "Single Women and Social Reform in Mid-Nineteenth Century England: The Case of Mary Carpenter," *Victorian Studies* 17 (March 1974): 308; Russell Lant Carpenter, ed., *Memoirs of the Life and Work of Philip Pearsall Carpenter, B.A., London, Ph.D., New York Chiefly Derived from His Letters,* 2nd ed. (London: C. Kegan Paul & Co., 1880), p. 65; Harry Lismer Short, *The Founding of the British and Foreign Unitarian Association,* Supplement to the *Transactions of the Unitarian Historical Society* 16 (October 1975): 24.

13. Henry Solly, *"These Eighty Years" or, The Story of an Unfinished Life* (London: Simpkin, Marshall, & Co., 1893), 2: 279, 338–39. The quotation is from p. 339.

14. William James, "Memoir of John Bishop Estlin, Esq., F.L.S., F.R.C.S.," *Christian Reformer* 11 (August 1855): 476; William McMillan, *A Profile in Courage [Henry Montgomery (1788–1865)]* (Newry: E. Hodgett, Ltd., 1966), pp. 13, 23; Herbert McLachlan, *The Unitarian Movement in the Religious Life of England* (London: George Allen & Unwin, Ltd., 1934), pp. 189, 211; [Robert Henderson], "Memoir of the Late Rev. George Armstrong, of Bristol," *Christian Reformer* 14 (August 1858): 470; Herbert McLachlan, *Records of a Family 1800–1933: Pioneers in Education, Social Service and Liberal Religion* (Manchester: Manchester University Press, 1935), p. 16; "American Slavery," *Inquirer,* 21 June 1851, p. 395.

15. McLachlan, *Records of a Family,* p. 18; "American Slavery," *Inquirer* 21 June 1851, p. 397; [Francis Bishop], "Key to Uncle Tom's Cabin," *Prospective Review* 9 (1853), p. 260.

16. Robert Kiefer Webb, *Harriet Martineau: A Radical Victorian* (New York: Columbia University Press, 1960), pp. 74–86.

17. Ibid., pp. 43, 58–65.

18. Martineau quoted by Short, *Founding of British and Foreign Unitarian Association,* pp. 24–25.

19. Webb, *Harriet Martineau,* pp. 142, 154–55, 171.

20. Harriet Martineau, *The Martyr Age of the United States* (Newcastle Upon Tyne: Finlay and Charlton, 1840).

21. Henderson, *Memoir of George Armstrong,* p. 458.

Bibliography

Manuscripts

Bristol Record Office—BRO
  Mary Carpenter Collection
Huntington Library, San Marino, California—CaSMH
  Thomas Clarkson Papers
  Francis Power Cobbe Papers
  Zachary Macaulay Papers
Dorset Record Office, Dorchester—DDRO
  Carpenter Autograph Collection
Library of Congress—DLC
  Frederick Douglass Papers
Meadville Theological Seminary—ICM
  William Ellery Channing Papers
British Library—LBL
  Thomas Clarkson Papers
  Lord Holland Papers
  Peel Papers
Dr. Williams's Library—LDW
  Bristol and Clifton Ladies Anti-Slavery Society Manuscripts
  Estlin Papers
Sydney Jones Library, University of Liverpool—LiU
  Rathbone Papers
Boston Public Library—MB
  Antislavery Letters
  Garrison Manuscripts
  May Papers
  Weston Papers
Radcliffe College Library—MCR
  Beecher-Stowe Papers
  Loring Family Papers
Houghton Library, Harvard University—MH
  Autograph File
  William Ellery Channing Papers

Lydia Maria Child Papers
James Freeman Clarke Papers
Ezra Stiles Gannett Papers
John Gorham Palfrey Papers

Andover-Harvard Theological Library—MH-AH
Joseph Henry Allen Papers

Massachusetts Historical Society—MHi
Bellows Papers

John Rylands University Library of Manchester—MJR
Unitarian Collection

American Antiquarian Society Library—MWA
Cheever Family Papers

Cornell University Library—NIC
Antislavery Collection

New York Public Library—NN
British and Foreign Unitarian Association Papers

Columbia University Library—NNC
Sidney Howard Gay Papers
David E. Smith Collection

Manchester College Library, Oxford—OMC
George Armstrong Papers
Lant Carpenter Papers
Carpenter Family Letters
Valentine D. Davis Manuscripts
Martineau Papers

Rhodes House Library, Oxford University—ORH
British and Foreign Anti-Slavery Society Papers

Alderman Library, University of Virginia—ViU
British Anti-Slavery Spokesmen Letters

Reports and Proceedings

Annual Reports of the American Anti-Slavery Society

American Slavery. Report of a Meeting of Members of the Unitarian Body, Held at the Freemasons' Tavern, June 13th, 1851, to Deliberate on the Duty of English Unitarians in Reference to Slavery in the United States. Rev. Dr. Hutton in the Chair, London: E. T. Whitfield, 1851.

Annual Reports of the American Unitarian Association

The First Report, Adopted at the General Meeting of the Anti-Slavery League, at Finsbury Chapel, May 19th, 1847, London: A. Munro, 1847.

Annual Reports of the British and Foreign Anti-Slavery Association

Annual Reports of the British and Foreign Unitarian Association

Reports of the Hibbert Trust

Annual Reports of the Massachusetts Anti-Slavery Society

Annual Reports of the National Anti-Slavery Bazaar

Report from Select Committee on the Extinction of Slavery Throughout the British Dominions: With the Minutes of Evidence, Appendix and Index, n.p.: Ordered by the House of Commons, to be Printed, 11 August 1832.

Reports of the Society for the Mitigation and Gradual Abolition of Slavery Throughout the British Dominions

Report of the Fiftieth Anniversary of the Southern Unitarian Society, Adopted at the Annual Meeting at Wareham, Dorsetshire, July 9, 1851,—the Rev. Hugh Hutton, A.M., in the Chair, n.p.: n.d.

Reports of the Half-Yearly Meetings of the Western Unitarian Christian Union

Newspapers and Periodicals

Anti-Slavery Advocate

Anti-Slavery Magazine

Anti-Slavery Monthly Reporter

Anti-Slavery Reporter

Anti-Slavery Reporter and Aborigines' Friend

Anti-Slavery Watchman

Appleton's Journal

Atlantic Monthly

British and Foreign Medico-Chirurgical Review

Christian Examiner

Christian Freeman and Record of Unitarian Worthies

Christian Inquirer

Christian Pilot and Gospel Moralist

Christian Pioneer

Christian Reflector and Theological Inquirer

Christian Reformer

Christian Register

Christian Teacher, and Chronicle

Contemporary Review

Eclectic Magazine

Edinburgh Review

Fraser's Magazine

Household Words

Inquirer

Irish Friend

Irish Unitarian Magazine

Liberator

Littell's Living Age
Manchester Guardian
Modern Review
Monthly Miscellany of Religion and Letters
Monthly Religious Magazine
Monthly Repository
National Anti-Slavery Standard
National Review
New England Magazine
People's Journal
Pitman's Popular Lecturer and Reader
Popular Science Monthly
Prospective Review; A Quarterly Journal of Theology and Literature
Quarterly Journal of the American Unitarian Association
Theological Repository
Theological Review; A Journal of Religious Thought and Life
Unitarian
Unitarian Almanac
Unitarian Chronicle, and Companion to the Monthly Repository
Unitarian Herald
Unitarian Magazine and Chronicle
Unitarian Review
Western Messenger
Westminster Review

Contemporary Books, Pamphlets, Letters, Sermons, Biographies, and Collections

Abdy, E. S. *Journal of a Residence and Tour in the United States of North America, from April, 1833, to October, 1834.* 3 vols. London: John Murray, 1835.

An Address from the undersigned Unitarian Ministers of Great Britain and Ireland, to their Ministerial Brethren of the Unitarian Churches in the United States of North America. Bristol: Philp and Evans, 1843.

Armistead, Wilson. *Resolutions Passed at a Committee of the Leeds Anti-Slavery Association, September 25th, 1855.* n.p.: n.d.

Armstrong, George. *A Discourse, Delivered in Lewin's Mead Chapel, Bristol, on the Morning of November 6th, 1842, being the Sunday next after the Intelligence had arrived of the Death of Dr. Channing.* London: J. Green, [1842].

———. *A Sermon on the Death of John Bishop Estlin, Esq., F.L.S.,*

F.R.C.S. . . . Delivered at Lewin's Mead Chapel, Bristol, June 17th, 1855. Bristol: Evans and Arrowsmith, [1855].

Armstrong, Richard Acland. *Henry William Crosskey, LL.D., F.G.S., His Life and His Work.* Birmingham: Cornish Brothers, 1895.

Aspland, R. Brook. *The Funeral Sermon Preached in the Church of the Divine Unity, Newcastle-On-Tyne, on Sunday Morning, Jan. 1st, 1860, on Occasion of the Death of the Late Rev. George Harris, Pastor of the Church. To Which is Prefixed, the Address at the Interment, Delivered in the Chapel of the Jesmont Cemetery, on Thursday, Dec. 29th, 1859.* London: Edward T. Whitfield, 1860.

————. *Memoir of the Life, Works and Correspondence of the Rev. Robert Aspland, of Hackney.* London: Edward T. Whitfield, 1850.

Barclay, Alexander. *An Address to Philanthropists Generally, and to Our Brethren of African Origin, in Particular: To Which Are Appended, Remarks on Emigration to Jamaica, Addressed to the Coloured Class of the United States, by Peter Gallego: with a Statement of Wages, and Other Advantages, Offered to Laborers and Tradesmen Emigrating to Jamaica.* Montreal: Lovell and Gibson, 1844.

————. *A Practical View of the Present State of Slavery in the West Indies; or, An Examination of Mr. Stephen's "Slavery of the British East India Colonies": Containing More Particularly an Account of the Actual Condition of the Negroes in Jamaica: with Observations on the Decrease of the Slaves Since the Abolition of the Slave Trade, and on the Probable Effects of Legislative Emancipation: Also Strictures on the Edinburgh Review, and on the Pamphlets of Mr. Cooper and Mr. Bickell.* London: Smith, Elder, & Co., 1826.

Beard, John Relly. *The Cotton Crisis. A Discourse. . . . Disciples Ministering to Their Needy Brethren.* London; E. T. Whitfield, [1862].

————. *Extinction of Slavery. A Discourse in Commemoration of the Extinction of Slavery in the British Colonies, On the 1st of August, 1838.* London: Smallfield and Son, 1838.

————. *The Life of Toussaint L'Ouverture, The Negro Patriot of Hayti.* London: Ingram, Cooke, and Co., 1853.

————. *The People's Dictionary of the Bible.* 3rd ed. London: Simpkin, Marshall & Co., 1859.

————. *Unitarianism Exhibited in Its Actual Condition; Consisting of Essays by Several Unitarian Ministers and Others; Illustrative of the Rise, Progress, and Principles of Christian Anti-Trinitarianism in Different Parts of the World.* London: Simpkin, Marshall & Co., 1846.

Bickell, R. *The West Indies as They Are; or a Real Picture of Slavery: But More Particularly as It Exists in the Island of Jamaica. In Three Parts. With Notes.* London: J. Hatchard & Son, 1825.

Binns, William. *A Sermon on the Death of President Lincoln Preached by the Rev. W. Binns, in the Unitarian Chapel, Birkenhead, On Sunday Evening, April 30th, 1865.* Birkenhead: J. Oliver, 1865.

[Blanco y Crespo, Jose Maria]. *Bosquejo del Comercio de esclavos y reflexiones sobre estre trafico considerado moral, politica y christianamente.* London: Ellerton and Henderson, 1814.

Bowring, John. *Autobiographical Recollections of Sir John Bowring.* With a Brief Memoir by Lewin B. Bowring. London: Henry S. King & Co., 1877.

[Bradburn, Frances H.] *A Memorial of George Bradburn.* Boston: Cupples, Upham and Co., 1883.

Bristol and Clifton Ladies' Anti-Slavery Society. *Statements Respecting the American Abolitionists; by Their Opponents and Their Friends: Indicating the Present Struggle between Slavery and Freedom in the United States of America.* Dublin: Webb and Chapman, 1852.

British and Foreign Anti-Slavery Society. *Address from the Committee of the British and Foreign Anti-Slavery Society to the Women of England.* [London: 184–]

———. *American Slavery and British Christians. A Tract Containing Reprints of the Address to Christians of All Denominations, and Especially to Christian Ministers, Issued by the Committee of the British and Foreign Anti-Slavery Society in April, 1853 and 1854. . . .* London: British and Foreign Anti-Slavery Society, 1854.

———. *The Crisis in the United States.* No. II, Tracts on Slavery in America. London: British and Foreign Anti-Slavery Society, 1862.

Brown, William Wells. *Sketches of Places and People Abroad.* Boston: John P. Jewett and Co., 1855.

"A Cambridge Man" [pseud.]. *Free Blacks and Slaves. Would Immediate Abolition Be a Blessing? A Letter to the Editor of the Anti-Slavery Advocate.* London: Arthur Hall Virtue & Co., 1853.

Carmichael, Mrs. *Domestic Manners and Social Condition of the White, Coloured, and Negro Population of the West Indies.* 2 vols. London: Whittaker, Treacher, & Co., 1833.

Carpenter, Joseph Estlin. *James Martineau Theologian & Teacher: A Study of his Life & Thought.* London: Philip Green, 1905.

———. *The Life and Work of Mary Carpenter.* 2nd ed. London: Macmillan & Co., 1881.

Carpenter, Lant. *A Discourse on Christian Patriotism: Delivered to the Society of Protestant Dissenters in Hanover Square, Newcastle-Upon-Tyne, on the Sunday after the Coronation of Her Majesty; Printed at Their Request, and Dedicated by Permission, to Her Royal Highness, the Duchess of Kent.* London: Longman, Orme, Brown, Green, and Longmans, 1838.

———. *Sermons on Practical Subjects.* Bristol: Philp and Evans, 1840.

Carpenter, Philip Pearsall. *"The Cup of the Lord, and the Cup of Devils." A Lecture on the Use of Intoxicating Wine at the Lord's Supper.* London: Job Caudwell, 1863.

———. *The Oberlin Tracts.* Warrington: Oberlin Press, n.d.

[———]. *Words in the War: Being Lectures on "Life and Death in the Hands of God and Man": By A Christian Teacher.* London: W. & F. G. Cash, 1855.

Carpenter, Russell Lant. *Discourses and Devotional Services.* London: E. T. Whitfield, 1849.

————. *A Farewell Lecture To the Friends of Temperance, Pledged and Unpledged, in Halifax.* Halifax: T. J. & F. Walker, Printers, 1865.

————. *A Fast Day Sermon Preached in Christ Church Chapel, Bridgwater.* London: J. Chapman, 1847.

————. *Free Blacks and Slaves.* From the *Christian Reformer* for August, 1853, n.p.:n.d.

————. *Imprisonment and Enslavement of British Coloured Seamen; Illustrated in the Case of John Glasgow.* Leeds Anti-Slavery Series, No. 89, n.p.:n.d.

————. *In Memory of Mary Carpenter, of 24 Regent Street, London, Who Died October 30th, 1877, Aged 90 Years.* [Bristol: Arrowsmith, 1878?]

————. "A Lecture on Tobacco . . . Delivered before the Mayor and People of Bridport, England," Abiel Abbot Livermore, *Anti-Tobacco.* Boston: Roberts Brothers, 1888.

————. *Memoirs of the Life and Work of Philip Pearsall Carpenter, B.A., London, Ph.D., New York, Chiefly Derived from His Letters.* 2nd ed. London: C. Kegan Paul & Co., 1880.

————. *Memoirs of the Life of the Rev. Lant Carpenter, LL.D., with Selections from His Correspondence.* Bristol: Philp and Evans, 1842.

————. *Observations on American Slavery, After a Year's Tour in the United States.* London: Edward T. Whitfield, 1852.

————. *Personal and Social Christianity. Sermons and Addresses,* J. Estlin Carpenter, ed., With a short memoir by Francis E. Cooke. London: Kegan Paul, Trench, Truebner & Co., 1893.

Carpenter, William Benjamin. *Nature and Man. Essays Scientific and Philosophical,* With an Introductory Memoir by J. Estlin Carpenter. New York: D. Appleton and Co., 1889.

————. *Principles of Human Physiology, with Their Chief Applications to Pathology, Hygiene, and Forensic Medicine.* 3rd ed. Philadelphia: Lea and Blanchard, 1847.

————. *Sketch of the Life and Work of Mary Carpenter of Bristol.* Bristol: Arrowsmith, 1877.

————. "Varieties of Mankind." *The Cyclopaedia of Anatomy and Physiology,* Robert B. Todd, ed., vol. 4, part 2. London: Longman, Brown, Green, Longmans, & Roberts, 1849–1852.

Channing, William Ellery. *An Address delivered at Lenox, on the First of August, 1842, the Anniversary of Emancipation in the British West Indies.* Lenox, Mass.: J. G. Stanly, 1842.

————. *Emancipation.* Boston: E. P. Peabody, 1840.

————. *Slavery.* Boston: James Munroe & Co., 1835.

————. *The Works of William E. Channing, D.D.* Boston: American Unitarian Association, 1878.

Channing, William Henry. *The Civil War in America; or, the Slaveholders' Conspiracy. An Address. . . .* Liverpool: W. Vaughan, [1861].

————, ed. *Memoir of William Ellery Channing, with Extracts from His*

Correspondence and Manuscripts. 3 vols. 3rd ed. Boston: Wm. Crosby & H. P. Nichols, 1848.

Chapman, Maria Weston, ed. *Harriet Martineau's Autobiography and Memorials of Harriet Martineau.* 2 vols. Boston: James Osgood & Co., 1877.

Clapp, Theodore. *Autobiographical Sketches and Recollections, during a Thirty-five Years' Residence in New Orleans.* Boston: Phillips, Sampson & Co., 1857.

[Clarke, James Freeman]. *American Slavery. A Protest Against American Slavery, by One Hundred and Seventy-Three Unitarian Ministers.* Boston: B. H. Greene, 1845.

———. *Anti-Slavery Days.* New York: R. Worthington, 1884.

Cobbe, Frances Power. *Life of Frances Power Cobbe as Told by Herself, With Additions by the Author and Introduction by Blanche Atkinson.* Posthumous ed., London: Swan Sonneschein & Co., Ltd., 1904.

———. *The Red Flag in John Bull's Eyes.* Tract No. 1, Ladies' London Emancipation Society. London: Emily Faithfull, 1863.

[———]. *Rejoinder to Mrs. Stowe's Reply to the Address of the Women of England.* London: Emily Faithfull, 1863.

Conway, Moncure Daniel. *Addresses and Reprints, 1850–1907.* Boston: Houghton, Mifflin & Co., 1909.

———. *Autobiography Memories & Experiences.* 2 vols. Boston: Houghton, Mifflin & Co., 1904.

———. *Centenary History of the South Place Society Based on Four Discourses Given in the Chapel in May and June, 1893.* London: Williams and Norgate, 1894.

———. *Testimonies Concerning Slavery.* London: Chapman and Hall, 1864.

———, and James M. Mason. "Abolitionism and Southern Independence." *William and Mary College Quarterly* 21 (April 1913): 221–23.

Cooper, Thomas. *Correspondence between George Hibbert, Esq., and the Rev. T. Cooper, Relative to the Condition of the Negro Slaves in Jamaica, Extracted from the Morning Chronicle: Also, A Libel on the Character of Mr. and Mrs. Cooper, Published, in 1823, in Several of the Jamaica Journals; with Notes and Remarks.* London: J. Hatchard and Son, 1824.

———. *Facts Illustrative of the Condition of the Negro Slaves in Jamaica: with Notes and an Appendix.* London: J. Hatchard and Son, 1824.

———. *A Letter to Robert Hibbert, Jun., Esq., in Reply to His Pamphlet, Entitled, "Facts Verified Upon Oath, in Contradiction of the Report of the Rev. Thomas Cooper, Concerning the General Condition of the Slaves in Jamaica," etc., To Which Are Added, A Letter from Mrs. Cooper to R. Hibbert, Jun. Esq., And an Appendix, Containing an Exposure of the Falsehoods and Calumnies of that Gentleman's Affidavit-Men.* London: J. Hatchard & Son, 1824.

Cordner, John. *The American Conflict: An Address, Spoken Before the New-England Society of Montreal, and a Public Audience, in Nordheimer's Hall, Montreal, . . . 22nd December, 1864.* Montreal: John Lovell, 1865.

———. *Canada and the United States: An Address, on the American Conflict, Delivered at Montreal, on Thursday Evening, December 22, 1864.* Manchester: A. Ireland and Co., 1865.

———. *Twenty-five Sermons. A Memorial of Twenty-five Years' Ministry.* Montreal: John Lovell, 1868.

Craft, William. *Running a Thousand Miles for Freedom; or, the Escape of William and Ellen Craft from Slavery.* London: William Tweedie, 1860.

Crozier, John A. *The Life of the Rev. Henry Montgomery, LL.D., Dunmurry, Belfast; with Selections from His Speeches and Writings.* vol. I [vol. 2 never published.]. London: E. T. Whitefield, 1875.

Dana, Mary. *Letters Addressed to Relatives and Friends, Chiefly in Reply to Arguments in Support of the Doctrine of the Trinity.* Boston: James Munroe Co., 1845.

The Debates in Parliament—Session 1833—on the Resolutions and Bill for the Abolition of Slavery in the British Colonies, with a Copy of the Act of Parliament. London: 162, Piccadilly, 1834.

Dewey, Orville. *Autobiography and Letters.* Mary E. Dewey, ed. Boston: Roberts Brothers, 1833.

———. *On American Morals and Manners.* Boston: William Crosby, 1844.

Dickson, S. Henry. *Remarks on Certain Topics Connected with the General Subject of Slavery.* Charleston, S.C.: Observer Office Press, 1845.

Douglass, Frederick. *Life and Times of Frederick Douglass Written by Himself* Hartford, Ct.: Park Publishing Co., 1882.

———. *My Bondage and My Freedom.* New York: Miller, Orton, & Mulligan, 1855.

Drummond, Robert Blackley. *President Lincoln and the American War. A Funeral Address Delivered on Sunday, April 30, 1865.* Edinburgh: W. P. Nimmo, 1865.

[Estlin, John Bishop]. *A Brief Notice of American Slavery, and the Abolition Movement.* Bristol: H. C. Evans, 1846.

———. *A Brief Notice of American Slavery, and the Abolition Movement.* 2nd ed., rev. London: William Tweedie, 1853.

———. *Reply to a Circular Issued by the Glasgow Association for the Abolition of Slavery Recommending a Discontinuance of British Support to the Boston Anti-Slavery Bazaar.* Paris: E. Briere, 1850.

Frothingham, Octavius Brooks. *Memoir of William Henry Channing.* Boston: Houghton, Mifflin & Co., 1886.

Furness, William Henry. *The Declaration of Independence. A Discourse Delivered in the First Congregational Unitarian Church in Philadelphia, June 29, 1862.* Philadelphia: C. Sherman & Son, 1862.

————. *A Discourse Delivered on the Occasion of the National Fast September 26th 1861 in the First Congregational Unitarian Church in Philadelphia.* Philadelphia: T. B. Pugh, 1861.

————. *England and America. A Discourse Delivered by W. H. Furness, Minister of the First Congregational Unitarian Church, Sunday, December 22, 1861.* Philadelphia: C. Sherman & Son, printers, n.d.

————. *Our American Institutions. A Thanksgiving Discourse Delivered in the First Congregational Unitarian Church in Philadelphia, August 6th, 1863.* Philadelphia: T. B. Pugh, 1863.

Gannett, William C. *Ezra Stiles Gannett. Unitarian Minister in Boston. 1824–1871.* Boston: Roberts Brothers, 1875.

Garrison, Wendell Phillips, and Francis Jackson Garrison. *William Lloyd Garrison 1805–1879. The Story of His Life Told by His Children.* 4 vols. New York: The Century Co., 1885–89.

Garrison, William Lloyd. *The Letters of William Lloyd Garrison.* Walter M. Merrill and Louis Ruchames, eds. 4 vols. Cambridge, Mass.: The Belknap Press of Harvard University Press, 1971–75.

Gill, Thomas H. *The Triumph of Christ. Memorials of Franklin Howorth.* London: Hodder and Stoughton, 1883.

Godwin, Benjamin. *Lectures on Slavery.* Boston: James B. Dow, 1836.

"Guilty or Nor Guilty?" A Few Facts and Feelings Regarding the Religious Bodies of America in the Matter of Slavery; Being a Report of an Anti-Slavery Meeting Held in Belgrave Chapel, Leeds, December 10th, 1855. Containing Addresses of Parker Pillsbury, Esq., and the Rev. G. W. Conder: Revised from the Columns of the Leeds Mecury. 2nd ed. with Additions. Leeds: Edward Baines & Sons, 1855.

Hargrove, Charles. *In Memoriam: Joseph Lupton, Who Died Suddenly, Unwarned Not Unready, January 17th, 1894. A Sermon Preached at Mill Hill Chapel, Leeds.* Leeds: Samuel Moxon & Son, 1894.

Harris, George. *Tracts and Sermons in Vindication of Christian Liberty, Righteousness, and Truth (Published on Various Occasions).* Glasgow: James Hedderwick & Son, 1836.

Haughton, James. *A Lecture on British India, Delivered Before the Dublin Mechanics' Institute, on Monday, 1st November, 1858.* Dublin: R. D. Webb, 1859.

————. *Progress of the British West Indian Colonies under Freedom: and the Inexpediency of Legislative Interference with Immigration into Them [and] Immigration into the British West Indian Colonies. Two Papers, Read before the Dublin Statistical Society, March 25th, 1859, and February 26th, 1860.* Dublin: Hodges, Smith, and Co., 1860.

————. *Slavery Immoral; Being a Reply to a Letter in Which an Attempt is Made to Prove that Slavery is Not Immoral.* Dublin: James McGlashan, 1847.

————. *Statistics of Free and Slave Labour in the United States of America. A Paper Read in the Dublin Statistical Society, on the 8th January, 1859.* [Dublin: 1859].

————. "A Voice from Erin." *Liberty Bell.* Boston: Massachusetts Anti-Slavery Fair, 1842, pp. 59–63.

Haughton, Samuel. *Memoir of James Haughton. With Extracts from His Private and Published Letters.* Dublin: E. Ponsonby, 1877.

Henderson, Robert. *A Memoir of the Late Rev. Dr. George Armstrong . . . .* London: Edward T. Whitfield, 1859.

[Hibbert, George.] *Brief Remarks on the Slave Registry Bill; and upon a Special Report of the African Institution, Recommending that Measure.* London: J. M. Richardson, 1816.

————. *Correspondence between Mr. George Hibbert and The Society of Friends.* n.p.: 1833.

————. *The Substance of Three Speeches in Parliament, on the Bill for the Abolition of the Slave Trade, and on the Petition Respecting the State of the West-India Trade, in February and March, 1807.* London: Lane, Darling, & Co., 1807.

Hibbert, Robert. *Facts, Verified Upon Oath, in Contradiction of the Report of the Rev. Thomas Cooper, concerning the General Condition of the Slaves in Jamaica; and More Especially Relative to the Management and Treatment of the Slaves upon Georgia Estate, in the Parish of Hanover, in that Island.* London: John Murray, 1824.

————. *Hints to the Young Jamaica Sugar Planter.* London: T. and G. Underwood, 1825.

Hopps, John Page. *Southern Independence: A Lecture.* London: Whitfield, Green, and Son, 1865.

James, William. *The Grateful Remembrance of Departed Ministers. A Sermon Delivered on Sunday Morning, August 16th, 1857, in Lewin's Mead Chapel, Bristol, On the Occasion of the Death of the Rev. George Armstrong, B.A.* London: Edward Whitfield, 1857.

————. *Memoir of John Bishop Estlin, Esq. F.L.S., F.R.C.S.* London: Charles Green, 1855.

————. *Memoir of the Rev. Thomas Madge, Late Minister of Essex Street Chapel, London.* London: Longmans, Green, and Co., 1871.

Le Breton, Anna Letitia, ed. *Correspondence of William Ellery Channing, D.D., and Lucy Aikin, From 1826 to 1842.* Boston: Roberts Brothers, 1874.

Lincoln, Abraham. *The Collected Works of Abraham Lincoln.* Roy P. Basler, ed. 8 vols. and Index. New Brunswick, N.J.: Rutgers University Press, 1953.

[Macaulay, Zachary]. *Negro Slavery; or, A View of Some of the More Prominent Features of that State of Society as It Exists in the United States of America and in the Colonies of the West Indies, Especially in Jamaica.* London: Hatchard and Son, 1823.

[————]. *The Slave Colonies of Great Britain; or a Picture of Negro Slavery drawn by the Colonists Themselves; Being an Abstract of the Various Papers Recently Laid before Parliament on that Subject.* London: J. Hatchard & Son, 1825.

McLachlan, Herbert. *Letters of Theophilus Lindsey.* Manchester: The University Press, 1920.

———. "A Liverpool Lady's Journal a Century Ago (11 February 1841–November, 1858)." *Transactions of the Unitarian Historical Society* 11 (1955–58): 1–19.

M'Queen, James. *The West India Colonies; the Calumnies and Misrepresentations Circulated Against Them by the Edinburgh Review, Mr. Clarkson, Mr. Cropper, etc., etc., Examined and Refuted. . . .* London: Baldwin, Cradock, & Joy, 1824.

[Markland, James H.] *A Sketch of the Life and Character of George Hibbert, esq., F.R.S., S.A., and L.S.* [London]: Printed for Private Distribution, 1837.

Martineau, Harriet. *A History of American Compromises.* London: John Chapman, 1856.

———. *The Hour and the Man. An Historical Romance.* 2 vols. New York: Harper & Bros., 1841.

———. "Introduction." *Right and Wrong Amongst the Abolitionists of the United States* by John A. Collins. Glasgow: George Gallie, 1841, pp. 3–5.

———. *The Martyr Age of the United States of America.* Newcastle Upon Tyne: Finlay and Charlton, 1840.

———. *Retrospect of Western Travel.* 3 vols. London: Saunders & Otley, 1838.

Martineau, James. "Letters of James Martineau to Joseph Henry Allen." *Publications of the Colonial Society of Massachusetts* no. 67 Transactions, 1889, 1900. Boston: Published by the Society, 1904, pp. 416–54.

———. "The Slave Empire of the West." *National Review* 4 (January 1857): 212–35.

May, Samuel J. *The DUTY of the UNITED KINGDOM towards the SLAVES of the UNITED STATES. A Letter by the Rev. Samuel J. May, of Syracuse State of New York.* Bristol: I. Arrowsmith, [1860].

———. *Emancipation in the British W. Indies, August 1, 1834. An Address, Delivered in the First Presbyterian Church in Syracuse, on the First of August, 1845.* Syracuse: J. Barber 1845.

———. *Some Recollections of Our Antislavery Conflict.* Miami, Fla.: Mnemosyne Publishing Co., 1969 [1st ed., 1869].

A Memoir of the Late Edward Tagart, Who Died 12th October, 1858, n.p.: n.d.

Memorials of Robert Spears 1825–1899. Belfast: Ulster Unitarian Christian Association, 1903.

Memorials of William Benjamin Carpenter, n.p.: n.d.

Mott, James. *Three Months in Great Britain.* Philadelphia: J. Miller M'Kim, 1841.

Mott, Lucretia. *Slavery and "the woman question"; Lucretia Mott's diary of her visit to Great Britain to attend the World's Anti-Slavery Convention of 1840*. Frederick B. Tolles, ed. Haverford, Pa.: Friends' Historical Association, 1852.

Murch, Jerom. *Memoir of Robert Hibbert, Esquire, Founder of the Hibbert Trust, with a Sketch of Its History*. Bath: William Lewis, 1874.

Nicholls, John Ashton. *In Memoriam. A Selection from the Letters of the Late John Ashton Nicholls, F.R.A.S., etc.* Sarah Nicholls, ed. N.p.: Printed for Private Circulation Only, 1862.

O'Connell, Daniel. *The Correspondence of Daniel O'Connell*. Maurice R. O'Connell, ed. 3 vols. Dublin: Irish University Press, 1974.

———. *Daniel O'Connell upon American Slavery: with Other Irish Testimonies*. Anti-Slavery Tracts, New Series, No. 5. New York: American Anti-Slavery Society, 1860.

Opinions of American Ministers on Slavery and the Fugitive Slave Bill, Selected from recent American Publications. Briggate, Leeds: Moxon and Walker, n.d.

Peabody, Andrew P. *Memoir of Rev. Samuel Kirkland Lothrop, D.D.*, [Reprinted from the *Proceedings of the Massachusetts Historical Society*]. *LL.D.*, Cambridge: John Wilson and Son, 1887.

"Philanthropos" [pseud.]. *Slavery Not Immoral: A Letter to James Haughton, Esq., Dublin*. Dublin: James McGlashan, 1847.

Porter, J. Scott. *Sermons by the Late Rev. W. H. Drummond, D.D., M.R.I.A., with Memoir*. London: E. T. Whitfield, 1867.

Price, Richard. *Richard Price and the Ethical Foundations of the American Revolution*. Bernard Peach, ed. Durham N.C.: Duke University Press, 1979.

Priestley, Joseph. *A Sermon on the Subject of the Slave Trade; Delivered to a Society of Protestant Dissenters at the New Meeting, in Birmingham; and Published at Their Request*. Birmingham: Printed for the Author, by Pearson and Rollason, 1788.

———. *The Theological and Miscellaneous Works of Joseph Priestley, LL.D., F.R.S., etc., with Notes*, John Towill Rutt, ed. 25 vols. London: George Smallfield, 1806–[32?].

Prichard, James Cowles. *The Natural History of Man; Comprising Inquiries into the Modifying Influence of Physical and Moral Agencies on the Different Tribes of the Human Family*. London: H. Bailliere, 1843.

———. *Researches into the Physical History of Mankind*. 2nd ed. 2 vols. London: John & Arthur Arch, 1826.

Rathbone, Eleanor F. *William Rathbone: A Memoir*. London: Macmillan & Co., 1905.

Riland, John. *Memoirs of a West-India Planter*. London: Hamilton, Adams, & Co., 1827.

Robinson, Henry Crabb. *Diary, Reminiscences, and Correspondence of Henry Crabb Robinson, Barrister-at-Law, F.S.A.* Thomas Sadler, ed. 2 vols. New York: Hurd and Houghton, 1877.

Roscoe, Henry. *The Life of William Roscoe.* 2 vols. Boston: Russell, Odiorne, and Co., 1833.

Roscoe, William. *The Wrongs of Africa. A Poem.* Part the First, Part the Second. London: R. Faulder, 1787, 1788.

Shaen, Margaret. *William Shaen. A Brief Sketch,* London: Longmans, Green, & Co., 1912.

Smith, A. Cobden. *Rev. S. Alfred Steinthal, 1826–1910. A Memorial Address Delivered to the Congregation of the Lower Mosley Street Sunday School, Manchester, on Sunday Evening, 8th May, 1910.* Manchester: Co-Operative Printing Society, Ltd., 1910.

Solly, Henry. *"These Eighty Years" or, the Story of an Unfinished Life.* 2 vols. London: Simpkin, Marshall & Co., 1893.

Spears, Robert. *Memorable Unitarians Being a Series of Brief Biographical Sketches.* London: British and Foreign Unitarian Association, 1906.

Steinthal, Samuel Alfred. *Address on the Assassination of Abraham Lincoln, Delivered at Platt Chapel on the Morning, and in the Ashton Town Hall on the Afternoon of Sunday, the 7th May, 1865.* London: Whitfield, Green, & Son, 1865.

————. *"American Slavery. A Sermon, Preached at Christ Church Chapel, Bridgwater, on Sunday, May the First, 1853.* Bridgwater: J. Whitby, 1853.

Stephen, James. *The Slavery of the British West India Colonies Delineated, as It Exists Both in Law and Practice, and Compared with the Slavery of Other Countries, Ancient and Modern.* 2 vols. London: Joseph Butterworth and Son, 1824.

Stowe, Harriet Beecher. *A Key to Uncle Tom's Cabin; presenting the Original Facts and Documents upon which the Story is founded, together with corroborative Statements verifying the Truth of the Work,* London: Sampson Low, Son, & Co., 1853.

Substance of the Debate in the House of Commons, on the 15th May 1823, On a Motion for the Mitigation and Gradual Abolition of Slavery Throughout the British Dominions. With Preface and Appendixes, Containing Facts and Reasonings Illustrative of Colonial Bondage. London: Ellerton and Henderson for the Society for the Mitigation and Gradual Abolition of Slavery Throughout the British Dominions, 1823.

Tayler, John James. *Letters Embracing His [the] Life of John James Tayler, B.A.* John Hamilton Thom, ed. London: Williams and Norgate, 1872.

Thom, John Hamilton. *Distress in the Manufacturing Districts. A Sermon Preached on Sunday, 7th December, 1862, in Renshaw Street Chapel, Liverpool.* London: E. T. Whitfield, [1862].

Thomas, Christopher James. *Some Account of the Rise and Progress of the Ancient Society of Protestant Dissenters, Worshipping in Lewin's Mead, Bristol.* Bristol: Stephens & Eyre, 1891.

Trimble, Robert. *The Negro, North and South: The Status of the Coloured Population in the Northern and Southern States of America Compared.* London: Whittaker & Co., 1863.

————. *The Present Crisis in America*. London: Whittaker & Co., 1865.

————. *A Review of the American Struggle, in Its Military and Political Aspects, from the Inauguration of President Lincoln, 4th March, 1861, till His Re-election, 8th November, 1864*. London: Whittaker & Co., 1864.

————. *Slavery in the United States of North America. A Lecture Delivered in Liverpool, December, 1861*. London: Whittaker & Co., 1863.

Turner, William. *Lives of Eminent Unitarians*, London: The Unitarian Association, 1840.

Ward, Samuel Ringgold. *Autobiography of a Fugitive Negro: His Anti-Slavery Labours in the United States, Canada, & England*. London: John Snow, 1855.

"A West Indian" [pseud.]. *The Rev. Mr. Cooper And His Calumnies Against Jamaica, Particularly His Late Pamphlet In Reply to Facts Verified On Oath*. Jamaica: publisher not known, 1825.

White, Joseph Blanco. *The Life of the Rev. Joseph Blanco White, Written by Himself; with Portions of His Correspondence*. John Hamilton Thom, ed. 3 vols. London: John Chapman, 1845.

Wicksteed, Charles. *The Englishman's Duty to the Free and the Enslaved American. A Lecture, Twice Delivered at Leeds, in January, 1853*. London: W. & F. G. Cash, 1853.

————. *The Law of Conscience, In Its Action on Nations and Individuals. A Sermon, Preached at Essex-Street Chapel, London, on Wednesday, May 18th, 1842, Being the Seventeenth Anniversary of the British and Foreign Unitarian Association*. London: The Unitarian Association, 1842.

Wicksteed, Philip Henry, ed. *Memorials of the Rev. Charles Wicksteed, B.A.* London: Williams and Norgate, 1866.

Wilberforce, William. *A practical view of the prevailing religious system of professed Christians, in the higher and middle classes in this country, contrasted with real Christianity*. London: T. Cadell, jun., & W. Davies, 1797.

Williamson, John. *Medical and Miscellaneous Observations, Relative to the West India Islands*. 2 vols. Edinburgh: Alex. Smellie, 1817.

Secondary Works

Abel, Annie Heloise, and Frank J. Klingberg, eds. *A Side-Light on Anglo-American Relations, 1839–1858*. N.p.: Association for the Study of Negro Life and History, 1927.

Adams, Oscar Fay. *A Dictionary of American Authors*. Boston: Houghton Mifflin Co., 1904.

Allen, Katherine Gibbs, ed. *Sketches of Some Historic Churches of Greater Boston*. Boston: Beacon Press, 1918.

Anstey, Roger. *The Atlantic Slave Trade and British Abolition 1760–1810*. London: Macmillan Press, 1975.

————. "Capitalism and Slavery: a Critique." *Economic History Review*. 2nd Series, 21 (1963): 307–20.

Baker, John Milton. *Henry Crabb Robinson of Bury, Jena, The Times, and Russell Square.* London: George Allen & Unwin, 1937.

Berger, Max. "American Slavery as Seen by British Visitors, 1836–1860." *Journal of Negro History* 30 (April 1945): 181–202.

Bloore, Stephen. "Miss Martineau Speaks Out." *New England Quarterly* 9 (September 1936): 403–16.

Bolt, Christine. *The Anti-Slavery Movement and Reconstruction: A Study of Anglo-American Cooperation 1833–1877.* London: Oxford University Press, 1969.

———. *Victorian Attitudes to Race.* London: Routledge & Kegan Paul, 1971.

Booth, Charles. *Zachary Macaulay: His Part in the Movement for the Abolition of the Slave Trade and of Slavery.* London: Longmans, Green and Co., 1934.

Brauer, Kinley J. "The Slavery Problem in the Diplomacy of the American Civil War." *Pacific Historical Review* 46 (August 1977): 439–69.

Briggs, John, and Ian Sellers, eds. *Victorian Nonconformity.* New York: St. Martin's Press, 1974.

Brooks, Arthur A. *The History of Unitarianism in the Southern Churches.* Boston: American Unitarian Association, n.d.

Burn, W. L. *Emancipation and Apprenticeship in the British West Indies.* London: Jonathan Cape, 1937.

Burton, Anthony. *Josiah Wedgwood: A Biography.* New York: Stein and Day, 1976.

Carter, George. *Unitarian Biographical Dictionary, Being Short Notices of the Lives of Noteworthy Unitarians, and Kindred Thinkers, Brought Down to the Year 1900.* London: Unitarian Christian Publishing Office, 1902.

Chadwick, Owen. *The Victorian Church.* Part 1. London: Adam & Charles Black, 1966.

Chandler, George. *William Roscoe of Liverpool.* London: B. T. Batsford, 1953.

Clark, G. Kitson. *The Making of Victorian England.* Cambridge, Mass.: Harvard University Press, 1962.

———. "The Romantic Element—1830 to 1850." *Studies in Social History: A Tribute to G. M. Trevelyan.* John Harold Plumb, ed. Freeport, N.Y.: Books for Libraries Press, 1969 [1st edition, 1955], pp. 209–39.

Claussen, Martin P. "Peace Factors in Anglo-American Relations, 1861–1865." *Mississippi Valley Historical Review* 26 (March 1939–40): 511–22.

Commanger, Henry Steele. *Theodore Parker.* Boston: Beacon Press, 1967 [1st edition, 1936].

Coupland, Reginald. *The British Anti-Slavery Movement.* London: Frank Cass & Co., 1964 [1st ed., 1933].

Cowherd, Raymond G. *The Politics of English Dissent.* New York: New York University Press, 1956.

Crone, John S. *A Concise Dictionary of Irish Biography.* Dublin: Tabot Press, 1937.

Crook, D. P. "Portents of War: English Opinion on Secession." *Journal of American Studies* 4 (1970): 163–79.

Davies, Horton. *The English Free Churches.* 2nd ed. London: Oxford University Press, 1963.

———. *Worship and Theology in England. From Newman to Martineau, 1850–1900.* Princeton, N.J.: Princeton University Press, 1962.

Davis, David Brion. "The Emergence of Immediatism in British and American Antislavery Thought." *Mississippi Valley Historical Review* 49 (September 1962): 209–30.

———. *The Problem of Slavery in Western Culture.* Ithaca, N.Y.: Cornell University Press, 1966.

———. *The Problem of Slavery in the Age of Revolution 1770–1823.* Ithaca, N.Y.: Cornell University Press, 1975.

Davis, Richard W. *Dissent in Politics 1780–1830. The Political Life of William Smith, MP.* London: Epworth Press, 1971.

Denton, Charles Richard. "An American War That Unitarians Approved: The American Civil War." *Proceedings of the Unitarian Historical Society* 17, part 1 (1970–72): 46–56.

Drescher, Seymour. "Capitalism and the Decline of Slavery: The British Case in Comparative Perspective." *Annals of the New York Academy of Sciences* 292 (1977): 132–42.

———. *Econocide: British Slavery in the Era of Abolition.* Pittsburgh: University of Pittsburgh Press, 1977.

Drummond, James. *The Life and Letters of James Martineau, LL.D., S.T.D., Etc.* 2 vols. New York: Dodd, Mead & Co., 1902.

Dubofsky, Melvyn. "Myth and History." *Reviews in American History* 1 (September 1973): 396–400.

Eliot, Samuel Atkins. *Heralds of a Liberal Faith.* 4 vols. Boston: The American Unitarian Association and Beacon Press, 1910–52.

Ellison, Mary. *Support for Secession: Lancashire and the American Civil War.* With an epilogue by Peter d'A. Jones. Chicago: University of Chicago, 1972.

Filler, Louis. *The Crusade Against Slavery, 1830–1860.* New York: Harper Torchbooks, Harper and Row, 1960.

Fladeland, Betty. *Men and Brothers: Anglo-American Antislavery Cooperation.* Urbana, Ill.: University of Illinois Press, 1972.

Foote, Henry Wilder. "Theodore Clapp." *Proceedings of the Unitarian Historical Society* 3 part 2 (1934): 13–39.

Fredrickson, George M. *The Black Image in the White Mind: The Debate on Afro-American Character and Destiny, 1817–1914.* New York: Harper Torchbooks, 1972.

Fulkerson, Gerald. "Exile as Emergence: Frederick Douglass in Great Britain, 1845–1847." *Quarterly Journal of Speech* 60 (February 1974): 69–82.

Galpin, W. Freeman. "Samuel Joseph May. 'God's Chore Boy.'" *New York History* 21 (April 1940): 139–50.

Gay, John D. *The Geography of Religion in England.* London: Gerald Duckworth & Co., 1971.

Gilbert, Alan D. *Religion and Society in Industrial England: Church, Chapel, and Social Change, 1740–1914.* London: Longman, 1976.

Gohdes, Clarence. "Some Notes on the Unitarian Church in the Ante-Bellum South: A Contribution to the History of Southern Liberalism." *American Studies in Honor of William Kenneth Boyd.* Durham, N.C.: Duke University Press, 1940.

Goring, Jeremy, and Roger Thomas, eds. *English Presbyterianism: From Elizabethan Puritanism to Modern Unitarianism.* London: George Allen & Unwin, Ltd., 1968.

Gow, Henry. *The Unitarians.* London: Methuen & Co., 1928.

Hamer, Philip M. "British Consuls and the Negro Seamen Acts, 1850–1860." *Journal of Southern History* 1 (1935): 138–68.

———. "Great Britain, the United States, and the Negro Seamen Acts, 1822–1848." *Journal of Southern History* 1 (1935): 3–28.

Hammond, J. L. and Barbara Hammond. *James Stansfeld: A Victorian Champion of Sex Equality.* London: Longmans, Green and Co., 1932.

Harris, John. *A Century of Emancipation.* London: J. M. Dent & Sons, 1933.

Harrison, Royden. "British Labor and American Slavery." *Science and Society* 25 (1961): 291–319.

———. "British Labour and the Confederacy." *International Review of Social History* 2 (1957): 78–105.

Harwood, Thomas F. "British Evangelical Abolitionism and American Churches in the 1830's." *Journal of Southern History* 28 (August 1962): 287–306.

———. "Prejudice and Antislavery: The Colloquy between William Ellery Channing and Edward Strutt Abdy, 1834." *American Quarterly* 18 (Winter 1966): 697–700.

Henriques, Ursula. *Religious Toleration in England 1787–1833.* Toronto: University of Toronto Press, 1961.

Hernon, Joseph M. "British Sympathies in the American Civil War: A Reconsideration." *Journal of Southern History* 33 (August 1967): 356–67.

Holt, Anne. *A Life of Joseph Priestley.* London: Oxford University Press, 1931.

———. *Walking Together. A Study in Liverpool Nonconformity 1688–1938.* London: George Allen & Unwin, Ltd., 1938.

———. "William Ellery Channing (1780–1842)." *Hibbert Journal* 41 (October 1942): 42–49.

Holt, Raymond V. *The Unitarian Contribution to Social Progress in England.* 2nd rev. ed. London: Lindsey Press, 1952.

Horsman, Reginald. "Origins of Racial Anglo-Saxonism in Great Britain Before 1850." *Journal of The History of Ideas* 37 (July–September 1976): 387–410.

Howe, Daniel Walker. *The Unitarian Conscience: Harvard Moral Philosophy, 1805–1861.* Cambridge, Mass.: Harvard University Press, 1970.

Hunt, John. *Religious Thought In England in the Nineteenth Century.* London: Gibbings & Co., 1896.

Hurwitz, Edith F. *Politics and the Public Conscience: Slave Emancipation and the Abolitionist Movement in Britain.* London: George Allen & Unwin, Ltd., 1973.

Inglis, K. S. *Churches and the Working Classes in Victorian England.* London: Routledge & Kegan Paul, 1963.

Isichei, Elizabeth. *Victorian Quakers.* Oxford: Oxford University Press, 1970.

Johnson, Allen, and Dumas Malone, eds. *Dictionary of American Biography.* 27 vols. New York: Charles Scribner's Sons, 1928–58.

Jones, Wilbur Devereux. "The British Conservatives and the American Civil War." *American Historical Review* 58 (April 1953): 527–43.

Jordan, Donaldson, and Edwin J. Pratt. *Europe and the American Civil War.* Boston: Houghton Mifflin Co., 1931.

Kielty, John. *British Unitarianism Past, Present, and Future.* The Minns Lectures, 1959. Boston: Minns Lectureship Committee, 1960.

Klingberg, Frank J. *The Anti-Slavery Movement in England: A Study in English Humanitarianism.* N.p.: Archon Books, 1968 [1st ed., 1926].

————. "The Evolution of the Humanitarian Spirit in Eighteenth-Century England." *Pennsylvania Magazine of History and Biography* 66 (1942): 260–78.

————. "Harriet Beecher Stowe and Social Reform in England." *American Historical Review* 43 (1937–38): 542–52.

Knutsford, Viscountess. *Life and Letters of Zachary Macaulay.* London: Edward Arnold, 1900.

Kraditor, Aileen S. *Means and Ends in American Abolitionism: Garrison and His Critics on Strategy and Tactics, 1834–1850.* New York: Pantheon Books, 1969.

Kraus, Michael. "Slavery Reform in the Eighteenth Century: An Aspect of Transatlantic Intellectual Cooperation." *Pennsylvania Magazine of History and Biography* 60 (1936): 53–66.

Landon, Fred. "The Negro Migration to Canada After the Passing of the Fugitive Slave Act." *Journal of Negro History* 5 (October 1920): 22–36.

Lincoln, Anthony. *Some Political and Social Ideas of English Dissent 1763–1800.* New York: Octagon Books, 1971 [1st edition, 1938].

Lindsey, David. *Americans in Conflict: The Civil War and Reconstruction.* Boston: Houghton Mifflin Co., 1974.

Litwack, Leon F. *North of Slavery: The Negro in the Free States, 1790–1860*. Chicago: The University of Chicago Press, 1969.

Lorimer, Douglas A. *Colour, Class and the Victorians: English attitudes to the Negro in the mid-nineteenth century*. [Leicester]: Leicester University Press, 1978.

———. "The Role of Anti-Slavery Sentiment in English Reactions to the American Civil War." *Historical Journal* 19 (1976): 405–20.

[Lyon, William Henry]. *The First Parish in Brookline: An Historical Sketch*. Brookline, Mass.: The Riverdale Press, 1898.

Machin, G. I. T. *Politics and the Churches in Great Britain 1832 to 1868*. Oxford: Clarendon Press, 1977.

McLachlan, Herbert. *The Methodist Unitarian Movement*. Manchester: The University Press, 1919.

———. *Records of a Family 1800–1933: Pioneers in Education, Social Service and Liberal Religion*. Manchester: Manchester University Press, 1935.

———. *The Unitarian Movement in the Religious Life of England*. London: George Allen & Unwin, Ltd., 1934.

McMillan, William. *A Profile in Courage [Henry Montgomery (1788–1865)]*. Newry: E. Hodgett, Ltd., 1966.

Mathieson, William Law. *British Slave Emancipation, 1838–1849*. London: Longmans, Green & Co., 1932.

———. *British Slavery and its Abolition, 1823–1838*. London: Longmans, Green & Co., 1926.

———. *Great Britain and the Slave Trade, 1839–1865*. London: Longmans, Green & Co., 1929.

Maynard, Douglas H. "The World's Anti-Slavery Convention of 1840." *Mississippi Valley Historical Review* 47 (December 1960): 452–71.

Mineka, Francis E. *The Dissidence of Dissent: The Monthly Repository, 1806–1838*. Chapel Hill, N.C.: University of North Carolina Press, 1944.

Morley, Edith J. *The Life and Times of Henry Crabb Robinson*. London: J. M. Dent and Sons, Ltd., 1935.

Muir, Ramsay. *William Roscoe: An Inaugural Lecture on Election to the Andrew Geddes and John Rankin Chair of Modern History at the University of Liverpool*. Liverpool: The University Press, 1906.

Nicholson, Francis and Ernest Axon. *The Older Nonconformity in Kendal*. Kendal: Titus Wilson, 1915.

Osofsky, Gilbert. "Abolitionists, Irish Immigrants, and the Dilemmas of Romantic Nationalism." *American Historical Review* 80 (October 1975): 889–912.

Park, Joseph H. "The English Workingmen and the American Civil War." *Political Science Quarterly* 39 (1924): 432–57.

Pease, William H. and Jane H. Pease. "Boston Garrisonians and the

Problem of Frederick Douglass." *Canadian Journal of History* 2 (September 1967): 29–48.

Perry, Lewis, and Michael Fellman, eds. *Antislavery Reconsidered: New Perspectives on the Abolitionists.* Baton Rouge, La.: Louisiana State University Press, 1979.

Quarles, Benjamin. "Ministers Without Portfolio." *Journal of Negro History* 39 (January 1954): 27–42.

Ragatz, Lowell Joseph. *The Fall of the Planter Class in the British Caribbean, 1763–1833. A Study in Social and Economic History.* New York: The Century Co., 1928.

———. *A Guide for the Study of British Caribbean History, 1763–1834 Including the Abolition and Emancipation Movements.* Washington, D.C.: United States Government Printing Office, 1932.

Riach, Douglas C. "Daniel O'Connell and American Anti-Slavery." *Irish Historical Studies* 20 (March 1976): 3–25.

Rice, C. Duncan. "Abolitionists and Abolitionism in Aberdeen: A Test Case for the Nineteenth-Century Anti-Slavery Movement." *Northern Scotland* 1 (December 1972): 65–87.

———. "The Anti-Slavery Mission of George Thompson to the United States, 1834–1835." *Journal of American Studies* 2 (April 1968): 13–31.

———. "Enlightenment, Evangelism, and Economics in the Interpretation of the Drive Towards Emancipation in British West India." *Annals of the New York Academy of Sciences* 292 (1977): 123–32.

———. "'Humanity Sold for Sugar!' The British Abolitionist Response to Free Trade in Slave-Grown Sugar." *Historical Journal* 13 (1970): 402–418.

———. *The Rise and Fall of Black Slavery.* New York: Harper & Row, 1975.

Routley, Erik. *English Religious Dissent.* Cambridge: Cambridge University Press, 1960.

Saywell, Ruby J. *Mary Carpenter of Bristol.* Bristol Branch of the Historical Association Local History Pamphlets, No. 9. Bristol: Bristol Historical Association, 1964.

Schroeder, William Lawrence. *Mill Hill Chapel Leeds 1674–1924.* Hull: Elson & Co., n.d.

Schupf, Harriet Warm. "Single Women and Social Reform in Mid-Nineteenth Century England: The Case of Mary Carpenter." *Victorian Studies* 17 (March 1974): 301–17.

Seller, Ian. "Unitarians & Social Change." *Hibbert Journal* 61 (October 1962; January 1963; April 1963): 16–22, 76–80, 122–80.

Shepperson, George. "Frederick Douglass and Scotland." *Journal of Negro History* 38 (1953): 307–21.

———. "The Free Church and American Slavery." *Scottish Historical Review* 30 (October 1951): 126–43.

———. "Harriet Beecher Stowe and Scotland, 1852–3." *Scottish Historical Review* 32 (April 1953): 40–46.

Short, Harry Lismer. *Dissent and the Community.* The Essex Hall Lecture, 1962. London: The Lindsey Press, 1962.

―――. *The Founding of the British & Foreign Unitarian Association.* Supplement to the *Transactions of the Unitarian Historical Society* 16 (October 1975).

Short, Kenneth R. M. "English Baptists and American Slavery." *Baptist Quarterly* 20 (April 1964): 243–62.

Short, L. Baker. *Pioneers of Scottish Unitarianism.* [n.p.: 1963].

Stampp, Kenneth M. *And the War Came:The North and the Secession Crisis 1860–1861.* Chicago: University of Chicago Press, 1968.

Stange, Douglas C. "Abolitionism as Maleficence: Southern Unitarians Versus 'Puritan Fanaticism'—1831–1860." *Harvard Library Bulletin* 26 (April 1978): 146–71.

―――. "Abolitionism as Treason: The Unitarian Elite Defends Law, Order, and the Union." *Harvard Library Bulletin* 28 (April 1980): 152–70.

―――. "From Treason to Antislavery Patriotism: Unitarian Conservatives and the Fugitive Slave Law." *Harvard Library Bulletin* 25 (October 1977): 466–88.

―――. *Patterns of Antislavery among American Unitarians 1831–1860.* Rutherford, N.J.: Fairleigh Dickinson University Press, 1977.

―――. "Teaching the Means of Freedom to West Indian Slaves, or, Failure as the Raw Material for Antislavery Propaganda." *Harvard Library Bulletin* (October 1981): 403–19.

―――. "United for Sovereignty and Freedom: Unitarians and the Civil War," *Proceedings of the Unitarian Universalist Historical Society* 19, part 1 (1980–81): 16–38.

Stanton, William. *The Leopard's Spots: Scientific Attitudes Toward Race in America 1815–59.* Chicago: The University of Chicago Press, 1966.

Staples, Laurence C. *Washington Unitarianism: A Rich Heritage.* Washington, D.C.: 1970.

Stephen, Leslie, and Sidney Lee, eds., *The Dictionary of National Biography.* 21 vols. Oxford: Oxford University Press, 1921–22.

Taylor, Clare. *British and American Abolitionists. An Episode in Transatlantic Understanding.* Edinburgh: Edinburgh University Press, 1974.

―――. "Notes on American Negro Reformers in Victorian Britain." *Bulletin of the British Association for American Studies.* 1961, pp. 40–51.

Temperley, Howard. "Anti-slavery." *Pressure from Without in early Victorian England.* Patricia Hollis, ed. London: Edward Arnold, 1974, pp. 27–51.

―――. *British Antislavery 1833–1870.* London: Longman Group Ltd., 1972.

―――. *British Politics and Slavery, 1830–1870. An Address . . . to the Anti-Slavery Society for the Protection of Human Rights at the House of Commons, Westminster on 29th October 1970.* London: The Anti-Slavery Society, n.d.

———. "Capitalism, Slavery and Ideology." *Past and Present.* No. 75 (May 1977): 94–118.

Thistlethwaite, Frank. *The Anglo-American Connection in the Early Nineteenth Century.* New York: Russell & Russell, 1971 [1st ed., 1959].

Thompson, David M., ed. *Nonconformity in the Nineteenth Century.* London: Routledge & Kegan Paul, 1972.

Tibbutt, H. G. "Robert Hibbert, Slaveowner Philanthropist." *Bedfordshire Magazine* 12 (Winter 1969): 117–19.

Trepp, Jean. "The Liverpool Movement for the Abolition of the English Slave Trade." *Journal of Negro History* 13 (July 1928): 265–85.

Walvin, James. "The Impact of Slavery on British Radical Politics: 1787–1838." *Annals of the New York Academy of Sciences* 292 (1977): 343–55.

Ward, William Reginald. *Religion and Society in England 1790–1850.* New York: Schocken Books, [1973].

Watts, Michael R. *The Dissenters.* Oxford: Clarendon Press, 1981.

Webb, Robert Kiefer. *Harriet Martineau: A Radical Victorian.* New York: Columbia University Press, 1960.

Whitridge, Arnold. "British Liberals and the American Civil War." *History Today* 12 (1962): 688–95.

Wigmore-Beddoes. Dennis G. *Yesterday's Radicals: A Study of the Affinity between Unitarianism and Broad Church Anglicanism in the Nineteenth Century.* Cambridge, Mass.: James Clarke & Co., 1971.

Wilbur, Earl Morse. *A History of Unitarianism in Transylvania, England, and America.* Boston: Beacon Press, 1969 [1st edition, 1945].

William Eric. *Capitalism and Slavery.* New York: Perigee Books, 1980 [1st edition, 1944].

Wright, Conrad. *The Beginnings of Unitarianism in America.* Boston: Starr King Press, 1955.

Wright, D. G. "Bradford and the American Civil War." *Journal of British Studies* 8 (1969): 69–85.

———. "Leeds Politics and the American Civil War." *Northern History* 9 (1974): 96–122.

Theses and Unpublished Materials

Billington, Louis. "Some Connections between British and American Reform Movements, 1830–1860, with Special Reference to the Anti-slavery Movements." M.A. thesis, University of Bristol, 1966.

Denton, Charles Richard. "American Unitarians, 1830–1865: A Study of Religious Opinion of War, Slavery, and the Union." Ph.D. dissertation, Michigan State University, 1969.

Dixon, Edward. "The American Negro in Nineteenth Century Scotland." M. Litt. dissertation, University of Edinburgh, 1969.

Harwood, Thomas Franklin. "Great Britain and American Antislavery." Ph.D. dissertation, University of Texas, 1959.

Rice, C. Duncan. "The Scots Abolitionists, 1833–1861." Unpublished manuscript, 1975.

———. "The Scottish Factor in the Fight Against American Slavery." Ph.D. dissertation, University of Edinburgh, 1969.

Sellers, Ian. "Liverpool Nonconformity, 1786–1914." Ph.D. dissertation, University of Keele, 1969.

———. "Social and Political Ideas of Representative English Unitarians, 1795–1850." B.Litt. thesis, Keble College, Oxford University, n.d.

Taylor, Clare. "Some American Reformers and Their Influence on Reform Movements in Great Britain from 1830 to 1860." Ph.D. dissertation, University of Edinburgh, 1960.

Index

251